I0127553

The Rise of the American Security State

The Rise of the American Security State

The National Security Act of 1947 and the Militarization of U.S. Foreign Policy

M. KENT BOLTON

Praeger Security International

BLOOMSBURY ACADEMIC
NEW YORK · LONDON · OXFORD · NEW DELHI · SYDNEY

BLOOMSBURY ACADEMIC
Bloomsbury Publishing Inc
1385 Broadway, New York, NY 10018, USA
50 Bedford Square, London, WC1B 3DP, UK
29 Earlsfort Terrace, Dublin 2, Ireland

BLOOMSBURY, BLOOMSBURY ACADEMIC and the Diana logo
are trademarks of Bloomsbury Publishing Plc

First published in the United States of America by ABC-CLIO 2018
Paperback edition published by Bloomsbury Academic 2024

Copyright © Bloomsbury Publishing Inc, 2024

Cover design by Silverander Communications
Cover photo: The view from President Bush's chair in the Situation Room of the White House in
Washington, DC, May 18, 2007. (AP Photo/Charles Dharapak)

All rights reserved. No part of this publication may be reproduced or
transmitted in any form or by any means, electronic or mechanical,
including photocopying, recording, or any information storage or retrieval
system, without prior permission in writing from the publishers.

Bloomsbury Publishing Inc does not have any control over, or responsibility for,
any third-party websites referred to or in this book. All internet addresses given
in this book were correct at the time of going to press. The author and publisher
regret any inconvenience caused if addresses have changed or sites have
ceased to exist, but can accept no responsibility for any such changes.

Library of Congress Cataloging in Publication Control Number: 2017024078 (print)

ISBN: HB: 978-1-4408-4319-8
PB: 979-8-7651-2107-8
ePDF: 978-1-4408-4320-4
eBook: 979-8-2161-4000-9

Series: Praeger Security International

To find out more about our authors and books visit www.bloomsbury.com
and sign up for our newsletters.

Contents

PART I

U.S. Foreign Policy and the Rise of the American Security State

The Rise of the American Security State is about the militarization of U.S. foreign policy starting about midway through the 20th century, increasing during the Cold War era and, somewhat surprisingly, continuing in the post-Cold War period. Part I asserts that something called the Cold War consensus emerged quickly after the end of World War II, during the first few years of what became the Cold War. One result of the Cold War consensus was a critical piece of legislation that created the Defense Department, what became the intelligence community (beginning with the CIA) and the National Security Council (NSC) inside the executive branch—that is the presidency.[1]

In the two chapters that constitute Part I, the Cold War consensus will be presented and compared to what preceded it. Also, the National Security Act of 1947 will be introduced to the reader. What is more, important terms used throughout the book are introduced and the main thesis presented.

Thereafter, the plan is to present Part II, the actual case studies used as empirical evidence of the thesis. Part II consists of three chapters of case studies. The case studies were chosen to fit a chronological typology employed with the first case studies coming from the Cold War's first decade. The second set of case studies comes from the main years of the Cold War. Finally, the third set of case studies tracks the transition from Cold War to post-Cold War and the post-Cold War era as distinct.

Finally, Part III will be a look back at what evidence the case studies provided and an attempt to generalize from the case studies.

CHAPTER 1

Understanding U.S. Foreign Policy

PRÉCIS OF WORLD POLITICS 1940–1944

On May 10, 1940, Hitler's Nazi Germany invaded the "low countries" (Holland, Belgium, and eventually France) commencing what became Germany's attempt to control Western Europe. After making a pact with Russia (then, the USSR), Hitler broke the pact and invaded the USSR in late June 1941 beginning a two-front war that would eventually become World War II.

In a couple of short years, the United States was transformed from a quasi-isolationist power to one that was immersed in World War II, thence on its way to hegemony. Isolationism was a powerful movement in the United States on Capitol Hill and among various societal interests that reflected the founding father's reluctance to create a powerful presidency. Indeed, it is fair to say that the Congress held rather more power in terms of foreign policy than the presidency until World War II. The balance (and what eventually became an imbalance) between Congress and the presidency began to change with Hitler's May 1940 attacks on Western European powers and again in the summer of 1941 when Germany abrogated its pact with the USSR to keep Germany and the USSR from war. Operation Barbarossa, Hitler's surprise attack on the USSR commenced on June 22, 1941.

An ethos of isolationism persisted from the United States' founding until World War II. Isolationism was a movement fueled by World War I—but which dated back to the Revolution and the War of 1812—that held that Americans ought not to involve themselves in European affairs. On Capitol Hill, key members of both the House of Representatives and, importantly, the Senate fought many battles with Franklin D. Roosevelt (FDR) over isolationism. Senator Bennett Clark (Missouri) and Gerald P. Nye (North Dakota), among others, battled with FDR through a series of neutrality acts prohibiting the president and U.S. private interests from intervening in European affairs.

Capitol Hill passed a series of neutrality acts in 1935, 1936, 1937, and again in 1939 restricting what the president could do. The 1939 act prohibited the United States from shipping supplies or people to belligerent ports in Europe. Thus, FDR as well as private interests were precluded from involving the United States even indirectly with European powers at war.

However, President Franklin Roosevelt believed America had to jettison isolationism for a more activist foreign policy. FDR believed the United States needed to consider the future if Hitler overwhelmed Europe. He was convinced that a successful Germany would eventually threaten the United States. FDR made a series of famous speeches building support slowly but steadily for America's eventual intervention in World War II.

Just weeks after Germany's invasion of Western Europe, President Roosevelt began a series of speeches and fireside chats that proved crucial in shaping public opinion to reject isolationism. On May 26, 1940 (some three weeks after Germany invaded Western Europe), the president spoke of millions of Europeans forced to flee their homes creating despair and misery in Europe. FDR addressed isolationism by asserting those who once thought the Atlantic Ocean protected them from Europe were naive. Indeed, there were "many among us who closed their eyes, from lack of interest or lack of knowledge; honestly and sincerely thinking that the many hundreds of miles of salt water made the American Hemisphere so remote that the people of North and Central and South America could go on living [amid] . . . their vast resources without reference to, or danger from, other continents of the world." FDR noted an "approaching storm."[1]

On December 29, 1940, FDR gave a speech that began thus: "This is not a fireside chat on war. It is a talk on national security." He then continued "the whole purpose of your president is to keep you now, and your children later, and your grandchildren much later, out of a last-ditch war for the preservation of American independence" and "all the things American independence means to you and me and to ours."[2] FDR reminded Americans that on September 27, 1940, by an agreement signed in Berlin, Italy and Japan had joined Germany's belligerence against Europe and the world and the United States must prepare to avoid war itself.

Among other things, the president committed the United States to helping the British and USSR against German and Italian fascism that FDR saw engulfing Europe and subsequently the world. Only by helping America's allies in Europe could America forego the scourge of war itself, so he argued. FDR called for "all Americans" to "stop being deluded by the romantic notion" that "Americas can go on living happily and peacefully in a Nazi-dominated world." Using a Wild West metaphor, FDR asserted that "when you see a rattlesnake poised to strike, you do not wait until he has struck to crush him."

These speeches and others, as well as press conferences slowly built pressure for the United States' intervention in world affairs and a rejection of isolationism. But it was not until Japan attacked Pearl Harbor that President Roosevelt was given a gift by Japan. In that single instant, FDR rallied the American people together behind the cause of war of retaliation against Japan. In so doing it, FDR (wittingly or not) changed the balance between foreign policy prerogatives of Congress versus the presidency. What is more, the balance has since favored the presidency at the expense of Congress, sometimes for better and other times for worse.

Between Pearl Harbor (just over 75 years ago) and today, the balance has continued to favor the presidency. The question is why so few Americans know how or why? The answer involves an interesting story that begins with World War II, continues through the Cold War and the creation of weapons of mass destruction (WMD), and continues in today's post-Cold War era. It involves the creation of new institutions (the U.S. Defense Department, the intelligence community under civilian leadership, and the NSC inside the White House) and new legislation (The National Security Act of 1947) that created the said institutions.

On December 7, 1941, FDR said, "Yesterday, December 7, 1941—a date which will live in infamy—the United States of America was suddenly and deliberately attacked by naval and air forces of the Empire of Japan." What is noteworthy is what followed those famous words. After telling the American people that Japan also invaded Malaysia (then Malaya) and Hong Kong (then still a British colony) as well as the Philippines, FDR called on Congress to do its job by declaring "war since the unprovoked and dastardly attack" the previous day.[3]

Interestingly, since Pearl Harbor, Congress has been reluctant to assert its Constitutional prerogatives and the presidency has become more powerful in the nearly eight decades since. It is this change in balance that has resulted in American foreign policy becoming more militarized. The powerful presidency and relatively weaker Congress that resulted from the events has rarely been examined in detail. (During presidential election cycles every four years, the argument is made that the imbalance needs to be examined but little is done substantively thereafter.)

Consider the post-Cold War presidencies of George W. Bush and Barack H. Obama, 43rd and 44th presidents, respectively. Without politicizing either, it is reasonable to ask what wars the United States has involved itself in without a formal declaration of war from Congress. Of course, after 9/11 President George W. Bush had massive support to attack al Qaeda, the transnational Jihadist movement that was then hosted by the Taliban government of Afghanistan. That war began in October 2001 (fewer than

30 days after 9/11). The war in Afghanistan continues today with some 10,000 U.S. troops in Afghanistan. President Obama continued the war, "surged" U.S troops there after his speech on December 1, 2009. In so doing, he followed the model set by President George W. Bush who invaded Iraq in March 2003 and "surged" U.S. troops there in 2006–2007. Thus, the war in Iraq must also be counted.

Additionally, during these two presidencies, the United States went to war (albeit, largely covertly) in Yemen, Syria, Libya, Somalia, Chad, and Mali and in southern Africa near the Congo and possibly elsewhere. None of these wars has been blessed by a formal declaration of war or the request for one from Congress. Rather, presidents have increasingly asserted executive powers not mentioned in the plain words of the Constitution. Beyond where America has sent U.S. troops under the two administrations mentioned, the United States has UAVs (unmanned aerial vehicles) or drones across northern African and the Middle East (MENA), as well as in Central Asia (Afghanistan). Both presidents have claimed the power to define who America's enemies are and to have them killed by drones. The drones are often operated from adjacent friendly countries or even from the United States. In short, the imbalance that began in FDR (and Truman) administrations has been thoroughly bipartisan in nature, as the reader will shortly discover.

That is the state of the "balance" between the executive branch on the one hand and the legislative branch on the other. And few Americans seem to be aware of how or why this balance has changed. Since 9/11, the author has watched the reelection of George W. Bush for a second term, the election and reelection of President Obama for two terms, and the election of President Donald Trump. Yet, in all those presidential election cycles, little has been said about how and why the president has become so powerful and why U.S. foreign policy has become militarized. Americans have simply accepted the militarization as necessary. With a new president and one who some fear—perhaps with some justification—as lacking a certain decorum or judgment it is time to consider the train of events that resulted in this confusing situation.

INTRODUCTION TO U.S. FOREIGN POLICY

This book is about U.S. foreign policy and what has happened to it since the late 1940s, when World War II was ending and the Cold War was just beginning. Among the other points, the main thesis is that from the late 1940s through the entirety of the Cold War, U.S. foreign policy increasingly militarized. Then the Cold War ended somewhere between the Berlin Wall coming down in 1989 and a failed coup in the former USSR in August 1991. Interestingly (and somewhat paradoxically), U.S. foreign policy continued to militarize rather than return to the inward-looking nation that existed prior to World War II. The question is why?

In a book about U.S. foreign policy, it is incumbent upon the author to define foreign policy and what is meant by terms, such as the *militarization of U.S. foreign policy*. This introductory chapter is intended to clarify some of these important concepts and terms.

What Is Foreign Policy?

For present purposes, foreign policy (and particularly, U.S. foreign policy) is a fundamental concept. It is the dependent variable, the variable to be explained and/or described. (It is the dependent variable that has increasingly militarized.) It is useful to define U.S. foreign policy (y-dependent variable) conceptually such that the reader may easily understand and conceptualize y for himself or herself. Some years ago, Charles Kegley and the late Eugene Wittkopf[4] defined U.S. foreign policy conceptually as follows. Kegley and Wittkopf asserted that U.S. foreign policy was the *goals and/or objectives* that policy makers sought to achieve abroad, the *values* that shaped the said objectives (affected them, constrained them, etc.), and the *instruments* used to accomplish them. It is as good as any definition and will be used hereafter.

The Kegley-Wittkopf definition had the virtue of simplicity. (In truth, many books on foreign policy never bother to define it, thus leaving the reader to infer the definition indirectly.) The Kegley-Wittkopf definition, though simple, included three main concepts (think of them as indicators of the dependent variable, y). The three indicators are (1) *goals or objectives* (whatever word the reader prefers), (2) the *values* that affect those objectives over time (one may think of this as America's *ethos*), and (3) the *instruments* by which the objectives are carried out or put into motion.

The Kegley-Wittkopf text asserted that five categories of inputs— independent variables—caused U.S. foreign policy to change or not change over time. For inputs (independent or x variables), Kegley and Wittkopf turned to James Rosenau's pre-theory construct. Accordingly, the following fivefold set of inputs affected U.S. foreign policy over time: external-systemic, societal, governmental, individual, and finally role inputs.[5]

Without belaboring the inputs, the reader should understand, briefly, what is meant by each. Any nation-state (or other actor) has things external, events outside its borders to which it reacts and responds: invasions, economic crises, various kinds of wars, balances of power, and the like, which cause policy makers to respond. Such events constitute *external-systemic inputs* of foreign policy.

Pluralistic societies such as the United States have societal inputs like public opinion, transmitters of public opinion (news media), special interest groups that lobby for both domestic and foreign policy (American Israel Public Affairs Committee [AIPAC], pro-Arab groups), elections and political parties, and so on. These constitute *societal inputs*. For example, the ubiquity of cable news networks that must churn out news constantly—or at least package events as news even when they have ceased being news—affects U.S. foreign policy (domestic policy too), as do presidential elections. Just consider how Donald Trump's jump into the GOP's pool of candidates drove other candidates to react to Trump's border wall (both a foreign policy and domestic issue). Societal inputs are complex and interconnected in a pluralistic society like the United States. However, even a closed society or closed polity such as North Korea (the DPRK) likewise has societal inputs, just far fewer. In the DPRK, the military, for instance, constitutes a massive special interest group.

Additionally, a nation-state like the United States has a large foreign policy bureaucracy (or rather, competing bureaucracies) including the defense and state departments, the intelligence community (from CIA to NSA to Naval intelligence), and others—commerce, agriculture, so forth—that affect making U.S. foreign policy. (The foreign policy behemoth of the United States probably implements foreign policy more often than makes it, but its influence is felt in many ways. Bureaucracy often constrains rapid or dramatic change, for instance.) Think of these *government inputs* as bureaucracy conforming, largely, to the rules of bureaucracy everywhere. Bureaucracy can create an impetus for change or it can constrain foreign policy—mostly the latter.

In the United States, key members of the president's cabinet—as will be seen—secretaries of state and defense, the president's advisers for security and counterterrorism, and Joint Chiefs of Staff—regularly meet with the president to address foreign policy challenges. (The reader will soon see a set of these advisers is called the National Security Council principals and the NSC was created by something called the National Security Act of 1947, an important focus of the present study.) Each presidential adviser has personality and management idiosyncrasies and those differences have the potential to affect U.S. foreign policy (particularly in the NSC setting but elsewhere too). These are *individual inputs* of U.S. foreign policy and they include, importantly, individual presidents and their idiosyncratic differences.

By contrast to individual inputs, however, each of the mentioned positions has *role expectations* also. The American people expect the president and secretary of defense (and others) to behave in certain ways and those roles come to shape the individual, often more than the individual shapes the office or role. In addition to role expectations by the public when a candidate becomes president and nominates cabinet and NSC advisers, several of these positions also have role expectations and role shapes the office holder as often as the office holder shapes the role. These constitute *role inputs*.[6]

Each of these five inputs (all inputs should be considered independent—x—or exogenous variables) all have the potential to affect U.S. foreign policy at a given time. So if the dependent variable (y) is U.S. foreign policy as defined previously, then the various inputs (x-external-systemic, x-societal, *x*-governmental, *x*-individual, and *x*-role) cause U.S. foreign policy—its goals and objectives, the values that shape them, and so forth—to be what it is at any given time.

Kegley and Wittkopf conceptualized U.S. foreign policy as a funnel into which all five sets of inputs flowed *mixing given* over time and circumstance—what they called process—and ultimately creating U.S. foreign policy as output. They wisely included feedback loops such that their readers understood that the foreign policy of a previous administration (call it Time One) affects the foreign policy of its successors (call it Time Two). Each new president inherits the foreign policy positions of his predecessor and unless and until the new administration changes those policies, they are still in effect. For present purposes, this should prove sufficient to conceptualize foreign policy as a relatively simple input-output device with inputs going in and any change in objectives the output.

In accepting the Kegley-Wittkopf definition of U.S foreign policy, it is important to discuss briefly values and instruments. *American values* tend to be enduring things that last over multiple generations. That is not to say they are unimportant—they are very important. But only over very long periods of time would one expect them to change and therefore to change goals and/or objectives. *Instruments*, by contrast, change as often as technology changes. However, it turns out presidents tend to use the same groups of instruments over four or eight years of a presidency just as the previous president did. (The only instrument not included is nuclear weapons, used only by President Harry S. Truman to end World War II.)

Both American values and the instruments of U.S. foreign policy are important in understanding foreign policy. But for present purposes, neither values nor instruments tell us much about the potential for *change* in *y* (U.S. foreign policy output). In this study, a principal thesis is that U.S. foreign policy changed beginning with World War II and as the Cold War began, neither values nor instruments are likely to account for much of said change. Put differently, as asserted earlier, U.S. foreign policy has become militarized over two periods: the Cold War and post-Cold War periods. Each year, U.S. foreign policy became incrementally more militarized than the previous year. Thus, values and instruments are likely to be less important in explaining why this continuity began shortly after World War II and continued through various phases of the Cold War and since. After all, if values accounted for the militarization of U.S. foreign policy, then one might expect to see militarization long before the 20th century.

The argument made next is that U.S. foreign policy changed beginning with World War II (hardly a surprise) but continued to change even more as the Cold War commenced. During the Cold War, new patterns of U.S. foreign policy—reflecting changing *objectives*—emerged, and these new objectives help account for the militarization of U.S. foreign policy from the late 1940s through the present. Beyond the Cold War, it is argued herein that the patterns evidenced during the Cold War continued, so the

Cold War alone cannot account for the militarization of U.S. foreign policy. Otherwise, it should have ceased sometime after the Cold War ended. Instead, the militarization of U.S. foreign policy continued and, indeed, increased to some extent. In short, once fascism and communism were slain, U.S. policy makers found new monsters to warrant U.S. attention.[7] The principal focus of this book is to discover why these periods of militarization occurred and therefore goals and objectives likewise changed, *strike me, as the appropriate focus of the definition used.*

THE CONTINUITY OF U.S. FOREIGN POLICY

A peculiarity of the United States' democracy is that Americans tend to assume that each time a new president is elected (every four or eight years) U.S. foreign policy must perforce change. I suppose it is because we hold so much stock in elections and in exercising our franchise to elect our leaders. Thus, it has become intuitive that most Americans simply assume that foreign policy changes with each new president.

In fact, if one begins to look at specific goals or objectives, one is struck by how constant goals or objectives are over time. Since the United States became an important world power (beginning in the late 19th century and maturing into a superpower by the end of World War II), many of its foreign policy objectives have remained constant. During the Cold War, a key goal was to prevent the USSR from expanding beyond its sphere of influence. That has not changed very much in the post-Cold War era (though the focus is now Russia not the USSR). In recent years, the United States recommenced its containment of Russia and the Russian federation— something the United States did openly of the USSR during the Cold War. Nor is its containment limited to Russia. The United States now contains the People's Republic of China in East Asia and various "rogue states," such as Iran and North Korea. Since the 1990s, myriad transnational threats have arisen, and the United States seeks to disrupt and contain them as well.

While it may seem counterintuitive at first blush, it is not so unusual that U.S. foreign policy changes only slowly, incrementally, and largely on the margins. If U.S. foreign policy underwent radical change every four years, it would be difficult for an ally or an enemy to adapt. Also, while it is theoretically possible for presidents to have different personality types or management styles, it does not take long to realize that presidents have much more in common than different. The U.S. presidents tend to be lawyers, tend to have gone to Ivy Leagues Schools, and tend to be WASPY (notwithstanding President Obama being the first African American president). They, therefore, tend to be socialized in similar ways.

What about the terrible things presidential candidates say about each other when campaigning? First, when candidates are campaigning, they are acting as candidates rather than presidents (the role, as noted earlier, is quite different). Second, foreign policy is not defined herein in such a way as to expect campaign rhetoric to affect foreign policy. Third, and as suggested in discussing role, once in office presidents join a pretty exclusive club and observation shows that they tend to adapt themselves rather quickly to their predecessor's views of things. They learn how difficult it is to be president, how little real power they have to change things and, of course, they typically are cautious during their first four years to ensure they get the opportunity to be president their second four years. (It will be interesting to see whether President Trump fits the post-World War II and post-Cold War pattern?)

In fact, if one thinks just a little bit about the inputs (the five sets of x variables affecting U.S. foreign policy), it becomes clear why change—by which change in U.S. foreign policy objectives is meant—is the exception rather than the rule. From external-systemic standpoint, the United States has been a superpower or hegemonic power since early in the Cold War: the four-plus decades of the Cold War and now the two-plus decades since. Accordingly, the United States is vested in the system it helped to create. The United States helped to create both the UN system (in which the United States is one of five powers with an exclusive veto vote in the UN Security Council, the P-5) and the Bretton Woods system (in which the United States is the dominant shareholder).

One useful way to think about U.S. foreign policy is to concede that the United States has many foreign policy objectives but it has one main, overriding foreign policy objective. To wit, the United States is interested and active in maintaining the status quo of the systems it helped create and in which it plays a key role. During the Cold War and since, the United States has been vested in maintaining the status quo, as it is a system in which the United States is a very important player. The status quo during the Cold War was a bipolar system in which both the United States and the USSR found advantages. Both superpowers began with a view of vanquishing its competitor but once nuclear annihilation became possible, each found it advantageous to maintain the bipolar system that existed.

The United States certainly spends a great deal of energy monitoring the external-systemic world but since its foreign policy objectives are those of a status quo power, U.S. behavior is quite predictable. That is probably why it seems hypocritical to critics of the United States at times. The United States will occasionally act on some principle but it more often acts in its own self-interest and most often it finds that its self-interest and preserving the status quo are one and the same. (No value judgment about the United States is intended. Rome sought to preserve the system it once dominated and the UK did likewise centuries later. The United States is simply doing what others have done; indeed, the United States has often maintained the status quo relatively benignly.[8])

The point is that if maintaining the status quo is critical to the United States then other foreign policy objectives are secondary or perhaps tertiary. They come after the status quo in terms of import. That is not to say that the domestic sources of U.S. foreign policy (societal, governmental, individual, and role inputs) are unimportant in affecting U.S. foreign policy. But, it is possible that they too have a tendency toward stasis. Let us quickly consider the possibility.

Bureaucracy (government inputs) may likewise constrain change in foreign policy objectives for multiple reasons. The bureaucracy is also maintaining the status quo, insofar as it makes choices. The Defense Department, for instance, is working to ensure the external-systemic inputs do not adversely affect the United States' position as a status quo power, just as the State Department attempts to do the same thing in its own peculiar way. (Defense is tasked with defending the United States once engaged in war; state is tasked with diplomacy or avoiding war when possible.) Moreover, the bureaucracy is so massive, so behemoth that it operates according to standard operating procedures (SOPs). For the most part, the bureaucracy slow walks change, prevents change, and even fears change (insofar as it thinks about it at all). Bureaucracies are notorious for constraining rapid or dramatic change.

Consider societal inputs likewise. Societal inputs have the potential to cause change, by their very nature. However, as most of us who study foreign policy understand, Americans are very badly informed about foreign policy. Many Americans consider it esoteric, arcane, and in any case, most Americans are interested in what is best for their individual interests and not what is in America's interest. Americans like to criticize presidents vehemently (including presidents' foreign policy objectives, insofar as they understand foreign policy), but survey after survey demonstrates Walter Lippmann's old maxim about Americans being the bewildered herd was not too far amiss.

That Americans remain relatively ignorant of foreign policy is not a very positive commentary of the media either. What else can be observed about the media and foreign policy? First, there is not a lot of reporting on foreign policy per se. In fact, the media do not do well (as a group) on knowing the difference between foreign and domestic policy. Moreover, the media play the role of a gadfly. They like to muck things up and play "got you," but they often do little serious analysis of foreign policy. In fact, the media are like most Americans. The media may shape public opinion in some ways, but they seldom educate or enlighten Americans about U.S. foreign policy. If they did, Americans could not be so poorly informed.[9]

Finally, consider the average American. He or she is busy working and taking care of his or her family. It is common to have both parents work these days and Americans work more hours and have insufficient time to worry about their families, much less U.S. foreign policy. Given the demand on his or her time, he or she simply does not find much time to read about foreign policy thereby relegating his or her sense of what is happening in foreign policy to television. And the television media are among the worst offenders in terms of helping Americans understand foreign policy.

Consider the cable news format with its 24-hour time horizon during which television media repeat the same stories hour after hour (and have the temerity to call it breaking news). All media in the United States (with very few exceptions) are owned by corporations and the media are, therefore, far from a public service that educates and enlightens. In fact, the old axiom that "If it bleeds, it leads" is not far from the truth in today's media conglomerates. For every conservative cable television network, there is an equal and opposite reaction from a liberal or progressive television network and vice versa. Frankly, it has long produced a race toward the bottom.

That the media perform so poorly in terms of informing the public about foreign policy is not a minor concern. Nor is the fact that Americans fit Lippmann's bewildered herd so readily. Among other things it means that the American experiment in democracy is not working well, at least when it comes to foreign policy. Surely, it is important for the world's most important democracy to have an informed public. Surely, it matters whether the public understands how foreign policy works (even if does not immerse itself in the details). Surely, it is important for Americans to realize that since the Cold War, American foreign policy has developed recurring trends and patterns. Surely, it matters that the public knows that despite (in fact, in some ways because) the lack of the USSR to focus our attention, U.S. foreign policy has continued to militarize. Surely, it is important even today for Americans to know enough about foreign policy to carrying on an intelligent conversation about it.

Finally, what about individual and role inputs? As noted earlier, they are almost opposite sides of the same coin. That is, individual inputs are dependent on cabinet members (actually, NSC principals and deputies as will be seen) having different management styles and idiosyncratic personality traits that find their way into U.S. foreign policy objectives. To be sure, they sometimes do. President Reagan's famous aloof management style resulted in lower-level NSC staffers running foreign policy based on their understanding of what they thought Reagan wanted. (See the Iran-Contra case study, for instance.)

As already mentioned, presidents tend to be more alike than different and the same can be said generally for other top positions, with some exceptions. They are socialized similarly leading to much more in common than differences between them. But role tends to dominate the NSC, as will be seen later. While there are unique times—for example, foreign policy crises—when individuals have the opportunity to affect U.S. foreign policy objectives in a dramatic way, it is actually rare in practice.

That is because role tends to cancel out individual idiosyncrasies. Both the Democratic and Republican parties have "stables" of foreign policy experts who are apprenticed—in effect—when their party is in power. They fill the positions in State and Defense Departments and others bureaucracies (including the NSC) and role expectations strongly influence these "experts" from both parties.

One need only consider the Cold War or America's involvement in the Vietnam War to confirm continuity. The Vietnam War had equal numbers of Republican and Democratic administrations and yet their foreign policies (vis-à-vis Vietnam) were remarkably alike. For the Democrats, Presidents Truman, Kennedy (JFK), and Johnson (LBJ) kept Americans increasingly involved in Vietnam. For the Republicans, Eisenhower's two terms (with Vice President Richard Nixon), followed by Presidents Nixon and Ford likewise kept the United States involved until Congress forced their hands. The same is true of the Cold War: roughly equal numbers of Republicans and Democrats were part of the Cold War consensus that caused the United States to jettison its isolationist mind-set and to become a hegemonic power.

WHO MAKES FOREIGN POLICY?

Before moving forward, it is useful to say something about who makes foreign policy? The idealized answer, the one learned in civics class, is something like this. The president, in consultation with the Senate (who has advise and consent responsibilities per the Constitution) and with the funding of Congress (from whence all appropriations arise), make foreign policy. Moreover, in a democracy the people elect the president, and both chamber in Congress and, hence, they too have indirect influence in making foreign policy.

The problem with that answer is this. The National Security Act of 1947 affects the question of who makes foreign policy making the answer much more complicated. Certainly, Congress affects foreign policy through the aforementioned means, and the citizenry have the opportunity every two or four years to endorse or reject foreign policy as well as public policy. However, since about 1950 (the Korean War) it will be seen that the NSC makes foreign policy and Congress has deferred to it over time. To be sure, there are important Senate committees—the Senate Armed Services, Senate Select Intelligence Committee, and the Senate Foreign Relations Committee that debate foreign policy and affect it here and there—but the office of the presidency has grown very powerful from 1950 until the present day.

Frankly, Congress has largely deferred to the power of the presidency for many reasons. During the Cold War, nuclear annihilation was possible and in its wisdom Congress realized 535 persons organized in committees and subcommittees with rules of seniority and the rest simply was too cumbersome. Thus, Congress deferred to presidents time and again due to the threat of nuclear war. Likewise, Congress found it was somewhat liberating to allow the presidency to seize more and more power as few representatives of senators are elected based on their foreign policy acumen (the American people are far more informed and interested in domestic matters).

Beyond Capitol Hill's reasons for deferring, presidents of both Republican and Democratic administrations have seized more power for their own reasons. George W. Bush was not the first to assert the unitary theory of executive power. Indeed if not President John Adams then certainly President Jefferson made similar claims of presidential prerogatives.[10] During the Cold War, president after president found it convenient to dream up new ways to present what amounted to rewriting the Constitution's balance between executive and legislative branches. Finally, presidents who are stymied and frustrated with compromise and defeat in domestic politics learn they can have their way very often in foreign policy, and this too has led to greater presidential power in foreign affairs.

As will be seen in the next chapter, the NSC is where this power has resided since around 1950. Specifically, the National Security Council principals committee has evolved and become the apex of U.S. foreign policy making, though the deputies committee and NSC staffers too have powers in foreign policy few Americans realize.

THE PRINCIPAL THESIS

A principal thesis of this book is that the National Security Act of 1947 is understudied and poorly understood *benchmark* in U.S. foreign policy. Next, it will be asserted that the National Security Act created the necessary conditions (though not sufficient) for the rise of the American Security State. The reader will find that the act marked a turning point in U.S. foreign policy. In fact, the act created the unified Defense Department, the Permanent Intelligence Community and, importantly, the NSC inside the presidency because of what both Republican and Democratic policy makers believed: Soviet expansionism was a grave threat that the United States felt compelled to oppose. The broad-based support for containing the USSR is part of what is called the Cold War consensus that began to take shape in late 1945 and was fully formed by 1947 or 1948. The USSR had been a World War II ally but quickly went from being an ally to enemy number one as surrenders were taken at the end of World War II.

Both Republicans and Democrats were sufficiently exercised by what they saw as Soviet aggression that they created new institutions in U.S. foreign policy. That is, the consensus was bipartisan. The National Security Act and the institutions it created were neither a secret nor hidden. There was plenty of time for the public to find out about the statute and the new institutions it created. For whatever reasons—and there are many—the public did not delve deeply into the act nor did the public care much about the institutions created. The atmosphere was of nuclear brinkmanship and potential crises so the act was passed and the institutions created with little fuss.

A principal result of these institutions has been *the militarization of U.S. foreign policy*. Those who comprised the Cold War consensus realized that U.S. foreign policy would necessarily become militarized and they held that such militarization was badly needed given the end of European hegemony (in particular, Pax Britannica). Without strong European states to hold Russia-USSR in check, the United States would perforce need to act so militarization was necessary.

DEFINING MILITARIZATION?

Already "militarization" has been used multiple times. What is meant by militarization precisely? The *Oxford English Dictionary* defines the verb to militarize as to "give (something, especially an organization) a military character or style: *militarized police forces*." Its secondary meaning is to "equip or supply (a place) with soldiers and other military resources: a militarized security zone."[11]

In what follows "to militarize" or the militarization of foreign policy is not a value judgment. Rather, it refers to the observation that the United States has increasingly used the military instruments of foreign policy (as opposed to nonmilitary ones) over the course of the Cold War and since. In the definition of foreign policy mentioned earlier, it was conceded that instruments were the means of effecting some foreign policy goal or objective. Therefore, militarization refers simply to an increased reliance on military instruments over other traditional instruments of statecraft such as diplomacy, foreign assistance, arms and other technology transfers, defensive security regimes, and the like. It also includes goals or objectives that require military instruments.

Put slightly differently, in maintaining the status quo, the United States helped create the bipolar system that prevailed during the Cold War, the UN system of joint governance, and the unipolar system since the Cold War ended, as well as parts of the Bretton Woods system; the U.S. has increasingly relied on military instruments to maintain the status quo. Prior to World War II, the United States was a relatively minor military power so that it confined its use of military power mostly to its own hemisphere (with a few notable exceptions). With World War II and the commencement of the Cold War, the United States became an important military power globally. It is hardly surprising, therefore, that it would increasingly rely on its military might to enforce the status quo. Nevertheless, few Americans appreciate these observations. The militarization patterns can be seen as follows.

First, in passing the National Security Act of 1947, the United States created a unified Defense Department (the Department of Defense) and as that bureaucracy has grown and required increasing annual appropriations, policy makers have come to rely on Defense, quite naturally, increasingly over other cabinet departments (State for instance). Interestingly, the two political parties agree on few things, domestic or in foreign policy. However, one thing they have both agreed to increasingly—and for different reasons often—is to send the military to achieve foreign policy goals. So, whether a Democrat or a Republican was in the White House and likewise whether Democrats or Republicans controlled Capitol Hill, policy makers have relied more on the Defense Department than other cabinet bureaucracies.

The Republican Party is ideologically inclined to tout the military for virtually every foreign policy issue or challenge. Republicans in both the House and Senate have close relationships with defense contractors and Pentagon sources and they mutually reinforce one another's tendencies. Since the mid-1990s, the Vulcans or neoconservative wing of the GOP has explicitly stated that the United States needs to be prepared to use its military power for effecting positive outcomes in world politics, such as democratization. Though some backlash to that position has been seen recently (both Ron and Rand Paul), the Vulcans have strong influence over the GOP in terms of foreign policy.

The Democrats, particularly beginning with President William Clinton were determined not to be painted as "weak" on defense issues or defense spending. While they have touted multilateralism (whereas the GOP sometimes touts unilateralism), they have also embraced various kinds of "nation building" for political and ideological reasons. Certainly, from Clinton to President Obama, the Democrats have attempted to shape an image of willingness to use military instruments when necessary.

The result is militarization of U.S. foreign policy: both parties agree to send the military for nearly every kind of problem that the United States faces in world politics. Not just challenges from other states' militaries but from transnational threats that have grown since the 1990s. Given that deploying the military suits either party for different reasons makes it the default option often times. If there is a tsunami in Asia, send the military. If there is an earthquake in Haiti, again the military is sent. (The Pentagon's logistics are spectacular.) If Saddam Hussein invades Kuwait, the United States sends the military. As we know from 9/11, the United States had sent the military into several parts of the Middle East and North Africa (MENA) to ensure U.S. interests.

Beyond the proclivity to send the military, the media have stopped functioning as the adversarial fourth estate. The major media have become corporate conglomerates with highly paid reporters who need access from both political parties as well as from the Pentagon with its massive annual appropriation. Some of the most important reporters in Washington, D.C., regularly allow the Pentagon to send them on what used to be called junkets. The media have become docile.

As noted earlier, the American people are incredibly poorly informed. Poll after poll, decade after decade demonstrates the American people know little about the world abroad. Self-identified experts on foreign policy (they exist in both parties) regularly defer to the military in theaters of war. The American people docilely take their cues from these sources in both parties.

If the American people are poorly informed, then it stands to reason that the United States' "free" media have become part of the problem. Instead of the adversarial role of the media, they have become "embedded" in relationships with the military and handfuls of self-identified military experts arisen in the media. To do otherwise would be to jeopardize their access to scoops leaked from the Pentagon (and from Capitol Hill, the White House, and parts of the Intelligence Community). Simply put, the media rarely raise issues such as the militarization of foreign policy. (Even when the occasional leak about surveillance or the national security sees the light of day, as with the Snowden leaks, the stories last relatively short times then disappear.)

But the story is even more complex than the rise of the Pentagon and the American Security State. As will be seen shortly, the National Security Act of 1947 created additional institutions that have hastened the rise of the American Security State. As this book goes to publication (2017), it will be 70 years since the National Security Act and the institutions thereby created have all contributed to the militarization of U.S. foreign policy (and arguably the diminution of Congress in foreign policy).

WHAT THE READER MAY EXPECT HEREAFTER?

In what follows, the reader will be introduced to the Cold War consensus, a bipartisan consensus about the Soviet threat following World War II. (The Soviets were allied with the United Kingdom and the United States against Nazi Germany from mid-1941 onward.) In a relatively short period of time, U.S. policy makers (both in the executive and legislative branches) came to view the Soviets as a threat to the democratic world and the United States in particular. The Cold War consensus accounts for this 180-degree change.

The Cold War consensus also explains why the National Security Act of 1947 was passed. Therefore, the National Security Act of 1947 and the critical institutions it created in U.S. foreign policy will be presented in some detail. These institutions led, quite directly, to the militarization of U.S. foreign policy.

Nor was it particularly unexpected that the said institutions would lead to the militarization of U.S. foreign policy. Indeed, as seen by many policy makers of the Cold War consensus, the problem was the old European balance of power system collapsed leaving little if anything to check Soviet expansionist tendencies. But beyond the collapse of Pax Europaea (and particularly Pax Britannica), many policy makers who formed the Cold War consensus believed the United States would necessarily have to check the Soviets, at least in the short to medium term. Coupled with lessons from Pearl Harbor, the Cold War consensus held that the United States must therefore fill the void left by the European power vacuum.

Though it will become clear in the next chapter, the Cold War consensus was both bipartisan and held by both ends of Pennsylvania Avenue (Capitol Hill and the White House). A question arises whether lawmakers intended to forego the powerful prerogatives Congress had held since the founding of the Republic? The answer appears to be in the affirmative. The reader might rightly wonder why? That answer is not simple but may be rendered relatively straightforward as follows.

First, consider the structure of the Congress. Congress is comprised of 100 senators (two for each state) along with 435 House members (divided into districts that get adjusted each decade by census). Both chambers have seniority rules and committee structures that permit the senior members to choose the plum positions (in domestic and foreign policy). Every senator or House member has staffers to grapple over difficult choices. The members have to spend time raising money for reelection.

For example, consider the average senator whose reelection campaign six years hence will require $20 million dollars. That means that every day of the senator's six years he or she must raise $9,133 for reelection. On top of that, one-thirds of the Senate is up for election every two years, thereby requiring two-thirds of the Senate to have run for reelection every four years (each presidential election year). The Congress is more problematic with all of Congress up for reelection each two years but the similar rules and exigencies are at work in both sides of Capitol Hill. Thus, members rely much more on their staffers for positions than the average American realizes. One result is deference with respect to foreign policy to the executive branch.

Additionally, given the brinkmanship and "crisis management" that permeated the Cold War, Congress easily slinked to the background relative to the presidency during the Cold War. By the end of the Cold War, a powerful presidency existed that the founders would not recognize. Indeed, the founders had carefully split powers, if anything, giving the Congress more power than the presidency in the Constitution.

For these reasons and others, lawmakers intentionally created a powerful presidency in terms of foreign policy, which necessarily diminished the power of Congress. Congress has occasionally attempted to wrest back some of the power it deferred but without success. (Interestingly, during the 2016 presidential campaign, Senator Rand Paul ran against the War Powers Act, as the cause of the imperial presidency. Candidate Paul mistakenly blamed the War Powers Act, which was an attempt by Congress to wrest power back, albeit an unsuccessful attempt.)[12]

ADDITIONAL EXPECTATIONS

The principal thesis of this book is that the National Security Act of 1947 created institutions that predictably resulted in the militarization of U.S. foreign policy. But there are other theses that will be considered.

One is that the American people—for any number of reasons—are largely ignorant of the *act* and its history or even the Cold War consensus.

Nor is there reason to believe those who passed it contrived to keep it secret. On the contrary, they debated it and in 1946 and 1947 the debate was held publicly. Thus, other reasons must explain why so few Americans know of the act of the three institutions it created and how they have affected U.S. foreign policy.

Another assertion is that the militarization of U.S. foreign policy during the Cold War was predictable and unsurprising (even if most Americans are ignorant of it). But once the Cold War concluded, a debate occurred about a "peace dividend" the presumed savings the United States could reprogram for domestic needs given the reality that the United States need no longer contain the USSR. (During the past few years, Russia and the United States, indeed the West, have returned to a state of tensions. But the USSR no longer exists. Still, many of the institutions created to contain the USSR—for example, the North Atlantic Treaty Organization or NATO—continued churning out policies that look as though the USSR continued to exist.) President George H.W. Bush decreased defense spending for three consecutive years as the Cold War ended.[13] But since then both Republican and Democratic presidents have increased spending steadily.

By the time President George H.W. Bush left office and President Bill Clinton took over, talk of a peace dividend had disappeared. First, the return of ugly nationalism in former Yugoslavia occupied the attention of policy makers, with some reason. Second, the rise of transnationalism (al Qaeda and like-minded groups) provided a new threat that challenged the traditional instruments of statecraft such as deterrence. (Deterrence requires [1] that the actor being deterred desires to live to fight another day and [2] that its return address is certain.)

So even with the Cold War over and the United States a world hegemonic power (whereas during the Cold War it had been one of two superpowers), the militarization continued. In the 24 or so years since the Cold War ended, the United States has continued to militarize its foreign policy. In fact, an interesting observation is that both Democrats and Republican presidents, irrespective of which party controls Capitol Hill, militarize U.S. foreign policy.

This leads to yet another supplemental thesis. Namely, U.S. foreign policy is remarkably similar over time (the continuity hypothesis already mentioned). If one divides U.S. foreign policy into a simple chronological typology—America's origins until about the 20th century, the rise of American power during World War II through the Cold War, and the post-Cold War period—the only significant change of objectives is traceable in the transition from period one to two. That is to say, even if one accepts that America's early years saw foreign policy that was introverted or isolationist, from about World War II forward, U.S. foreign policy is anything but introverted. On the contrary, the United States effectively supplanted the last of the European empires (Pax Britannica) and has sought to stay atop the heap since that time irrespective of which party controls the White House or Capitol Hill.

SUMMARY

In the next chapter, the reader will be introduced to the National Security Act of 1947 and why it was passed. I will develop the Cold War consensus and why both Republicans and Democrats believed they must act quickly and create institutions that were, in some sense, contrary to the Constitution.

Thereafter, a chronological typology will be employed—slightly different from above—and the case study chapters that form the basic data source for this analysis—presented. Case studies from the earliest years of the Cold War (when Truman and Eisenhower have tremendous flexibility to wrest power from Congress and improvise U.S. foreign policy), the main decades of the Cold War (1960s through 1980s), and the post-Cold War era (1991–2015) will be presented (Chapters 3, 4, and 5, respectively). The typology will help to make generalizable observations from the case study data.

Finally, two chapters are presented after the case studies to consider the evidence the case studies supply (Chapters 6 and 7). In those chapters, observations and generalizations will be drawn from the case studies. The book will conclude with some normative observations as well.

CHAPTER 2

The Cold War, the Cold War Consensus, and the National Security Act of 1947

PRÉCIS OF U.S. FOREIGN POLICY, 1944–1946

On April 12, 1945, at around 13:00 hours in Warm Springs, Georgia, President Roosevelt was preparing for luncheon. He had some visitors with him who saw Roosevelt wave his hand around his forehead and heard him complain of a terrible headache. Shortly thereafter, Roosevelt was in a sort of swoon then soon thereafter dead.[1]

Back in Washington, D.C., the new vice president, Harry S. Truman congregated on Capitol Hill with colleagues from his previous job as Senator Truman. As Congress debated "the Mexican water issue," Vice President Truman decided to write a letter home to Missouri. Senator Alexander Wiley (R-WI) finished his speech on the water issue just before 17:00 hours. Vice President Truman crossed the Senate's private lobby, headed to the vice president's office in the Capitol when somebody told Truman he needed to return a call from the White House. Truman returned the White House call whereupon Steve Early (FDR's pressman) requested the vice president to come immediately to the White House using the main entrance on Pennsylvania Avenue. It was about 17:15 hours. Upon entering the second floor, Eleanor Roosevelt, her daughter, and son-in-law, John Boettiger, and Early informed Truman that Roosevelt was dead. Vice President Truman had met with President Roosevelt (excluding cabinet meetings) only twice, once on March 8 and again on March 19, 1945.[2]

Just weeks before FDR died in Georgia, the president had attended the second of three Big Three meetings (United States, United Kingdom, and USSR) in Yalta, Ukraine (USSR). At Yalta, the Big Three bargained over the final disposition of troops, surrender of troops in Europe, and where the respective troops of the Big Three would be stationed for approximately two years, while Europe rebuilt. A third meeting was schedules for late July into August (1945) in Potsdam, East Germany (in Soviet-occupied Germany).

Interestingly, while meeting at Potsdam, President Truman would learn that the atom bomb (the Manhattan Project) was no longer theory but was a fact. In New Mexico, scientists and military personnel had tested an atom bomb and assembled two more for use in compelling a Japanese surrender (which they did later in August).

President Truman was inheriting a very different world from the one that had existed just a few months before. In the post-World War II world, Britain was prostrated and nearly bankrupt. The former empire, on which the sun never set, effectively ceased to exist. In fact, the former Europe-dominated world of colonial empires was no more, though it would muddle on for years trying to regain its former influence. In its place, a new world dominated by two new "superpowers" came to exist.

The United States with its capitalist mode of production and its representative democracy would soon be called the First World. The Soviet Union with its state-planned economy (with five-year plans and state-control economy) and its single-party polity (the Soviet Communist Party) would soon be called the Second World. Those aligned with neither superpower would soon be called the Third World (aka, the nonaligned movement).

The two superpowers dominated world politics and their respective foreign policies trumped others for the better part of the next five decades. Not until 1989–1991 when the USSR ceased to exist did the Cold War yield to something else. During the Cold War, the two superpowers built military behemoths that others could not rival. Nuclear deterrence became the principal force that tempered either the United States or the USSR, as each superpower viewed the other with deep mistrust and worked to destabilize the other, while seeking to avoid nuclear war.

The Cold War had begun. In a leftover residual of World War II, a movement began to unify the War Department under a secretary of defense. The said movement eventually became the National Security Act of 1947, as will be detailed below. It is likely similar changes occurred in the USSR, though both the USSR and today's Russia are beyond the current scope and purpose.

In April 1945, President Truman inherited the aforementioned. Indeed, Truman inherited a legacy of misunderstandings and growing concerns (from both Washington, D.C., and Moscow). Soon, the United States (with the United Kingdom, France, West Germany, and others) squared off against its former World War II ally across the abyss of a nuclear Cold War. The USSR reciprocated by building and maintaining a massive military presence throughout Europe (half of Germany and much of East Europe). Within two years (the middle of 1947), an emerging consensus in America (what is called the Cold War consensus hereafter) held the USSR as an extreme menace.

In 1946 and again in 1947, the Truman administration became alarmed at Soviet machinations in Turkey (soon to be a member of NATO) and Greece. In Berlin (the seat of government of East Germany or DDR), the allies squared off, each controlling sectors that would eventually precipitate the Berlin Airlift "crisis" by which time the National Security Act was law and the United States continued the militarization of U.S. foreign policy that had begun with World War II.

AMERICA AS AN UNINTENTIONAL SUPERPOWER

America did not start out as an empire, of course. Rather, America began as a colonial experiment of sorts. America's founding fathers descended from British subjects who fled the homeland for any number of reasons. Within a few generations, Americans were becoming tradesman, professionals (lawyers, doctors, clergy), and farmers. The American Revolution provoked an irreparable breach between Britain (King George II, later King George III) and the soon-to-be revolutionaries.

After the Revolution, America necessarily focused inward. The United States of America had modest foreign policy ambitions that turned around laissez-faire economics, freedom of navigation (necessary for capitalism), Americans' self-perception of isolationism, and eventually the Monroe Doctrine (dividing the European Hemisphere from our own), which memorialized American "isolationism." Whether the United States was ever isolationist beyond the War of 1812 is of little consequence for present purposes. That many Americans conceived of themselves as isolationists, including many members of Congress, is clear. Moreover, the United States eschewed European politics and focused on Latin America and eventually Asia as a Pacific power.

Where and when did America's modest foreign policy objectives change, therefore, becomes an interesting question? Some argue that the change came late in the 19th century. Certainly, President William McKinley and his peers conceived of the United States in more glorious and expansive terms than the founders. But the American people continued to harbor perceptions of isolationism after McKinley.

Nevertheless, by FDR's 1944 reelection (his fourth term), the United States had given up any pretenses of isolationism. (Loch Johnson thinks it may have been the Spanish-American War near the end of the previous century when America finally jettisoned isolationism. For present purposes it matters little whether it was the 1890s or the 1940s.)[3] Japan's invasion of Pearl Harbor on December 7, 1941, handed President Roosevelt a gift that allowed him to outmaneuver any residual isolationist sentiment in America. (Famous pilot Charles Lindbergh continued to assert isolationism even after Pearl Harbor, but the movement was a dead letter after Japan's invasion.) Somewhere between FDR and Truman, America rejected any pretense of isolationism once and for all. Thenceforth, U.S. foreign policy began to change, fairly dramatically.

As World War II neared its conclusion, some important decision junctures are worth mentioning. The summits at Yalta (early 1945) and Potsdam (July-August 1945) between the allies were two such turning points. The so-called Big Three (United States, Britain, and USSR) met at the summits to agree on how to accept the German surrender and how to coordinate efforts in the Pacific Theater following Germany's surrender. Eventually, Truman, Churchill (and Churchill's replacement, Clement Atlee), and Josef Stalin had to discuss similar terms for Japan's surrender.[4]

Nearly as soon as those agreements were made, mutual suspicions abounded between England and the United States and their nominal ally the USSR. (To be sure, suspicions had arisen earlier but the Yalta and Potsdam seem to have constituted turning points in the alliance of the Big Three.) Interestingly, FDR and Truman as well as Churchill all believed they were persuasive enough to change Stalin from his anti-West, anti-capitalist worldview. None of them succeeded. Stalin, it seems, was fated to harbor every kind of paranoid suspicion of both the British and the American leaders.[5]

Among other things, Stalin redrew the borders of Poland, and neither the British nor American leaders forced Stalin to back off from the new borders. Next, the borders of Germany were disputed. As World War II came to a conclusion in Europe, the Soviet army approached Berlin from the east; the other allies approached Berlin from the west. Germany was divided into two distinct spheres by Victory in Europe (VE) Day (May 8, 1945). It would not be unified again until 1989.

Without belaboring the precise agreements reached at Yalta and Potsdam, one key issue seemed to divide the Big Three. The three leaders agreed that the allies would necessarily have to stay in Europe for a time in order to accept the surrender of German troops. The questions were (1) how long the allies would stay and (2) what would happen at the end of that period?

From both FDR's and Truman's perspectives, the disaster of World War II provided a potential silver lining. Europe might finally move past its feudal and subsequent colonial history and become a source of democracy in the world. As the world's first democratic republic, the United States had long hoped all of Europe would reject monarchy and turn to democratization and republicanism.

Therefore, the United States came away from the summits believing that the Allies would stay about two years, after which elections would be held in the war-torn lands of Europe. The thinking was that in two years' time, sufficient infrastructure would be rebuilt and enough crops planted so that Europeans might finally turn to political reform. This proved a key misunderstanding among the Allies, in addition to others.

Beyond the summits, myriad issues began to exacerbate mutual suspicions that began late in the war. In the next two sections, a brief review of the early Cold War chronology is presented. The said chronology provides the reader with the context in which American lawmakers and policy makers eventually took actions to contain the USSR, a major volte-face as will be seen in U.S. foreign policy objectives.

THE COLD WAR CONSENSUS

In the previous chapter, the Cold War consensus was mentioned. In doing so, it was noted that the consensus was a bipartisan consensus, as well as a consensus between key lawmakers and key members of President Truman's White House. As suspicions of Soviet motives at Yalta and Potsdam grew in the United States, both ends of Pennsylvania Avenue became convinced of several critical premises concerning world politics and America's role therein. Since these premises formed the basis of containment of the USSR, they are worth noting.

First, a crucial member of the U.S. Senate who was peerless in terms of his isolationist credentials, Senator Arthur Vandenberg (R-MI), began changing his views as World War II neared its conclusion. Importantly, Senator Vandenberg chaired the powerful Senate Foreign Relations Committee and gave an important speech in which he said that under his leadership U.S. foreign policy must become bipartisan. Specifically, he used the phrase that politics in U.S. foreign policy must stop at the "water's edge."[6] Vandenberg's conversion to bipartisanship in foreign policy profoundly affected what became the Cold War consensus.

The following month, President Franklin Roosevelt attended Yalta where (at least from America's perspective) Stalin and Churchill struck bargains carving Europe into spheres of influence. (Within two years, the British would be insolvent and forced to retreat from their colonial empires.) Of course, President Roosevelt died in mid-April leaving his vice president, Harry S. Truman, in a difficult position. FDR had consulted with Truman a total of two times (apart from cabinet meetings) and had told Truman neither about FDR's plans for Manhattan (America's atom bomb program) nor the deals struck at Yalta.

What President Truman knew was that FDR had put America's prestige behind the United Nations. When Truman became president in April, VE Day was fewer than four weeks away. But the United States would thereafter shift its fighting almost entirely to the Pacific Theater until later in the year (August 1945), when two atom bombs ended Japan's continuation of World War II.

Over the next two years—and that chronology will be presented in detail in the following section—the outline of the Cold War consensus arose and it contained the following points of agreement. First, the Soviet Union—formerly an ally—represented a grave threat to the United States and the democratic world the United States supported. (The previous year, the United States and other democratic states formed the Bretton Woods Agreement in order to foster laissez-faire economics.) In 1945, the United States and others would draft the United Nations charter leading to creation of a liberal political system. From Washington, D.C., both the *economic* and *political* systems the United States backed were challenged by the Soviets.

Second, the Cold War consensus held that given Europe's atrophy in terms of world power (much of Europe was razed by war) the United States must necessarily lead world politics, at least in the short to medium term. Whether Europe would regain its one dominant role was never carefully examined by policy makers in Washington, though many expected Europe would. That the United States would fill the gap in the interim was critical to the Cold War consensus. Of course, U.S. leadership was contrary to America's previous isolationism.

Third, the consensus held that containment would be the preferred means of checking Soviet expansion. Though the United States had an atom bomb monopoly, no one doubted the Soviets would eventually catch up. Therefore, at some point the Soviets would likely reach parity in terms of weapons of mass destruction (WMD). (It was not until late 1949 that the United States confirmed the Soviets tested their own atomic weapon. And it was not until a couple of years later the Soviets detonated a thermonuclear weapon, or hydrogen bomb. That the Soviets would follow suit, however, was not in doubt.) Given the eventuality of parity, the only reasonable means of checking the Soviets would be to *contain* them, meaning erecting a physical barrier around the periphery of the USSR and setting trip-wire deterrence to make any Soviet expansion very costly.

Fourth, the United States must lead in terms of defense of the "democratic" world. This meant creating various collective security regimes such as NATO, SEATO, CENTO, and others. It also meant creating a group of like-minded allies inside the United Nations. It meant the United States would use "soft" power as well as hard power in containing the USSR.

Eventually, and fifth, the consensus held the United States must create a nuclear deterrent against the Soviets ever breaking containment. By the early 1960s, U.S. nuclear "blackmail" over the Soviets gave way to mutually assured destruction (MAD), a policy premised on both sides having ample first-strike capability to destroy the other. In turn, this led the United States and the USSR to focus on second-strike capability, so that if either side was foolish enough to launch a first strike, the other side would destroy the initiator with its second strike held in reserve. This led to additional nuclear arms spirals such as MIRVing missiles—putting multiple warheads on one ICBM—and deploying each side's deterrence on airplanes, land, and at sea or the nuclear triad.

These five points of agreement constituted the Cold War consensus that was increasingly held by the foreign policy elites of either political party and held by lawmakers and policy makers at Capitol Hill and the White House. The leadership of Republican Vandenberg in the Senate coupled with the Democratic president, Harry Truman created a bipartisan era of foreign policy which would last decades, through most of the Cold War.[7]

THE BEGINNING OF THE COLD WAR: A BRIEF CHRONOLOGY

As noted, suspicions between the allies were mutual and becoming pervasive as World War II neared conclusion in Europe. Tensions began to emerge between the western part of Germany (soon to be West Germany) and the Soviet-controlled eastern part of Germany (soon to be East Germany). But the suspicions were broader than Germany.

Late in the war the Soviets had moved into the Balkans, creating consternation in London and Washington, D.C. By 1946, it became clear that the Soviets were attempting to manipulate events and politics in Turkey. By 1947, it was both Greece and Turkey that alarmed the United States and United Kingdom.

In fact, the British government made the determination that it could no longer hold up its administrative duties in Greece by early 1947. Representatives from the United Kingdom's foreign ministry traveled to Washington to inform their State Department counterparts of the news. Apparently, the British thought it important enough to allow Washington to decide whether it would replace the British and England's duties in Greece. As many readers know, the direct result of these events was what eventually became known as the Truman Doctrine (more on it later).

By mid-1947, America increasingly assumed what were once England's responsibilities in the post-World War II architecture. The next flashpoint would be Germany again, this time Berlin.

Another part of the agreements made at the summits was that Berlin was sufficiently important—as the seat of the German government—that even though it lay entirely in the part of Germany controlled by the Soviets, Berlin would be a special case. Thus, Berlin was divided into sectors with the Allies each controlling real estate in Berlin. By early 1948, an array of issues rose to the forefront.

In any case, in reaction to what the Soviets perceived as provocative movements by the United States and the United Kingdom, the Soviets cut off access to the west to the sectors agreed to earlier. The Soviets perceived both the Truman Doctrine and the Marshall Plan (1947 and 1948 respectively) as grave provocations. Ultimately, the Soviets closed rail and road access to Berlin, in effect, making Berlin a Soviet-only city. President

Truman had come to realize he had little influence over Stalin after all. Indeed, Truman believed he must act lest the Soviets think the West apathetic and weak.

President Truman said as much in his memoirs of the period. "Russia was caught off guard by the Marshall Plan" (i.e., the U.S. plan to help Europe rebuild with financial assistance). He goes on to write that Moscow realized that it would be difficult for the Soviets to "communize" Western Europe. What Truman calls an even "more provocative move" was "to risk a military incident in Berlin, designated to test our firmness and our patience."[8]

President Truman's response was to airlift supplies into the sectors of Berlin to which the Soviets closed Western access. Everything from coal to food staples to currency was flown into Berlin, and the Berlin Airlift lasted over a year. It was costly but an effective way for Truman to demonstrate Washington's resolve to Stalin.

The policy of containment had already been formulated in 1946 and 1947. The Truman Doctrine memorialized the method by which the United States would seek to keep the Soviets from additional expansion. In 1949, the North Atlantic Treaty Organization (NATO) alliance was formed. From Moscow's viewpoint, Washington committed another grave provocation. The alliance was explicitly a collective defense regime that called for members to treat any Soviet invasion of any particular member as an invasion of all members.

In fact, 1949 was an important year for multiple reasons. Not only was NATO formed but the Chinese Communist Party—from Washington's perspective, an appendage of the Communist Party in the USSR—prevailed over the Nationalists (KMT) in China's civil war. The KMT fled to Formosa where it created the Republic of China (ROC) as an alternative to the People's Republic of China (PRC) on the mainland. In Washington, a new term was coined: *monolithic*. The USSR and the PRC were one and the same. The Soviets had accomplished an expansion into Asia despite containment.

Last but not least, late in 1949, the United States determined the USSR had detonated an atomic weapon (noted earlier), thereby voiding America's previous nuclear monopoly. No longer could Washington cow Moscow into desirable behavior—it really never had but that was beside the point. If the United States threatened retaliation with atomic weapons, the Soviets could match the threat, if not in 1949 soon enough. This was seen as a grave event in Washington.

Next, the Korean War began in June, 1950. Like other parts of the war-torn world, Asia had been divided between the Allies. Above what eventually became the 38th parallel on the Korean Peninsula, the Soviets and Chinese held sway. Below, the United States and Western allies held sway. When war began in June, the interpretation in Washington was clear.

Truman is clear and explicit in his memoirs about Korea. In spring 1948, as Truman discussed the disposition of Korea with his advisers, he and his advisers "knew that [Korea] was one of the places where the Soviet-controlled Communist world might choose to attack." Two years later in late June 1950, Truman analyzed the North Korean invasion across the parallel in the following terms. "I told my advisers that what was developing in Korea seemed to me like a repetition on a larger scale of what had happened in Berlin [meaning 1948]." The Communists ("Reds") "were probing for weakness in our armor; we had to meet their thrust" and do so without provoking World War III.[9]

By 1947, President Truman believed the Soviets would probe and thrust any number of places to check America's resolve. The previous alliance was in name only. In fact, of the Big Three, the Soviets, it was clear, was the new tyranny that had to be stopped from Washington's perspective. The United Kingdom was on the verge of bankruptcy and did not have the economic wherewithal to contribute to America's effort to contain the USSR, and the United States therefore began a new trajectory in U.S. foreign policy requiring new foreign policy objectives. (The British supported the United States through much of the Cold War but England became a secondary or even tertiary actor in the Cold War drama.)

Since Potsdam, the world had changed rapidly and definitively. The old European system that kept world politics in equilibrium from the mid-17th century through the early 20th century was finished. A new "bipolar" system of two "superpowers" with allies-like satellites around the centers (one in Washington, the other in Moscow) had emerged. A titanic struggle had commenced and the United States must find a way to measure up to the test. How it chose to do so is of direct interest for present purposes.

THE TRUMAN DOCTRINE, THE RISE OF THE AMERICAN SECURITY STATE, AND THE NATIONAL SECURITY ACT OF 1947

Containment was discussed earlier. I need not go into great detail to assure the reader of containment's provenance. Russian expert and State Department personnel in American embassy in Moscow, George Kennan, gets much of the credit and deservedly so. He wrote a telegram to his bosses in Washington trying to explain how the Russians had long behaved, well before the Bolshevik Revolution in 1917.

Among other things, Russian leaders had long sought access to warm-water ports. The Bolsheviks were only the latest brand of Russian leader and they would follow the pattern of their predecessors. They had unique attributes as well but mostly insofar as in helping the West to understand their unique paranoia of the West and potential enemies.

Stalin, and those whom he led in the struggle for succession to Lenin's position of leadership, were not the men to tolerate rival political forces in the sphere of power which they coveted. Their sense of insecurity was too great. Their particular brand of fanaticism, unmodified by any of the Anglo-Saxon traditions of compromise, was too fierce and too jealous to envisage any permanent sharing of power.[10]

The most basic of the compulsions of the Kremlin under the Bolsheviks was in seeing capitalism as a menace everywhere. Since "capitalism no longer existed in Russia and since it could not be admitted that there could be serious or widespread opposition to the Kremlin springing spontaneously from the liberated masses under its authority, it became necessary to justify the retention of the dictatorship by stressing the menace of capitalism abroad."

Kennan continued to explain Soviet "realities." Truth for the Soviets, Kennan argued, "is not a constant but is actually created, for all intents and purposes, by the Soviet leaders themselves. It may vary from week to week, month to month. It is nothing absolute and immutable—nothing which flows from objective reality. It is only the most recent manifestation of the wisdom of those in whom the ultimate wisdom is supposed to reside, because they represent the logic of history."

Soviet aggression "can be effectively countered not by sporadic acts which represent the momentary whims of democratic opinion but only by intelligent long-range policies on the part of Russia's adversaries—policies no less steady in their purpose, and no less variegated and resourceful in their application, than those of the Soviet Union itself." This became the essence of containment.

Finally, Kennan recommended how to approach Soviet behavior: contain the USSR-Russians. Kennan's peroration advised Washington how to contain Soviet aggression. He argued, "Soviet pressure against the free institutions of the Western world is something that can be contained by the adroit and vigilant application of counterforce at a series of constantly shifting geographical and political points, corresponding to the shifts and maneuvers of Soviet policy, but which cannot be charmed or talked out of existence."[11]

As a practical matter, the United States and its allies would erect a steady perimeter around the areas into which the Soviets were likely to try to expand in the future. Both NATO and the Marshall Plan were elements or instruments of the policy. NATO formed a physical barrier the Soviets must cross at the risk of their own destruction. Assistance for Europe to rebuild was an investment in America's NATO allies as well as an investment in America's future trade partners. Whether for humanitarian reasons or simple self-interest, both made sense to contain Soviet aggression.

Given America's history and Constitution, the question became how would physical barrier be applied to the Soviets with patience? Who would apply the said barrier? The Constitution gave the president the important prerogative of becoming the commander in chief, "when called into the actual Service of the United States," which seems to imply the clause in Article I, where Congress was given the power to "declare War, grant Letters of Marque and Reprisal, and make Rules concerning Captures on Land and Water."[12]

The Rise of the American Security State

To contain the USSR, the United States could no longer count on a European balance of power system, which many Americans loathed in any event. Rather, the United States must necessarily step in where previously it had been quite reluctant to venture: in the heart of Europe. To do that meant a new *ethos* for America, one not based on isolationism but on activism, internationalism, and even interventionism. The problem was an active, interventionist foreign policy was anathema to the way many Americans thought. Thus, new thinking was needed!

Indeed, what was needed was entirely new thinking about who responded to foreign policy threats in America. During America's first 100-plus years, powers were split between Congress and the president. The founders were certain they wanted no single branch of government to be able to take America to war without the consensus of at least one other branch. Lawmakers on Capitol Hill and policy makers in the White House were dealing with a Soviet threat that was altogether different from earlier ones. Threats from the Soviets materialized with almost no warning. They materialized rapidly. Soviet threats required deft handling. How could 500-plus members of Congress be informed in a timely way of what the Soviets were doing? The United States had entered the age of "crisis" management and new institutions and procedures were needed.

Fortunately, a residual issue leftover from World War II (parochialism in the Navy and Army) provided a way to address several issues at once. That the Army and Navy had worked at cross-purposes during World War II was hardly news. MacArthur's war in the Pacific Theater, for instance, was at variance with Admiral Nimitz's views and so on. FDR was thought to favor the Navy at the Army's expense. Thus, an effort began after World War II to unify the military under a single command.

This effort simmered along for several months before being joined by key advisers to President Truman in 1946 onward. (Thus, just as the Cold War chronology began to gain momentum, so too did the unification effort move from the Pentagon to the White House.) Two of Truman's key advisers were Dean Acheson (Truman's second-in-command at the State Department under Secretary Marshall, who eventually succeeded Marshall) and presidential adviser and utility man (speechwriter, general adviser) Clark Clifford.[13]

Acheson and Clifford agree on the particulars of the origins of the National Security Act of 1947. But Clifford had an inside seat being a speechwriter and Naval aide for FDR and again as a presidential adviser for President Truman when the legislation was drafted. Clifford sat in on many of the meetings that eventually recommended the legislation.

According to Clifford, Secretary of the Navy James Forrestal had been tasked with bringing together the titans of the military with respect to unification. As Navy secretary, Forrestal's was the lead department. The eventual National Security Act created the National Military Establishment (NME) with a civilian secretary of defense. Congress passed the statute on July 9, 1947. The Marines, dominated by Navy for so long finally were now able to exercise some independence. "The Navy, however, still had not finished protecting itself," wrote Clifford.

According to Clifford, the position of secretary of defense—which would supplant the old war secretary—was created, but it was made far too weak by the statute. The secretary of defense had no deputy and "almost no staff," which was largely due to Forrestal's machinations. Clifford asserts that Forrestal did not desire to have a secretary of defense except in name and Forrestal ensured it was a position that could not order any other division to do anything.[14]

Again, taking Clifford's word for it, both he and Truman hoped to strengthen the secretary of defense over time but decided to accept the small victory they had accomplished with the unified NME. Despite Truman's disappointment about the weakened secretary of defense, the National Security Act did multiple important things that were imperative for thwarting Soviet aggression after 1947.

Despite its flaws the National Security Act contained tremendous innovation and remains one of the most important pieces of legislation passed since World War II. The bill not only formally established the Joint Chiefs of Staff, it also created the Air Force, the position of Secretary of Defense, and civilian secretaries for all three services. In addition, it created the Central Intelligence Agency and the National Security Council. Much remained to be done, though.[15]

Just as the Senate passed the legislation, Truman wished to fly home to Missouri to see his sick mother, for he feared she would not live long. Truman waited at the airport, while Clifford and others expedited the paperwork so Truman could sign it before leaving for Missouri. (As it turned out, his mother died while he was in the air flying home.)

"For the same reason that he signed the National Security Act as soon as it passed, the President wanted to announce the name of the first Secretary of Defense without delay" (to wit, to show the Soviets that the United States was responding with resolve to Soviet provocations). Forrestal was not Truman's first selection, perhaps because of how powerful Forrestal had become, says Clifford. Rather, Patterson was Truman's first choice. But Patterson had served for six years in Washington and wanted and needed to return to private practice to make some money. "This left the choice wide open," wrote Clifford. "Finally, the President decided to choose the man who had most opposed creating the position and who had succeeded in weakening it,"—James Forrestal.[16]

Despite Forrestal's opposition to the secretary of defense position when the negotiations were being conducted earlier in 1947, he immediately accepted the position once offered to him. Clifford wrote, "I think he sensed his dilemma as soon as he was offered the position; he now had to deal with the problems he had done so much to create." In fact, Clifford says that Forrestal came to tell Clifford and others the position was devoid of real influence. Forrestal's work to ensure Navy and others continued their powerful influence ensured his own dissatisfaction with the new position of secretary of defense.

"But we were, in fact, only at the midpoint in the long road towards unification [of defense]. Once again, the central figure was Forrestal. He should have been pleased, for he had won a decisive victor over the Army and had created a structure that had fully protected the Navy and the Marines." Clifford remarked in his memoirs that Forrestal was as powerful as anyone in Washington, at that moment, except the president and his then secretary of state, George Marshall.[17]

In fact, what happened next became a recurring motif in the evolution of the National Security Act of 1947. First, in 1949 and then several times since, the National Security Act was amended. The 1949 amendment (sometimes, referred to as the Reorganization Act) rectified the weaknesses Forrestal has ensured plagued the secretary of defense in 1947.

According to Clifford, in the summer of 1948, Forrestal came to Clifford and essentially surrendered. "Forrestal made a startling statement to [Clifford]: 'Clark, I was wrong. I cannot make this work. No one can make it work.'" Clifford says he realized how difficult it was for Forrestal to admit it to Clifford. But Clifford told him he'd done his best and he should go to Truman and tell the president.

But before Forrestal was ready to see the President, he convened a series of evening meetings at his office in the Pentagon with high-level officers, asking them ways to improve the NME. I participated in some of these discussions and also kept myself informed through Forrestal, Symington, Eisenhower, and others. For the first time, Forrestal told me, he was finding that he trusted some senior Army generals more than his former Navy colleagues. Eisenhower and Omar Bradley, in particular, had risen in his estimation. After these meetings, Forrestal said he was ready to see the President.[18]

By late 1948, Forrestal conceded defeat to Truman. President Truman did not gloat, according to Clifford. He accepted Forrestal's change in mind magnanimously but the relationship was in trouble. It was an election year and Forrestal was certain—as were many others—that Truman would not be reelected.

Truman accepted Forrestal's change of heart in a matter-of-fact manner, with no gloating. With the election only a month away, Forrestal, who had already told [Clifford] he believed Dewey's victory was certain, may have regarded his discussion as academic. But the President asked him to head up a new legislative drafting team, and asked me and Frank Pace Jr. the Director of the Bureau of the Budget [today's OMB] to work with Forrestal.[19]

The National Security Act of 1947 (and the 1949 Reorganization Act) was part and parcel of containment and the deference of Congress to the presidency in terms of "crisis" management. Without the events of the early Cold War, the support for empowering the presidency would never have existed. Without the events of the early Cold War, the rejection of America's "isolationism" past would not have occurred. Without Europe's prostration from World War II (and World War I), two new superpowers would not have likely emerged. But events conspired to change U.S. foreign policy in the late 1940s and none of the events alone explains this change of trajectory of U.S. foreign policy. It required many things to fall into place.

THE NATIONAL SECURITY ACT OF 1947 AND THE IMPORTANT INSTITUTIONS IT CREATED

Though it did more than three things, the main three things the National Security Act of 1947 created were these (along with the 1949 revision). First, it rejected America's past history of ad hoc entities for defending America's national security and instead created a permanent, unified Defense Department. The War Department was gone and its way of creating ad hoc responses to potential threats disappeared with it. The Defense Department has grown into the most powerful of executive bureaucracies, replacing the State Department's former prominence. (In order to keep civilian control of the new Defense Department, the act created a civilian secretary of defense who would report to the National Security Council [NSC] inside the executive.)

Second, it created a permanent intelligence entity (actually, it combined former tactical intelligence from Navy, and other parts of the military with a civilian-led Central Intelligence Agency [CIA]) and created a civilian director of national intelligence, ostensibly to be atop all of America's disparate intelligence agencies. Today, this collection of intelligence agencies has grown into 17 distinct (though occasionally redundant) entities, each of which terminates in the civilian-led NSC inside the presidency.

Third, it created the NSC, the apex of U.S. foreign and national security policy making. Originally, what became the National Security Council was not envisioned inside the White House but the Defense Department. However, as events and time proved, placing the NSC inside the presidency was probably fortuitous. (From a purely parochial perspective, however, the NSC inside the presidency has led to a powerful presidency at the expense of Congress.)

The NSC consists of three main parts. The first part is the NSC principals (after 1991 called the principals committee). The principals committee includes the advisers and members articulated in the National Security Act of 1947 (president, vice president, secretary of state, secretary of defense, what has become the national security adviser but began as an executive secretary) and a few others, such as the chairman of the Joint Chiefs of Staff (CJCS) and the head of civilian intelligence (originally the DCI but today called the Director of National Intelligence [DNI]). Presidents are allowed by statute to include others as they deem necessary. Sometimes a president will include the attorney general, director of homeland defense, and others.[20]

Slightly less august is the NSC deputies (called the deputies committee since 1991). Most of the positions included in the NSC principals have deputies (e.g., the number two in Defense is the deputy secretary of defense) who run the day-to-day business of the department or bureaucracy. The NSC deputies committee meets more frequently than the NSC principals and tries to anticipate upcoming challenges to U.S. foreign policy. The deputies committee often will meet for preliminary discussion in order to prepare options to eventually be decided by the principals themselves.[21]

The third and final part of the NSC is the NSC staff. NSC staffers are experts from various other executive agencies of the U.S. federal government such as Defense, State, the intelligence community (IC), Treasury, and others who are seconded to the NSC staff for limited time frames (two years or so). NSC staffers are invariably going to return to their home agency at some future point but they pass through the NSCs of different administrations for the expertise and for the sake of continuity.

It is important to note that these three entities have not always existed in the NSC. Rather, they evolved over time. Initially, the National Security Act of 1947 created a group of members *and* advisers who have evolved into the principals committee in modern times as well as an executive secretary who evolved into the NSC adviser. The *members* were originally the president, the vice president, both secretaries of state and defense, and the NSC adviser. (The NSC adviser is actually called the special assistant to the president for national security affairs. When the position was the executive secretary of the NSC, it was a relatively weak paper pusher. By the time of the Kennedy administration, however, a relatively powerful NSC adviser evolved.) The *advisers* were initially the chairman of the Joint Chiefs of Staff and the then director of central intelligence, known as the DCI. (In the 2004 Intelligence Reform and Terrorism Prevention Act, IRTPA, the former DCI was recreated as simply the head of CIA, while a new Director of National Intelligence, DNI was created to oversee the entire Intelligence Community or IC.)

Together, the members and advisers have evolved into the NSC principals. Apart from the president and vice president who do not have deputies, the other members all have deputies who are the number two position in the particular bureaucracy; so there is a deputy secretary of state and deputy secretary of defense and so forth. These deputy members eventually evolved into the deputies committee (again by the H. W. Bush administration). The NSC staff began as just a few persons who worked for the executive secretary of the NSC. By the early 1960s, the NSC staffers had increased many times. During the post-Cold War era, the NSC staffers numbered scores of persons, typically seconded from another executive agency for finite periods of time.

Thus, all three bureaucracies created by the National Security Act of 1947 (the NSC, department of defense, and today's intelligence community) evolved into rather substantial bureaucracies. Given the laws of bureaucratic inertia and momentum, all three have grown and made themselves invaluable to the president in the conduct of foreign policy. As we move into the case studies, the heart of the evidence presented, terms like *the NSC principals* will be used notwithstanding the fact that the principals committee did not fully emerge until the 1990s. Though not called the NSC principals originally, what eventually evolved as the NSC principals went through several iterations. For example, during the Cuban Missile Crisis, the "ExComm" or executive committee of the NSC met. The "ExComm" was essentially a meeting of the NSC principals along with some participation by others that we would today consider NSC deputies or ad hoc members (as opposed to statutory members) of the NSC. In each of the case studies in Part II, the same criteria or questions will be applied: whether the NSC (including the principals, deputies, and staff) have been used in a novel or unique way. The reader must understand that in some cases during the 1950s and even later, only NSC members and advisers (according to the National Security Act of 1947) met. Nevertheless, the structured questions asked of each will use the phrase NSC principals and NSC deputies.

Another curious issue arises when comparing the NSC of different administrations over time. Some presidents use the NSC differently. For instance, while several administrations make decisions using the NSC principals—whether the formal committee existed or not—other presidents prefer formal NSC meetings in which both NSC principals and what we would call deputies (and others occasionally) meet. A good example is President Obama during his first year, 2009. While Obama's first NSC adviser, Jim Jones, ran the NSC, Jones regularly held principals-only meetings wherein the NSC principals minus the president met to flesh out options. Jones used the principals-only meetings as "dress rehearsals" following which the full NSC would meet (that day or the next) with President Obama. The National Security Act of 1947 never specified precisely how the NSC is to be used and therefore different presidents with different management styles use it somewhat differently. It is important to bear in mind such matters of management style as opposed to novel or unique uses of the NSC.

All three of the main creations of the National Security Act of 1947—Defense, the IC, and the NSC—have contributed in various ways to the militarization of U.S. foreign policy begun during World War II; each of the three continues to affect foreign policy today. A major thesis of this book is that the three have contributed to the militarization of U.S. foreign policy and the case studies will be used to demonstrate the said thesis. The case studies will attempt to chronicle those changes over time using a threefold typology of U.S. foreign policy eras or epochs. The three are (1) the early Cold War (the 1950s), (2) the main Cold War years (the 1960s through the 1980s), and (3) the post-Cold War era.

The NSC has become the apex of U.S. foreign policy making and the NSC is terribly understudied and underappreciated in academic and journalistic circles. Few foreign policy experts write about it or the power that has accrued to the presidency since its creation. Though the NSC was never considered a secret, and in fact Congress debated it in 1947, it has escaped proper scrutiny. (That the NSC is understudied and underappreciated is clear from a search of the literature. However, a few crucial exceptions exist.)[22]

SUMMARY

In this chapter, some important events following World War II were presented. Two changed the role America played in world politics and in U.S. foreign policy. America has long wrestled with its appropriate role in world affairs, but only after the National Security Act of 1947 created new permanent and powerful institutions inside the U.S. bureaucracy did the United States begin to become the National Security State it grew into over time.

As has been demonstrated, Soviet behavior and Western perceptions of it fueled a bipartisan consensus among policy-making elites (both lawmakers and policy makers) at either end of Pennsylvania Avenue. The Cold War consensus called for new thinking about how to respond to the USSR and that in turn led to the creation of the National Security Act of 1947. The act created a permanent Defense Department, a permanent IC, and the NSC inside the executive office of the presidency.[23]

Additionally, these institutions have led to a great deal of foreign policy continuity. For instance, from President Truman to President Ford, equal numbers of Democratic (Truman, JFK, LBJ) and Republican (Eisenhower, Nixon, and Ford) presidents involved the United States in a war in Vietnam. Or roughly, equal numbers of Democratic (add Carter to previous list) and Republican (add Reagan to the previous list) presidents kept the United States involved in the Cold War. In other words, something about these institutions has led to the militarization of U.S. foreign policy over time, irrespective of which party holds the White House (or for that matter, which party is ascendant on Capitol Hill). It remains to demonstrate the said militarization systematically. The next three chapters will do so using selected case studies of U.S. foreign policy.

PART II

Case Studies from the Cold War

In Part II of *The Rise of the American Security State*, a threefold typology of the Cold War is employed to present the case studies. The case studies presented are divided chronologically as follows. The 1950s comprised the first two presidencies of the Cold War (Presidents Truman and Eisenhower), when precedents were set for the remainder of the Cold War. Chapter 3 presents those case studies.

Chapter 4 presents several case studies from the 1960s through the 1980s, the main part of the Cold War (from the Vietnam War to Iran-Contra affair). For analytical purposes, the main part of the Cold War became more routine from either America's or the Soviets' perspective. The United States clearly identified the USSR as the principal enemy to be contained and vice versa. Precedents initiated in the 1950s became the routine behavior of either actor during the main part of the Cold War: proxy wars, covert and paramilitary operations, intense spying, and so forth.

Finally, Chapter 5 presents case studies from the post-Cold War period. For analytic purposes, it is necessary to demonstrate that in the wake of the Cold War the militarization of U.S. foreign policy continued, largely unabated. While some talked of a New World Order—including then President George H.W. Bush—the new order was simply a system in which the United States was no longer tempered by its Soviet rival, making the system a unipolar or hegemonic one. However, Chapter 5 begins with two case studies from the transitional phase of the Cold War to the post-Cold War era. Both case studies come from the George H.W. Bush administration.

The reader will discover that those who created the Cold War machinery—those who were *Present at the Creation*, as Dean Acheson famously coined the phrase—did not claim to know how long the Cold War might last. They simply believed that the USSR presented a grave threat to the capitalist-democratic West and had to be opposed, whatever the cost. They, therefore, created the institutions and machinery to accomplish what they believed was an imperative of U.S. foreign policy. No claims about their motivations are imputed here, other than they were reacting to the threat of the Soviet Union as they perceived it.

Nevertheless, few who created the said machinery believed then that the United States ought to become a world hegemonic power or empire. On the contrary, they believed, as did many Americans, that the United States preferred to stay aloof of the European system it eventually supplanted. None of them, as far as was discovered herein, believed the American Security State was permanent. (Indeed, as President Eisenhower famously lamented in his farewell address, the United States had become world power with a military-industrial complex second to none and that circumstance presented challenges for America's democracy.) Thus, once the Cold War ended (between 1989 and 1991), there was at least a potential for the United States to return to its previous position in world politics, while not exactly isolationist, one in which the United States was not the dominant hegemonic actor in world politics.

The post-Cold War era thus becomes an important part of the chronology for purposes of the main thesis. In Chapter 5, cases from the transition to the post-Cold War and the post-Cold War era are presented giving the reader the opportunity to compare the three periods.

METHOD: FOCUSED, COMPARATIVE
CASE STUDY ANALYSIS

Given the nature of case studies—they tend to constitute a small N and a certain amount of interpretation is involved in considering them—it is important that a method be used that minimizes potential problems. Some years ago the late foreign policy scholar, Alexander George, employed what he called a "controlled, structured" comparative case study.[1] Another foreign policy scholar Richard Melanson used the same method of structured comparative case studies in his work on the Vietnam War and foreign policy consensus.[2]

Herein a structured, focused case study comparison will be used in an effort to mitigate subjectivity. The case studies were selected based on time frame—to fit the Cold War typology used herein—as well as to feature the three principal institutions created by the National Security Act of 1947. The reader will soon see that the National Security Act is a principal focus of this study and why.

However, for now it is critical to specify the structured case study questions that will be asked of each case study in the following chapters (3, 4, and 5). The questions is: Did the administration use, in the case study under consideration, any of the three entities created by the National Security Act of 1947 in a novel or an unusual (extraordinary) way creating a new precedent?

1. Did the administration use the National Security Council (NSC) in a novel or unique way? (By the NSC I mean what we today think of as the NSC principals, the NSC deputies, and/or the NSC staff.)[3]
2. Did the administration use, in the case study under consideration, the Defense Department in a novel or unique way? (Including the uniformed armed forces, the uniformed military leadership, and/or the civilian leadership.)
3. Did the administration use, in the case study under consideration, the Intelligence Community (IC) in a novel or unique way?
4. Did the case study make the argument for militarization of U.S. foreign policy as defined elsewhere?
5. Did the case study make the argument for any other evidence of militarization of U.S. foreign policy as defined elsewhere?

CHAPTER 3

The Early Cold War: The 1950s

INTRODUCTION

As seen in Chapter 2, the Cold War consensus was a bipartisan consensus (both major parties) among policy makers and lawmakers (i.e., in the executive branch and on Capitol Hill). The consensus began in the late 1940s and continued through several presidential administrations, from Truman through at least Lyndon Johnson (arguably, through Reagan).

Truman became the president, suddenly after April 12, 1945, when FDR died while away from Washington (resting in Georgia). Vice President Truman had not been included in the inner workings of the Roosevelt administration. Roosevelt held only two perfunctory meetings with Truman,[1] treating Vice President Truman as other presidents have treated other vice presidents. (To be specific, Truman was largely kept out of the loop of decision-making responsibilities.)

When Harry S. Truman inherited the presidency, he was, understandably, overwhelmed. In his memoirs, Truman wrote about his first full day as president (April 13, 1945) when he arrived at the White House early and encountered *Associated Press* reporter Tony Vaccaro (whose beat was Capitol Hill). President Truman told Vaccaro "that few men in history equaled the one into whose shoes [Truman] was stepping and that [he] silently prayed to God that [he] could measure up to the task."[2] McCollough's biography of Truman generally confirms the particulars adding that Truman looked "absolutely dazed," according to then secretary of war Henry L. Stimpson.[3]

Though World War II was not over, it was nearly so in Europe (VE Day coming in May) and would end later that year in Asia (August). Nevertheless, Truman inherited the presidency at a time when America was at war and when Truman had several critical decisions to make, including which programs of FDR's to continue and which, if any, to stop. Within the first few hours of his presidency, he was briefed on America's ultra-secret program to build and use an atomic weapon. As a senator, Truman had threatened to investigate cost overruns in Washington State and elsewhere associated with Manhattan but as president, Truman saw the program through to its logical conclusion. Of course, it was President Truman who made the ultimate decision to use atomic weapons to end World War II in the Pacific Theater.

Truman, of course, inherited much else from FDR. He inherited Roosevelt's cabinet, the war, the summits at which decisions had already been made by the Big Three (Yalta and Tehran), and the upcoming Potsdam summit, which Truman would attend later in 1945. Truman also inherited two important elements of reform: unification of the military into the Defense Department (formerly, War) and what would become the National Security Act of 1947 as the Cold War heated up.

THE TRUMAN ADMINISTRATION AND TRUMAN'S NSC PRINCIPALS

In the previous chapter, it was demonstrated how extraordinary the National Security Act of 1947 was, given America's early republican history and its mythology of isolationism. It was an extraordinary law passed during extraordinary times to allow the United States, particularly the U.S. president (the presidency), to take extraordinary actions in response to the Soviet Union as the Cold War got underway and raged for decades. When these extraordinary measures were undertaken, no one knew how long the Cold War would last. Rather, they knew they needed to take action immediately to ensure the Soviets did not prevail in the foreseeable future. Beyond that there is little evidence that those who drafted the legislation thought much beyond the near term (roughly, the next five to ten years).

Of course, we know now that President Truman was elected in 1948, despite dire predictions to the contrary. (Recall, he came to office in 1945 as FDR's last vice president and therefore was only elected in his own right the first time in fall 1948.) The reader may recall an infamous newspaper cover that Harry Truman held up in which the newspaper called the election in favor of Truman's Republican opponent. (The *Chicago Tribune* cover of November 3, 1948, reads, "Dewey Defeats Truman" and Truman was shown holding up the newspaper cover in defiance.) Few pundits believed Truman would be elected in his own right.

President Truman would serve for four more years and would not be replaced until the election of 1952. Thus, while he filled most of FDR's fourth term—all but January through April 12—Truman ultimately served nearly two full terms of office, including FDR's fourth term and then one term of Truman's own. Then general (retired) Dwight Eisenhower replaced him in early 1953. When Eisenhower took over, a good deal more of the Cold War lay ahead.

Also, as noted earlier, the Soviets were testing their own atom bomb in the fall of 1949, and an ad hoc NSC committee informed Truman of the fact between late 1949 and early 1950. It is there that this chapter picks up the chronology, for 1950 was an important time for U.S. foreign policy. (In the chronological typology herein used, the 1950s were the years the Cold War became the central focus of U.S. foreign policy. The 1950s represent the early Cold War during which a principal objective of U.S. foreign policy became containing the USSR.)

In 1949, China's civil war ended in communist victory and the People's Republic of China was born, sending the nationalists (whom the United States supported) packing to Formosa (Taiwan). This caused grave concern in the United States. Among other things, policy makers assumed that "Communist China" and the USSR formed a monolithic political entity.[4] Also, in 1949, the United States created NATO along with other collective defense mechanisms (CENTO, SEATO, etc.). Finally, in 1949, the NSC undertook a study to determine whether the Soviets had built an atomic weapon and whether the United States should move to thermonuclear weapons (the hydrogen bomb) in consequence. In fact, once the determination was made that the Soviets had tested an atom bomb in fall 1949, within weeks the NSC decided to move ahead with the hydrogen bomb. In short, 1949 was a year in which the Cold War heated up considerably.

Interestingly enough, though President Truman was given the NSC as of mid-1947, he initially refused to use it thinking it was an intrusion on presidential prerogatives.[5] Not until the Korean War, did President Truman choose to attend NSC meetings—thus, the NSC met from 1947 through 1949 and passed on recommendations to Truman, but the president continued to make decisions more or less unilaterally. During this initial period, the NSC functioned as a clearinghouse of position papers reflecting the interagency process the National Security Act created (state, defense, NSC, intelligence, uniformed military). Prior to the National Security Act of 1947, the president met with his secretary of state and his other important advisers in a cabinet model for making foreign policy. Those cabinet officers, on whom Truman relied, included Secretary of State Marshall, followed in early 1949 by Secretary of State Acheson (recall, Acheson was Marshall's number two or what we call deputy secretary of state today), and Secretary of Defense Forrestal. (Before becoming America's first secretary of defense, Forrestal had served as secretary of the Navy. By late 1948, the Truman-Forrestal relationship was deteriorating quickly. Forrestal believed Truman would not be reelected and may have made entreaties to others whom Forrestal thought stood a better chance than Truman. In any case, the Truman-Forrestal relationship did not survive the election.)

Truman's first secretary of defense, James Forrestal, left office in March 1949, not long after President Truman's inaugural. Tragically, Forrestal committed suicide later ending a tumultuous but important start to the Defense Department. Louis Johnson became Truman's second secretary of defense and he lasted only until a couple of months after the Korean War began in mid-1950. George Marshall returned to Truman's inner circle to replace Johnson as secretary of defense in September 1949 but stayed almost exactly one year. (Thus, Marshall served both as Truman's secretary of state and subsequently as Truman's secretary of defense.) Truman's final secretary of defense was Robert Lovett. It may be that the Truman-Forrestal relationship discussed previously precluded much chance for a relationship between the president and the secretary of defense to evolve.

After the Korean War began, Truman began using the NSC differently and regularly attended meetings, giving the NSC more credibility. Whether a function of secretaries of defense or otherwise, the State Department continued to dominate input at the NSC principals level. Truman had particularly good relationships with both Secretary of State Marshall and Secretary of State Acheson. For whatever reason, Truman began the precedent of relying on ad hoc NSC advisers like Clark Clifford and Averill Harriman who did not head executive bureaucracies inside the federal government but were simply trusted advisers to Truman. The statute actually provides for the president to invite others to NSC meetings but the precedent once set has been followed by many other presidents. Harriman became a sort of roving ambassador for Truman and was involved with NSC as was Clifford.

Despite not relying on the newly created NSC for decisions until the Korean War (June 1950), Truman's NSC began a series of innovations. During the administration, the Psychological Strategy Board (PSB) was created in the NSC in 1951. The PSB was established by presidential directive of April 4, 1951, "to authorize and provide for the more effective planning, coordination, and conduct within the framework of approved national policies, of psychological operations."

The PSB was composed of the Undersecretary of State, the Deputy Secretary of Defense and the Director of Central Intelligence, or their designated representatives. The founding Presidential Directive instructed the PSB to report to the National Security Council on the Board's activities on the evaluation of the national psychological operations, including implementation of approved objectives, policies, and programs by the departments and agencies concerned.[6]

It is not entirely clear what the PSB did during the few years it existed, other than "national psychological operations." According to some accounts, it was hamstrung for bureaucratic reasons.[7] But it was the first in a series of NSC subcommittees that proliferated during the Cold War and the post-Cold War world.

Some accounts have the PSB creating plans for the postwar occupation of Japan, plans for political involvement in Europe (France, Italy) and in Yugoslavia (in the Soviet camp but not firmly so), and elsewhere. Its importance has more to do with the growing powers of the NSC over time. A *pattern* was created: Presidents introduced new innovations, and while particular innovations worked, once they are lashed onto the NSC, they are difficult to do away with. The interagency process often is messy with turf battles and no small degree of pettiness. Often, the NSC is where these battles get worked out and the PSB appears to be one of the early formats in which turf battles and other bureaucratic bottlenecks were compromised.[8]

TRUMAN'S NSC AND THE KOREAN WAR

President Truman's speech in 1947 to a joint session of Congress regarding threats to Turkey and Greece by Soviet-supported insurrection became known as the "Truman Doctrine." (The Truman Doctrine whereby the president challenged America to support free peoples whom Truman asserted were resisting Soviet subjugation is familiar to most readers and it need not be restated here.) Truman's misgivings about the Soviets continued to be voiced in major speeches. In his inaugural in early 1949—when Truman was elected in his own right—he devoted many of his comments to foreign policy. Most of Truman's speech was closely connected to what was happening in the NSC setting during the period. It was one of only a couple of interagency settings from which Truman received foreign policy advice. Again, in February 1949, Truman told another joint session of Congress that the situation in the world was dire and it was not a result of the world war. Rather, nearly

[T]hree years have elapsed since the greatest of all wars, but peace and stability have not returned to the world. . . . But the situation in the world today is not primarily the result of natural difficulties which follow a great war. It is chiefly due to the fact that one nation has not only refused to cooperate in the establishment of a just and honorable peace, but—even worse—has actively sought to prevent it . . .
   But that is not all. Since the close of hostilities, the Soviet Union and its agents have destroyed the independence and democratic character of a whole series of nations in Eastern and Central Europe.[9]

As noted above, the tragedy of Forrestal's suicide led Truman to select Louis Johnson as his second secretary of defense. Johnson proved problematic for various reasons. Louis Johnson was quickly approved by the Senate and nearly as soon as he assumed his duties, Secretary Johnson attacked the uniformed military he was supposed to lead. It is unclear why Johnson attacked the military but it may be due to Johnson's familiarity with Truman's own work as a senator on a committee that dealt with military waste. Whatever the reason, Johnson's tenure proved problematic.

As McCullough's biography on Truman makes clear, "Louis Johnson was possibly the worst appointment Truman ever made. In a little more than a year, many who worked with him, including Truman and Dean Acheson, would conclude that Johnson was mentally unbalanced. 'Unwittingly,' wrote General Bradley later, "'Truman had replaced one mental case with another.'"[10]

It is likely that the turnover at the secretary of defense position allowed Truman to do what he had done earlier: rely on his own counsel rather than turn to the NSC sooner. Nevertheless, in late summer or early fall 1949, Truman approved an interagency committee (called the Z committee) to be created in the NSC to determine how much progress the Soviets had made on atomic weapons. And it was at least partly because of a recommendation given by Truman's Atomic Energy Commission (AEC) to pursue a "superbomb" (or hydrogen bomb) that Truman called on Secretary of State Acheson to convene an NSC subcommittee to discuss the recommendation. Clearly, the NSC was created to foster interagency cooperation and coordination with respect to U.S. foreign and national security policy. (Convening subcommittees of the NSC was a precedent we shall see repeatedly.)

From November 1949 until January 1950, the so-called Z committee met and argued about the hydrogen bomb, about whether to go public and how, and about whether any lost chance of keeping nuclear weapons under some sort of civilian control was possible any longer. The AEC argued for civilian rather than military control, an understandable position given the AEC's civilian nature. Some in defense took the position that like any other weapon the military would be tasked to use, the military should control the hydrogen bomb.

The top-secret debate went on for three months, from November 1949 to the end of January 1950, and much of it in Acheson's immense fifth-floor office at the State Department—a room that reminded him, he said, of the cabin-class dining salon on one of the old North German Lloyd ocean liners. But the three-man Z Committee of Acheson, Johnson, and Lilienthal met only twice, due primarily, as Acheson said, "to the acerbity of Louis Johnson's nature." Johnson and Lilienthal [AEC] argued bitterly.[11]

The president made a decision about the hydrogen bomb but he also tasked a subcommittee of the NSC to undertake a study to see what to do about the budget and whether it needed to be submitted anew now that the United States was going to proceed with the hydrogen bomb. Thus was born NSC-68, the Z committee's recommendations about what was necessary for the sake of containing the USSR now that it had detonated its own atomic weapons. Containment without the necessary budget commitment was a thin reed on which to place U.S. foreign policy. Therefore, NSC-68 recommended both support for the hydrogen bomb and an increased budget to pay for its implementation. Truman accepted both decision. When it came to containment, henceforth, the United States would incur budget deficits in order to prevail. It would use the more menacing hydrogen bomb to show the Soviets the United States was as firm as Gibraltar.

Once the Korean War began, Truman began using the NSC differently and it soon became the apex of policy making at the executive level, supplanting the old cabinet model. After the outbreak of the Korean War, President Truman presided over the NSC meetings, even though he does not call them such in his memoirs. That he chose not to call them NSC meetings does nothing to diminish how important the NSC had become. Rather, it is probably because he was not used to seeing himself as presiding over the NSC. However, if one reads who attended the meetings, it becomes clear that these were early versions of what later became the NSC, principals and deputies meetings.

The outbreak of the Korean War changed President Truman's view of the NSC. Harry Truman's memoirs make it clear. In Chapter 21, he spends the bulk of the chapter talking about the disposition of Korea at the end of World War II, including meetings and understandings FDR had with the Big Three at Yalta and an earlier meeting in Tehran, Iran. Truman's intent seems to be to demonstrate how unreasonable the Soviets were after agreeing to (1) multi-allies' administration of Korea after World War II and (2) various Soviet schemes to circumvent previous agreements on Korea. He convincingly demonstrates that Stalin and Molotov (Soviet foreign minister) engaged in every sort of maneuver to get out of previous commitments by which they were bound. (Interestingly, like both FDR and Churchill, Truman too thought he could control Stalin. They all discovered otherwise.)

Then in the last couple of pages of the Chapter 21, Truman introduces the NSC, almost incidentally, as follows. First, Truman explains that the Soviets had established a People's Army in North Korea (above the 38th parallel) and that the Soviets had been infiltrating commissars and various other advisers into North Korea. He then writes,

In the spring of 1948 the National Security Council [NSC] had reported to me that [the U.S.] could do one of three things. [It] could abandon Korea; or [it] could continue [its] military and political responsibility for the country; or [it] could extend to a Korean government aid and assistance for the training and equipping of their own security forces and offer extensive economic help to prevent a breakdown of the infant nation. The Council recommended, however, that [the president choose] the last course and [Truman] gave his approval.[12]

It is important to note that President Truman acknowledges that he distrusted Syngman Rhee (the man the United States would eventually support against Soviet-controlled North Korea) because Rhee was associated with authoritarians of extreme, right-wing ideology that caused Truman concern. Truman's pattern was a precedent for virtually all Cold War presidents. Presidents would make decisions contrary to America's previous history and justify those decisions in the name of containing the Soviets from expanding.

Soviet machinations continued through summer of 1950 when things began to take on a different complexion in Korea. Throughout the spring of 1950, according to President Truman, CIA reports estimated that the Soviets and their allies in North Korea might turn from isolated forays across the 38th parallel into a substantial thrust of military power. The problem was intelligence reports showed the same thing in any number of places around the globe that had the Soviets and the Americans (former allies) squaring off across some land boundary. Thus, the actual outbreak of war seems to have caught Washington somewhat by surprise.

On June 24, 1950 (while Truman was again back in Missouri on family business), he received a phone call from Secretary of State Acheson at about 10:00 p.m., informing Truman that a military attack from the North across the parallel had indeed begun. Truman's first instinct was to return to Washington immediately but Acheson recommended waiting until a subsequent phone call by which time Acheson hoped to confirm the details of how big an attack North Korea had made. Acheson and Truman agreed to call for an emergency meeting of the UN Security Council (UNSC) to force action against what both saw as Soviet aggression in Korea.

When Acheson did phone back early the next morning (Sunday, June 25), he was able to report a substantial attack and that Acheson had arranged the emergency meeting of the UNSC and that Truman should head back to the capital. Truman "asked Acheson to get together with the Service Secretaries [secretary of the navy, army, so on] and the Chiefs of Staff and start working on recommendations for [Truman] when [he] got back." (He would have asked Acheson to call Secretary of Defense Louis Johnson too but Johnson had not yet returned from an inspection of the Far East.)[13]

When Truman finally landed in Washington, Secretary Acheson met him at the airplane (as did Secretary Johnson, who had just returned). The motorcade rushed straight to the Blair House (the White House was undergoing some refurbishing) where an NSC meeting was held. Present at the meeting were Secretary of the Army Frank Pace, Secretary of the Navy Francis Matthews, Secretary of the Air Force Thomas Finletter, the Joint Chiefs of Staff, including Omar Bradley and Army Chief General Collins along with Secretary Acheson and his new deputy (Deputy Secretary of State Dean Rusk), and a few others. This was, in effect, an NSC principals meeting with a slightly larger crowd than normal, based on the fact that war had occurred and the United States would likely be responding militarily.[14]

Thus, the initial response from the Truman administration to the outbreak of the Korean War was that the president met and presided over his NSC advisers for the first time, instead of simply receiving, ex post facto recommendations from the NSC. Truman's memoirs makes clear that the NSC convened as a body of advisers and that Truman not only used their recommendations but also made his own decisions as events warranted. The next day (Monday, June 26, 1950), "the reports from Korea began to sound dark and discouraging, and among the messages that arrived was one from Syngman Rhee asking for help in the telegraphic style of the State Department" messages.[15]

For present purposes it is enough to establish that the Korean War caused President Truman to turn to the NSC, an entity created by the

National Security Act of 1947 some two years earlier. The NSC replaced the former cabinet model of presidential policy making and the cabinet model would not return (with very few exceptions, detailed later). Henceforth, each new president would enter office with his own ideas about how to employ the NSC, but each would employ it as part of the portfolio of new institutions the Congress had empowered the presidency with in 1947.

Structured Case Study Questions for Truman

The question is whether Truman's use of the NSC was novel or unique (and similarly, whether his use of the unified military under Defense or the intelligence community, all created by the National Security Act, were novel)?

Question 1 (A, B, and C). First, we consider the NSC. Truman allowed the NSC to function prior to 1950 and even read and was influenced by the work product the NSC produced. (The special subcommittee to determine whether to create the "superbomb" or hydrogen bomb comes to mind.) Beginning with the Korean War, however, Truman began using the NSC regularly and that it supplanted the previous cabinet model is inarguable. Truman had, hitherto, only used the NSC as a sounding board of decisions he made. After the Korean War, President Truman began presiding over the NSC committees and using it as a policy-making entity (more aligned with its creation).

Truman created the PSB, for example, and it was tasked with what subsequently became various psychological programs (some of which were later debated in NSC-68) against the Soviets. The PSB along with various ad hoc subcommittees constitute novel uses of the NSC structure.[16]

Thereafter, the NSC became the main locus of foreign and national security policy making for the Truman administration. That is not to suggest that President Truman ever deferred his own decision-making prerogatives to NSC advisers, but he did use the NSC thereafter as an interagency advisory board to help him consider various options. This was a precedent that was novel, and it shaped every subsequent administration's use of the NSC.

(A template was created by Truman, which evolved further in the Eisenhower administration and it was what emerged by the Kennedy administration as the NSC principals—NSC members with some additions including some deputies—though they were not called the principals committee formally until the George H. W. Bush administration. What the Kennedy administration called the "ExComm," or executive committee, of the NSC was effectively a group that varied between NSC principals and a handful of others included and the full NSC.)

To be sure, there was a novel use of the NSC in the case study on the Korean War. The president changed from thinking of the NSC as interfering with his constitutional responsibilities to using it as the main forum in which to make decisions on foreign policy. It is unclear what exactly changed his views. It may be that the change was nominal. President Truman had always held close consultation with his secretary of state—whether Marshall or Acheson—and the secretary of defense was starting to become more important in terms of policy making than anyone had anticipated previously. Thus, the NSC setting was a natural setting for these two and a few other interagency advisers to meet and vet the president's decisions.

Questions 2 and 3. It should surprise no one that Truman used both the military and the intelligence community (then principally the CIA) in novel ways. The entire policy of containment was novel: the United States would thereafter contain Soviet machinations through collective defense regimes (like NATO and CENTO), and Truman began using the CIA in novel ways to thwart the Soviets.

The mere changes in use of defense and the intelligence community constituted the militarization of U.S. foreign policy. (Let us remember no pejorative meaning should be connected with militarization and it was defined simply as using military instruments rather than others.) Though not noted in the case examined, the Truman administration was the first to contain the USSR physically, with the creation of collective defense regimes such as NATO and others. It was also the first to begin using covert operations—propaganda and the like—and new methods of espionage against the USSR so it likewise contained the USSR (or checked it) psychologically. Indeed, the United States began trying to affect the outcomes of elections not just in Soviet satellites but in ally's elections (Italy, for example, where a legal communist party existed). Thus, it can clearly be stated that both the military and intelligence communities became much more involved in U.S. foreign policy and were used in unique ways to effect U.S. foreign policy objectives.

Questions 4 and 5. Prior to the National Security Act of 1947 (and the Reorganization Act of 1949), neither Defense Department nor the CIA existed as such. As noted earlier, the War Department and the Navy Department predated the National Security Act; so while there is nothing dramatic about the changes in using the newly created DoD and CIA, they were new institutions. Thus, technically, there is evidence that they were both used in novel ways, though one hesitates to make too big a deal about it at present.

Finally, the case studies in the 1950s are full of new precedents. Clearly, U.S. foreign policy was undergoing fairly dramatic militarization. The United States essentially took over the old European balance of power. Moreover, the new policy of containment of the USSR equated to the militarization of U.S. foreign policy. Whether one looks at NATO or the other collective defense regimes (SEATO, CENTO, so on), something the United States has heretofore eschewed as European and contrary to America's republican ideology, the military and intelligence communities were fortified and used robustly to contain the USSR, setting new precedents for either institution. The Cold War itself constituted novel uses of either and NSC-68 led to a proliferation of using either institution.

THE EISENHOWER ADMINISTRATION AND EISENHOWER'S NSC PRINCIPALS

If the National Security Council came to prominence in the Truman administration during the Korean War, it reached new heights during the Eisenhower administration's two terms in office. During Ike's tenure, the NSC became the center of gravity for national security and foreign policy decisions, much as what happened after Korea with the Truman administration. Additionally, the NSC became the apex of presidential decision-making in terms of America's covert war of attrition against the USSR. Indeed, during Ike's time, the NSC became precisely what those who passed the National Security Act of 1947 envisioned: an interagency group that coordinated domestic and national security policy making and made difficult decisions between trade-offs and opportunity costs.

The image of the Eisenhower presidency was somewhat one-sided for years. Early biographies portrayed Eisenhower as the "hidden-hand president," which often, erroneously, painted Secretary of State John Foster Dulles as the main mover behind decisions. The truth, however, was rather different.

Eisenhower, like virtually every other post-World War II president, took his constitutional responsibilities seriously. President Eisenhower certainly gave Secretary John Foster Dulles wide berth but when Eisenhower disagreed with Dulles, Ike made his disagreements clear and asserted his own prerogative. For instance, President Eisenhower and Secretary of State Dulles differed over helping the French at Dien Bien Phu (Vietnam) in 1954.[17] That Dulles was a major decision maker is clear. In fact, two Dulles brothers (John Foster at State and Allen Dulles as director of central intelligence, or DCI) sat in on NSC meetings. Clearly, President Eisenhower respected both Dulles brothers. But Eisenhower alone was commander in chief and made the decisions, when events warranted such a decision.

Charles "Charlie" Wilson was Eisenhower's secretary of defense much of Eisenhower's presidency (until October 1957), which for present purposes is the only secretary of defense we need know. Robert "Bobby" Cutler was Eisenhower's NSC executive secretary and the executive secretary evolved into the prototype of the NSC adviser during Eisenhower's two terms.

The chairman of the Joint Chiefs of Staff (CJCS) was Admiral Arthur Radford (summer of 1953 until 1957) who was eventually replaced by General Nathan Twining who stayed until mid-1957. After Twining, General

Lyman Lemnitzer served into the first year plus of the Kennedy administration. (Lemnitzer served as CJCS from October 1, 1960, in Eisenhower's last year until September 30, 1962, near the end of Kennedy's first year in office.[18]) For the case studies during the Eisenhower administration, we need only concern ourselves with Admiral Radford.

Like his predecessor, Korea was the issue that dominated Eisenhower's NSC—at least initially—and Korea became an intense focus for Robert Cutler (Ike's NSC adviser) even during the transition between Truman and Eisenhower. For instance, the Dwight D. Eisenhower Library and Museum houses a collection of NSC documents divided into boxes or discrete collections. The dates listed on the summary of those NSC files lists 1952 (when Ike was president-elect) to 1961 (when in January the transition between Eisenhower and John Kennedy occurred) as a discrete collection. Thus, even while president-elect, Eisenhower and the NSC began working on the Korea problem.

Before looking more closely at Eisenhower's use of the NSC (and the other entities created in the 1947 statute), it is useful to understand Eisenhower's relationship with his Secretary of State John Foster Dulles (until early 1959 when he was incapacitated by cancer) and Robert Cutler, the man Ike would appoint to run Eisenhower's NSC and bring it into "military" shape. Both men were critical parts of the Eisenhower NSC system.

The simpler of the two relationships is Robert Cutler's relationship with Eisenhower. Eisenhower specifically brought Cutler "down" from Boston to put his NSC into proper trim, so that it functioned more like Ike's headquarters had functioned during World War II. Eisenhower "brought Robert Cutler down from Boston" so as "to give some form, direction, and organization to the work of the National Security Council" so that it functioned more like SHAEF had during the war.[19] Eisenhower was frustrated to discover that neither his NSC nor his administration had contingency plans when Stalin unexpectedly died in 1953. Cutler was not a military man but a Harvard-educated lawyer whom Eisenhower had come to respect. But the serendipity of Stalin's death made Cutler invaluable to Eisenhower.

Cutler's own remarks on what he did for Eisenhower, as the NSC adviser, are interesting. According to Cutler (writing in 1956 or when the NSC was just eight years old), the NSC had "held 273 meetings and at them" it had taken some "1,508 separate policy actions." Cutler continued, "[o]f these totals, 128 of the meetings were held and 699 of the policy actions were taken in the five and one-quarter years of the Truman Administration and 145 of the meetings and 809 of the policy actions were recorded in the three years of the Eisenhower Administration." Cutler went on to say that during Eisenhower's first 115 weeks, "the Council met 115 times (compared with 82 Cabinet meetings for the same period)."[20] In short, the function of the cabinet during Eisenhower's first two years diminished as the NSC gained prominence.

According to Cutler, when Eisenhower "became President, General Eisenhower transformed the Council into a forum for vigorous discussion against a background of painstakingly prepared and carefully studied papers," which Cutler averred suited Eisenhower's personality and management style. The evidence is ample that Cutler's description was accurate. Indeed, both the NSC and certain NSC members (notably Secretary of State Dulles) were constantly arguing with Eisenhower in NSC meetings over how much to do. Dulles and others seemed to think the United States was affluent enough to do all things everywhere, whereas Eisenhower was deadly serious about holding defense spending down and balancing the budget. Therefore, there was tension between the activist Dulles and the president, but the president had his way.

A good deal has been written about Secretary of State John Foster Dulles and there is little need to rehash it here. What is clear is that he was a strong-willed secretary of state with strong feelings about Communism.[21] Eisenhower seemed content to have Dulles offer his opinions and even argue strenuously in behalf of them. Nevertheless, the evidence shows that Eisenhower made the decisions and *once made*, Secretary Dulles fell into line behind decided policy.

To cite just one example, early during the first year of Eisenhower's tenure, balancing the budget came up several times. At an NSC meeting to discuss the trade-offs of a balanced budget and national security, "Dulles was opposed to making a balanced budget top priority. He warned Eisenhower that if the United States cut back on defense spending, it would have the effect of saying the crisis [in Europe] was over (meaning the post-war crisis of rebuilding Europe). The Europeans would then feel that in that case, they too could cut back on military expenditures. This, he gravely warned, 'would take the heart out of NATO.' " Eisenhower immediately took issue with Dulles. "There could be no security, he told Dulles, without a sound economy, which was dependent upon a balanced budget. Dulles charged that the decision to balance the budget was made in a vacuum."[22] But Ike prevailed.

EISENHOWER'S NSC PRINCIPALS AND COVERT, PARAMILITARY OPERATIONS

We have already reviewed evidence that the NSC became a high-level policy planning entity during the Eisenhower two terms. We have also seen that Eisenhower reserved for himself (i.e., the president) ultimate decisions, though he clearly saw the give and take of positions and the NSC's importance in helping him come to a decision. The record shows a broad range of issues covered at NSC meetings as already noted. Beginning with the Korean War (which Eisenhower had run on as one who would get things settled in Korea) to Stalin's death to Eisenhower's subsequent attempts to lure the post-Stalin USSR into self-restraint to the other areas, the first year of the Eisenhower presidency was filled with NSC meeting. Perhaps the most intriguing aspect, however, is Eisenhower's increased covert and/or paramilitary operations run out of the "5412 committee," a subcommittee of the NSC. The rest of this chapter will consider a couple of important examples of how and why Eisenhower turned to such operations during the 1950s and how the 5412 subcommittee of the NSC ran those operations.

Iran and Operation Ajax

The first of the covert operations (apart from espionage) the Eisenhower administration got involved in was a British initiative to remove the elected leader of Iran, Mohammad Mossadegh, from power. Mohammad Mossadegh came to power in Iran in 1951 as prime minister, with a vote in the parliament. Mossadegh and others had proposed nationalizing the British-Iranian Oil Company previously. However, in early May 1951, nationalization occurred and the British were thrown out of their previous monopoly in Iran's lucrative oil fields. By 1952 (mid-year), Mossadegh had consolidated power and the British were getting more desperate to regain their former colonial possession.

The British retaliated with a blockade of Iranian petroleum and began various other schemes to punish and/or persuade Mossadegh to back down; he did not. Inside Iran, things went from bad to worse with factions forming, some for the Shah (King) of Iran (who had been installed by the British) and some for Mossadegh. By fall of 1952, Mossadegh declared the British an enemy of Iran and this action as much as anything caused the British to act desperately.

Once Eisenhower was elected (November 1952), the British apparently became convinced they had a partner in Washington. Eisenhower was enormously popular in Europe and in the United Kingdom. Former prime minister Churchill apparently contacted the incoming Eisenhower administration in late 1952. Consultations between the incoming Eisenhower NSC members and the British continued in early 1953 with a plot forming by March. The British "told Ike that Mossadegh was a communist. Next, Anthony Eden (British foreign minister) visited the U.S. whereupon he proposed a joint venture between the British Secret Service and America's CIA to topple Mossadegh."[23]

According to the late historian Stephen Ambrose, Eisenhower was receptive to the proposal. Why might Eisenhower and his administration be more receptive to such a plot than Truman? Both Ike and Dulles believed the battle had shifted to the Third World (the first world being the industrialized West and the second world being the industrialized East). Eisenhower was already interested in U.S. assistance to the Third World as a means to bring more of it into the Western camp (preempting, wars of national liberation, the Soviet means of co-opting Third World leaders).

"With NATO in place, an armistice in Korea, the battleground for the Cold War had shifted to the so-called Third World. Latin America, India, Egypt, Iran, Vietnam—these were the places where the free world was being challenged, or so Eisenhower and Dulles believed."[24]

In meeting the challenge in the Third World, "Eisenhower intended to use the CIA in a much more active role than Truman had given it." The CIA had mostly committed espionage during Truman's tenure. Eisenhower planned to use it differently, in covert and paramilitary ways in which the U.S. backing could later be denied (known as "plausible deniability"). This would be a new means of taking on the Soviets that did not risk direct confrontation and the hazards of nuclear annihilation. Eisenhower held the fundamental belief that nuclear war was already unimaginable—both sides already held too many massive weapons making such an exchange obsolete.[25]

Thus, was born Operation Ajax. Ambrose says Ajax was planned by Secretary of State Dulles, his brother Allen Dulles along with Bedell Smith (Smith and Dulles were first and second directors of Central Intelligence, DCIs after the CIA's creation in 1947), and Charlie Wilson (Wilson was secretary of defense). Though the Eisenhower administration was very secretive about the "5412" committee, it became public near the end of the administration when Senator Scoop Jackson (D-WA) held hearings that critiqued the Eisenhower administration's NSC. We know it was where covert operations were approved within the NSC by subgroups of NSC principals with the "need to know" the details involved. It seems likely that Ajax was among America's first covert operations. The list of attendees shows it was a subcommittee of the NSC.[26]

The Ambrose biography concluded its discussion of Ajax with this peroration. "Eisenhower had ordered the Mossadegh government overthrown, and it had been done. It seemed to him that the results more than justified the methods." Moreover, covert operations such as Ajax constituted "an additional side of the man who had insisted on making peace in Korea and trying new approaches to Russia on disarmament. Where he thought it prudent and possible, he was ready to fight the Communists with every weapon at his disposal—just as he had fought the Nazis."[27] What is clear, moreover, is that Ike's fight against the Soviets would be conducted from the NSC either at regular NSC meetings or subcommittee meetings of NSC members with a need to know.

But Ajax would not be the last of covert operations. Indeed, so successfully did these operations appear at first blush that the Eisenhower administration turned increasingly to a series of such covert, paramilitary procedures. Avoiding direct confrontation with the Soviets was a major reason. Eisenhower had declared in his first year that nuclear war was a national suicide—it made no sense whatsoever. Plausible deniability was an underlying premise of covert operations and the need to keep the information between only those with a "need to know" provided another rationale. But the secrecy became a nearly irresistible aspect for President Eisenhower and subsequent presidents.

President Arbenz and Guatemala

During the last couple of years of the Truman administration, Jacobo Arbenz Guzman was elected president of Guatemala. Given the politics of the Cold War in the United States, it is not surprising that Arbenz (whatever he may have been objectively) was seen as leftist, which was analogous with being a communist. By the time of McCarthy's hearings and myriad charges of communism in the federal government, it was not likely that a cold warrior such as Eisenhower was going to see Arbenz any more positively than Truman had seen him.

In February 1953, Arbenz announced plans to expropriate a quarter million acres of United Fruit Company (UFCO) holdings in Guatemala. According to Eisenhower's own memoirs, the president believed Arbenz's expropriation of UFCO's holding unfair and discriminatory.[28] (Recall, Eisenhower was elected in November 1952 but inaugurated in January 1953 so this was during Ike's first month or so in office.) During the summer of 1953, a representative of UFCO (Thomas Corcoran) met with Undersecretary of State Walter B. Smith (sometimes called Bedell and even Beadle). This activity led to what one account cites as August meetings (1953) when the 5412 committee met and began planning for the overthrow of Arbenz.[29]

"If Eisenhower ever needed any convincing that an operation—now called PBSUCCESS and which had been planned over the previous months—was necessary, he was now convinced. Sometime in January (1954) he gave the first go-ahead nod for pushing ahead with what was shaping up as a covert plan to topple Arbenz. Eisenhower would reserve his final approval a little longer."[30] (This was Eisenhower's standard procedure, allowing planning to occur but reserving the right to veto it at any subsequent point if he felt anything about the plan looked weak or likely to point to the United States.)

During spring 1954, Eisenhower approved the operation. President Arbenz lived down to expectations by asking for help from the Soviet Bloc and the Soviets were happy to oblige. By April, the CIA learned the Soviet were shipping armaments to Guatemala at Arbenz's request. The ship arrived in port on May 17, 1954, when according to Eisenhower's own account "things came to a head."[31]

On May 19, there was an early morning White House meeting. (It is unclear whether it was an NSC or a subgroup of the NSC.) The president decided that the seriousness of the situation had to be underscored to both domestic and foreign audiences. Eisenhower would use that day's scheduled press conference to do so. Also, on May 19, Secretary Dulles, in an apparently coordinated attack, announced that "a government in which

Communist influence is very strong has come into a position to dominate militarily the Central American area."[32]

The actual operation is better covered elsewhere. It involved CIA, State, and the U.S. embassy in Guatemala, coordinating operations and plans to get rid of President Arbenz. Together with Ajax (Iran), the two covert operations took place in the first 15 months of the Eisenhower administration. They illustrate that Eisenhower was prepared to play hardball with the Soviets, while also being careful enough to avoid direct implication of the United States and direct confrontation, potentially, of the United States and USSR.

Eisenhower continued to use the NSC (and 5412) in creative ways during his two terms. The creation of the U-2 and one of the administration's biggest embarrassments (and setbacks), the failure of talks with the USSR over ratcheting down the Cold War confrontation and coming to agreement in terms of arms control inspections would also feature the NSC and its subgroup designated for covert operations. The secrecy of the Eisenhower administration would be copied in large measure by the Kennedy administration that followed Eisenhower. In fact, covert operations became a mainstay of U.S. containment of the USSR for subsequent presidents.

Structured Case Study Questions for Eisenhower

Question 1 (A, B, and C). Novel or unusual use of the NSC? In assessing the case studies involving the Eisenhower administration, one is struck by the various innovations of the administration. Before discussing them, however, let me first note that the NSC evolved during the Eisenhower years (at least during the early to mid-1950s). What began in the NSC during Truman's time with respect to how the NSC itself was used, is best seen as incremental evolution, not radical change. The NSC continued to evolve as the apex of foreign policy decision-making. That does not mean, however, there were no innovations under Eisenhower. In fact, quite the contrary is true.

In fact, the 5412 subcommittee itself was an innovation. We saw a subcommittee during Truman's times that studied whether to pursue the "superbomb" or hydrogen bomb, but it was a group whose work product (NSC-68) thereafter was disseminated by the NSC to others. By contrast, the 5412 subcommittee was a wholly new creation: it was limited to those with a need to know and the information was not disseminated to others in the NSC later. Clearly, the 5412 subcommittee constituted an innovation. It may be argued that it evolved out of Truman's Psychological Strategy Board. But even if it did evolve from the PSB, it was a new wrinkle in containment of the USSR.

Question 2 (A, B, and C). What about the use of the military structure created by the National Security Act of 1947? Again, under the Eisenhower administration, the military was used in a novel way: the use of the

military and CIA in combination to conduct paramilitary operations. Both
the Eisenhower administration's participation in the overthrow of Mossadegh government in Iran and its subsequent overthrow of the Arbenz
government in Guatemala were new and unique uses of the intelligence
community (IC) mostly with some logistics provided by the Pentagon.

Question 3. Evidence of novel uses of the intelligence community (IC)?
Again, plenty of evidence exists that U.S. foreign policy was changed under
the Eisenhower administration. The CIA was created by the National Security Act of 1947. By the end of the Truman administration, it had begun
to evolve into a more complex intelligence community. By the time Eisenhower came to Washington, the IC became a semisecret weapon of U.S.
foreign policy. Paramilitary and covert operations became critical to Ike's
method of containing the USSR and subsequent presidents pushed it even
further. Both case studies provide ample evidence of how the IC was used.

Questions 4 and 5. Did the two cases of covert action during Eisenhower's tenure demonstrate the militarization of U.S. foreign policy? The answer is clearly yes. (It is not surprising that both Truman and Eisenhower
did more than previous presidents to militarize U.S. foreign policy. The
Cold War consensus meant both the executive and legislative branches
demanded more action against the USSR, which in turn meant using the
new institutions created by the National Security Act of 1947 in new ways
to thwart what were perceived as Soviet machinations globally.) However,
the best evidence of the militarization of U.S. foreign policy came in Eisenhower's farewell speech, just before handing over the new machinery—
not more than a decade old—to the Kennedy administration.

Three days before handing over responsibilities to president-elect Kennedy, Eisenhower addressed the nation. After taking some time to explain
why the United States had to build up a permanent military establishment
after the trauma of World War II and of the looming threat posed by communism, Ike made conflicted claims. Though Eisenhower himself had done
even more than Truman to militarize U.S. foreign policy, it is interesting to
read of his ambivalence as he left office. President Eisenhower said this:
"Our military organization today bears little relation to that known by any
of my predecessors in peace time, or indeed by the fighting men of World
War II or Korea." He continued

Until the latest of our world conflicts, the United States had no armaments in-
dustry. American makers of plowshares could, with time and as required, make
swords as well. But now we can no longer risk emergency improvisation of national defense; we have been compelled to create a permanent armaments indus-
try of vast proportions. Added to this, three and a half million men and women
are directly engaged in the defense establishment. We annually spend on military
security more than the net income of all United State corporations.

This conjunction of an immense military establishment and a large arms indus-
try is new in the American experience. The total influence—economic, political,
even spiritual—is felt in every city, every state house, every office of the Federal

government. We recognize the imperative need for this development. Yet we must not fail to comprehend its grave implications. Our toil, resources and livelihood are all involved; so is the very structure of our society.

In the councils of government, we must guard against the acquisition of unwarranted influence, whether sought or unsought, by the military-industrial complex. The potential for the disastrous rise of misplaced power exists and will persist.

We must never let the weight of this combination endanger our liberties or democratic processes. We should take nothing for granted only an alert and knowledgeable citizenry can compel the proper meshing of huge industrial and military machinery of defense with our peaceful methods and goals, so that security and liberty may prosper together.[33]

Though it is sheer speculation, one gets the impression Eisenhower is concerned about the entire military-industrial-intelligence complex and the power that has accrued to the presidency dating back to the National Security Act of 1947. On reflecting as he prepared to hand over the powerful machinery to the incoming (and from Ike's perspective, very young) president and his advisers, Eisenhower is clearly uneasy about the tensions between democracy and America's increasing role in world politics. General (retired) Eisenhower was clearly concerned with the militarization of U.S. foreign policy and what it meant for the future of the Republic. Like others, however, Eisenhower could not see how to square the circle of republicanism and the threats of Soviet expansion.

SUMMARY

From mid-1950 through the end of 1960, the NSC grew in importance in terms of U.S. foreign and national security policy making. The old cabinet model was not entirely supplanted yet, but it increasingly took on issues of domestic policy whereas the NSC was dominated by foreign and national security, as well as prioritizing domestic programs that presented opportunity costs with the former. The modern NSC that would eventually emerge had not quite evolved yet, but it was a good deal closer to evolving than the early years of the NSC when Truman resented the NSC as what he saw as congressional interference. Its full evolution would be seen in the Kennedy administration and subsequent ones.

The Defense Department had, likewise, become a bureaucracy to reckon with. Indeed, by the end of Eisenhower's two terms, the president was frustrated with the rise of what he called the military-industrial complex. In one of Eisenhower's most widely known speeches, the president warned that the U.S. military bore "little relation to that known by any of my predecessors in peace time, or indeed by the fighting men of World War II or Korea."[34]

A careful reading of the entire speech suggests the possibility that Eisenhower was not simply talking about the Pentagon and the arms industries that lobby Capitol Hill and the White House. As Eisenhower was leaving office, he had plenty of reasons to be content with his tenure. He had prevented war between the United States and the USSR (along with others). He had announced both Atoms for Peace and Open Skies; that the Soviets balked took nothing way from his administration's innovation. He balanced the budget multiple times, while keeping the Soviets occupied with America's containment policy.

Nevertheless, he was concerned that a young, new president who would succeed him might not be as patient and might not be able to say "no" as Eisenhower had done, many times, to his NSC, his cabinet, and the Pentagon and CIA. He was offended by some of the campaign antics the Democrats had used including promising to spend much more on defense and domestic programs. Eisenhower believed defense spending, in particular, ought not to be used as political-domestic rhetoric and he had doubts about the incoming Kennedy administration's maturity (many of which proved prescient).

But Eisenhower also had the vantage point of eight years in which he made decisions and the last couple of years of the Truman administration in which President Truman made them since the advent of the National Security Act of 1947. There is every reason in the world to think his farewell speech was talking about the entire panoply of creations the 1947 statute provided the presidency. Eisenhower believed he had used those creations with temperance. He was not so sure about how the incoming Kennedy administration would use the same creations.

A plain reading of Eisenhower's farewell speech suggests Ike's unease with some of the institutions he inherited from Truman (from the National Security Act) and their influence in American politics. His unease proved surprisingly farsighted, as Americans would come to see during the Vietnam War. We turn next to the incoming Kennedy administration and its uses of the institutions created by the act.

CHAPTER 4

The Main Cold War Years: 1960s–1980s

INTRODUCTION

Chapter 3 focused on foreign and national security policies during the 1950s, the initial phase of the Cold War when policy makers had little sense of how enduring the confrontation with the USSR would prove. While policy makers realized early on—certainly by 1947-1948—that a competition with the Soviets had replaced the earlier alliance, it took time for the American people *and* the bureaucracy to apprehend that the Cold War was underway in earnest—that competition between former allies was the new normal. Presidents Truman and Eisenhower were the first two presidents to use the tools and institutions created by the National Security Act of 1947. After the outbreak of the Korean War, President Truman began using the NSC (as well as the CIA and Defense Department) in ways it had never been used during the first few years of his administration. For the first time the United States kept a permanent military establishment with a monumental supply chain, intentionally spread out among multiple states and congressional districts domestically so it would be difficult to undo later. Foreign policy became relatively constant "crisis" management between the United States and USSR under both Truman and Eisenhower. During the 1960s through 1980s, foreign policy continued to evolve.

Under President Eisenhower, a new entity was grafted onto the NSC (5412 committee or subcommittee) that involved a subgroup of what eventually became the NSC principals. The 5412 committee became a subcommittee with NSC "members" (and often advisers) with a "need to know" the details of America's various covert and paramilitary operations. The pace of covert operations accelerated during Eisenhower's two terms so that by the end of his administration, it was commonplace to plan to overthrow governments the United States considered unfriendly, to create new technologies (the U-2 and others) through the CIA and its contractors, and even to attempt assassinations of foreign leaders committee members determined were enemies of the United States. Perhaps a little less exciting but novel, nonetheless, was the evolution of the CIA's technical expertise in development of spying and espionage, such as the U-2 program, the SR-71, and eventually satellites and high-tech cameras.

Thus, when John F. Kennedy moved into the White House on January 20, 1961, a substantial structure of NSC committees-subcommittees awaited him. The U.S. Defense Department had already begun to surpass the State Department in terms of influence in U.S. foreign policy.[1] The intelligence community (IC) had grown considerably from CIA and a few tactical entities in Defense to an array of different agencies (although many of them secret) that divided intelligence work into human intelligence (HUMINT), signals intelligence (SIGINT), and other types of intelligence work product. The CIA had grown considerably over the previous decade, as had the larger IC.

This chapter will cover cases from multiple presidential administrations at the height of the Cold War. It begins with President Kennedy's shortened tenure (he was assassinated in November of his third year) followed by case studies from Lyndon Baines Johnson's time, Kennedy's immediate successor. After Johnson, a case from the Richard M. Nixon's administration will be presented. Nixon spanned the late 1960s into the 1970s. Finally, the chapter turns to a case from the Ronald Reagan administration in the early 1980s.

The cases range from the Cold War contest with Cuba (seen by the United States as a Soviet proxy) to various parts of what became the Vietnam War and cases conclude with America's renewed Cold War—after a respite of détente—in Latin America. One might argue about whether détente was achieved but there was at least a temporary retrenchment in U.S. foreign policy militarism after the Vietnam War (often thought of as détente). By the time Ronald Reagan became president (elected in November of 1980 but not inaugurated until January of 1981), the Cold War had returned with a vengeance. The case studies give the reader a chance to consider the evolution of the main institutions created by the National Security Act of 1947 and to assess what effect any evolution might have had on U.S. foreign policy, particularly the militarization thereof.

The reader will see that the NSC continued to evolve and new ad hoc institutions were created in it throughout the cases presented. Likewise, both the Defense Department and the IC grew and evolved into far more complex, massive institutions facilitating the militarization of U.S. foreign policy. Finally, as the new institutions created by the National Security Act evolved, so too did the power of the presidency, at the expense of the Congress. In short, the 1960s and 1970s represented a distinct phase of the Cold War for analytic purposes.

THE JOHN F. KENNEDY ADMINISTRATION AND
JFK'S NSC PRINCIPALS

President John F. Kennedy won by a narrow election margin against Richard Nixon (who had served Eisenhower for eight years as vice president) in November 1960. Among other things, Kennedy ran on the critique that (1) the NSC structure had become moribund under Eisenhower and that Ike's secretary of state, John Foster Dulles, ran U.S. foreign policy and (2) the Eisenhower administration had allowed a missile gap to develop between the U.S. ability to deliver nuclear weapons atop intercontinental ballistic missiles (ICBMs) to the USSR and the Soviet's capabilities to deliver them to America. Neither premise was particularly accurate.[2]

For Kennedy, it made political—by which I mean electoral politics—sense to paint Eisenhower as a tottering old general whose best days were well behind him. (By 1961, Eisenhower suffered multiple heart attacks making him a vulnerable target.) Senator Henry "Scoop" Jackson (D-WA, sometimes called the senator from Boeing) held hearings that overlapped with candidate Kennedy's campaign. The Jackson subcommittee examined how the Eisenhower administration had used the NSC and argued that Eisenhower had not used it to its full potential.[3] (Clearly, Senator Jackson was partial to candidate Kennedy but it is unclear if that was the only motivation for his subcommittee disparaging Eisenhower's NSC.) Furthermore, Senator Jackson's hearings again publicized the NSC, had Americans (regular citizens, journalists, academics, pundits) been interested in learning about the NSC and the statute that created it.

Among Kennedy's early decisions was the president's decision to select a high-profile secretary of defense. Robert S. McNamara filled the bill nicely. McNamara had been among the Pentagon's "whiz kids," or statistical control officers during World War II that helped assess U.S. bombing damage. According to McNamara's account (not written until 1995), Robert Kennedy phoned McNamara on December 8, 1960 (about a month after the election), at Ford headquarters (where McNamara had become president of Ford Motors) and asked him to discuss the president-elect's wish that McNamara become secretary of Treasury. After McNamara insisted he was not qualified, Robert Kennedy then said he was authorized to offer the secretary of defense instead. The Kennedy brothers wanted McNamara to meet their brother-in-law Sargent Shriver later that day and eventually McNamara agreed.[4] McNamara proved an incredibly important NSC member (and arguably an early NSC "principal"[5]) during the Kennedy administration who empowered the Defense Department even more than had occurred under his predecessors.

The other Kennedy appointees—those who would constitute what eventually became the NSC principals—were McGeorge Bundy, as the adviser to the president on National Security Affairs (NSC adviser) and Secretary of State Dean Rusk. Allen Dulles stayed on initially as the director of central intelligence (DCI) and chairman of the Joint Chiefs of

Staff (CJCS) General Lyman Lemnitzer, inherited from Eisenhower, was eventually replaced late in Kennedy's second year by General Maxwell Taylor. Allen Dulles was replaced at CIA by John McCone eventually, and by most accounts it had to do with the Bay of Pigs in spring 1961. (Though the attorney general was not a statutory member of the NSC, Attorney General Bobby Kennedy was clearly among Kennedy's NSC principals. The National Security Act of 1947 does not limit whom a president may include in his NSC.) Walt Rostow became McGeorge Bundy's deputy and eventually replaced Bundy in 1966 during the Johnson administration.

The National Security Council became, according to historian Arthur Schlesinger, "a supple instrument to meet the new President's distinctive needs."[6] Others have questioned just how crucial Secretary of State Rusk was in the Kennedy NSC meetings.[7] Former secretary of defense McNamara eventually threw Rusk under the bus in his memoirs on the Vietnam War. Among other things, he argued that Rusk was indecisive and easily circumvented by his underlings; he argued likewise that President Kennedy was prepared to dump Rusk in the second term. (Kennedy was assassinated in November 1963, a full year before he could run for a second term.)

Of Secretary Rusk, McNamara wrote: "It was not a secret that President Kennedy was deeply dissatisfied with Dean Rusk's administration of the State Department." McNamara went on to say that shortly after Kennedy's death McNamara was "surprised" to learn from Bobby Kennedy that the president intended to ask McNamara to serve as secretary of state beginning in the second term.[8] (Despite the growing influence of the secretary of defense, the secretary of state was still considered the preeminent cabinet position and the key NSC member, though the balance between the two positions was already changing in the NSC with the secretary of defense becoming very powerful indeed.)

According to multiple sources, the transition meeting between outgoing president Eisenhower and his replacement president John F. Kennedy was productive and focused on two regions: Laos in South East Asia (what would become the Vietnam War) and Cuba under Fidel Castro.[9] It is therefore unsurprising that these two issues came to dominate the Kennedy administration's foreign policy during Kennedy's 1,000 days in office. Vietnam had been shaping up as a proxy war between the United States and the Soviets for years. Some of President Kennedy's most controversial policies were with respect to Vietnam and Cuba. And as will be seen presently, these policies arose from the NSC inside the Kennedy administration (and particularly a few key members, including what we would call NSC principals and deputies today).

Cuba and the Bay of Pigs

With respect to Cuba, the Eisenhower administration already had a plan in place when John Kennedy became president. The Eisenhower plan had

included both a military and political component: the military component was a guerilla infiltration of Cuba only *after* an alternative government (the political component) that could speak for many Cubans was
established outside of Cuba. During the transition from Eisenhower to
Kennedy, the CIA had altered the guerilla infiltration to an amphibious
landing, thus changing partly the "plausible deniability" aspect of the operation, something both Eisenhower and Kennedy had insisted on having.
But the CIA was not alone in changing things as NSC members signed on
to the changes.

The key was keeping America's role small enough to conceal direct U.S.
responsibility. The problem was the media had already caught onto parts
of the story. As Schlesinger stated in his biography of Kennedy, the dilemma was this. If the United States "kept its role small enough to conceal
its responsibility, the operation might not have a fair chance of success;
while if it made its role large enough to give the operation a fair chance
of success, the responsibility could not be plausibly disclaimed in case of
failure."[10] This left the incoming administration in a predicament. If the
plans were left to proceed as such, Kennedy may well face the humiliation
of the failure of a plan he had approved (as had Eisenhower) or having to
send U.S. forces into the breach, obviating the covert nature of the assault.

The Bay of Pigs fiasco eventually became a "perfect failure."[11] It is worth
noting that the basic plan had been proposed by CIA's Allen Dulles and
Ted Bissell, under the Eisenhower administration. The Joint Chiefs were
informed only in January 1961, along with most of the other NSC participants. Moreover, as noted, the plan had begun to leak to various publications in the United States. *The Nation* published a piece titled "Are We
Training Cuban Advisers?" in November 1961. Both the *New York Times*
and others would soon be poking around the story. These leaks alone
should have stopped the momentum or at least slowed it down giving the
NSC members time to consider different options. The fact that plausible
deniability had already become problematic alone should have created
hesitation. Instead, the operation continued with NSC members all engaging in cognitive dissonance (or what might better be called groupthink);
in fact, in addition to the Bay of Pigs, the Kennedy NSC ended up autho-
rizing multiple assassination attempts of Fidel Castro resulting in spreading a massive Cold War confrontation to Cuba that threatened nuclear
war, the Cuban Missile Crisis (fall 1962).

On January 22, 1961, the Kennedy NSC principals were finally briefed
on the operation that would become known as the Bay of Pigs. (Note, this
is just two days after Kennedy became president.) On January 28, nearly a
week later, President Kennedy held his first NSC meeting on a plan to topple Fidel Castro. In attendance were Secretary of Defense McNamara, Secretary of State Dean Rusk, both Dulles and Ted Bissell from CIA and CJCS
General Lemnitzer. Also in attendance was Attorney General Robert Kennedy, President Kennedy's younger brother.[12] We may never know why
neither President Kennedy nor Attorney General Robert Kennedy or even

Secretary of Defense McNamara failed to question the plan more robustly or scrutinize its shortcomings. (Irving Janis, of course, makes the case that it was due to groupthink, a pathology associated with small group decision-making and he may well be right.)[13] Certainly, the NSC principals were a small group. But the new team was just that: new and that may have had much to do with it. For whatever reasons, the Kennedy administration moved forward with the plan tweaking it here and there and thereby making the plan more prone to failure. (For instance, Eisenhower had always maintained the plan could not be hatched until a government-in-waiting was in place but the Kennedy NSC approved it despite never identifying alternative Cuban leadership!)

Of course, the plan degenerated almost immediately after Kennedy gave the final go ahead on April 15-16, 1961. (Note, again, that the approval was fewer than three full months since Kennedy's inauguration.) Within days the Bay of Pigs debacle was seen as a failure of U.S. foreign policy and a massive humiliation for the new Kennedy administration. The failure would ultimately shade so much else the administration attempted, including how to respond in Vietnam where things were going from bad to worse and what would become the Cuban Missile Crisis the following year. Kennedy's humiliation made him desperate to find some credible way to stand up to Soviet "wars of national liberation," which made him even more desperate about Cuba. The Bay of Pigs debacle is terribly important because it says much about the transition from the Eisenhower NSC to the Kennedy NSC and about continuity in U.S. foreign policy (as well as about a potential recurring problem in presidential transitions).

The Structured, Comparative Case Study
Questions for Bay of Pigs

Question 1. Novel use of the NSC? The question at hand is whether the Bay of Pigs constituted a novel use of the institutions created by the National Security Act of 1947. Specifically, for Question 1, did it constitute a novel or improvised use of the NSC? Like previous Eisenhower covert operations, the Bay of Pigs was a combination of planning at the NSC level and execution at the military and, more important, paramilitary elements of the IC. The Bay of Pigs resulted in plans hatched at the NSC levels using Cuban immigrants living in the United States to attack a sovereign nation. It was quite true that Cuba was an enemy and the United States had poor relations with its leader, Fidel Castro. Nevertheless, to overthrow an extant government in America's backyard (90 miles from Florida's southern extremity) was novel as it was decided at the NSC principals level, not at a subcommittee level with a "need to know" the information. (Recall, decisions to overthrow government had been made by the 5412 subcommittee during the Eisenhower administration.) Likewise, the use of

CIA (paramilitary) was novel in the scope: military and paramilitary elements (both Defense and the IC) trained and advised Cuban émigrés in the United States and abroad (in Central America).

Soon Kennedy too would create a subcommittee similar to Eisenhower's 5412 subcommittee. In the Kennedy NSC, the subcommittee became known as the 303 committee and it would be involved in subsequent decisions in Vietnam. At this early juncture, however (and it is worth remembering that Kennedy had only been president just under three months when the Bay of Pigs was hatched), the NSC was still taking shape.

It is interesting to note yet again how precedents in one administration become normalized in subsequent ones. Eisenhower was the first president to use the CIA and other agencies of the federal government in covert and/or paramilitary ways. The Eisenhower precedent proved irresistible to subsequent administrations too. Kennedy followed Eisenhower's precedent by launching the Bay of Pigs fiasco. Though the planning was begun under Eisenhower, it was implemented and approved under Kennedy and the Kennedy NSC would live with the results for years to come.

Kennedy's NSC subcommittee that formulated and changed the Eisenhower plan for Cuba was novel, at least nominally. As noted, the precedent was set in the Eisenhower administration. However, there it had been quite small and confined to the NSC principals with a need to know—that is, a subgroup of NSC members and advisers with some reason to be briefed on the covert operation. In the Kennedy administration, it grew to include what would later be called NSC deputies and other "back benchers." Probably, that was due to Kennedy's relatively young age and lack of experience but it also had to do with Kennedy's management style. As would be seen again with the Cuban Missile Crisis, Kennedy liked a large group of advisers who advised on military, intelligence, as well as political matters. To cite two examples, Kennedy included his brother Robert Kennedy (the attorney general) and Arthur Schlesinger (an historian who would chronicle the presidency). Thus, technically, it was a novel use of the precedent created under Eisenhower.

Question 2. Novel use of the military? There is some evidence that the military was used somewhat uniquely. For instance, the military helped train Cuban refugees in Florida and then in Latin America. But it is probably more accurate to assert that it was an evolution of the military use, continuing with what was begun under President Eisenhower in covert and paramilitary operations. The conclusion in terms of novel use of the military therefore must be negative.

Question 3. Novel use of the IC? Like Question 2, it is difficult to call the cooperation between the military and IC in training Cuban refugees novel. It was a slightly different twist to something begun in the Eisenhower administration. In the case of Bay of Pigs, however, it was enough to conclude the military was used in a novel way. For instance, though the Bay of Pigs was supposed to have plausible deniability, the military became openly involved—though not as much as some military leaders hoped—in mitigating the worst of the negative consequences of the disaster.

Questions 4 and 5. Militarization of U.S. foreign policy? Yes, clearly there is evidence of the NSC militarizing U.S. foreign policy. New iterations of Eisenhower's 5412 committee appear to have functioned in the Bay of Pigs case and the result was spreading the Cold War confrontation to Cuba. Moreover, though not the focus of the Bay of Pigs, the evidence shows that Kennedy authorized assassination attempts of Castro, a sort of militarization—killing foreign leaders deemed troublesome—of U.S. foreign policy.

As noted earlier, the transition between Eisenhower and Kennedy focused on two foreign policy topics: Cuba and Laos. Laos was also inherited from Eisenhower. President Eisenhower had been unhappy with the situation in former French Indochina since 1955 (the Geneva Conference that reached an agreement on Indochina). The Eisenhower administration had begun undermining the agreement—although it was careful not to be a signatory to it—almost immediately. The administration's means of undermining it included the building of a covert paramilitary force in Laos among the Hmong (ethnic group who lived on subsistence agriculture in the mountains that divided Laos from Vietnam).

Vietnam: The Ngo Dinh Diem Coup

In documenting the Ngo Dinh Diem coup during the fall of 1963 (ironically, just weeks before President Kennedy was assassinated), two main sources were employed. Both agree on the main outlines of the NSC's involvement in the affair. The first source is the so-called *Pentagon Papers*.[14] The other is Defense Secretary Robert McNamara's memoirs on the Vietnam War, *In Retrospect*,[15] written two decades after the United States had departed Vietnam for good. The sources are somewhat redundant—which is a good thing in this case as they confirm each other in many particulars—but together give the researcher a good insider's perspective of policy making in the Kennedy (and subsequently the Johnson) administration's decisions on Vietnam.

Like Cuba, the Kennedy administration inherited Vietnam (originally, Laos and Vietnam) from the Eisenhower administration. President Eisenhower became involved—at least in earnest—in 1954 after the French were defeated at Dien Bien Phu. While Eisenhower considered using low-yield nuclear weapons to "save" the French, he ultimately decided against such madness. After all, the French were attempting to salvage what was left of their colonial possessions and most Americans considered colonialism a European pathology and something America would never undertake. (The British had begun research into atomic weapons prior to the United States and shared their research with the United States leading to an agreement between the two allies not to use atomic weapons without consulting the other. The British remained firm against using atomic weapons at Dien Bien Phu.)

However, the Eisenhower administration was also keen to take a stand against Soviet wars of national liberation, and President Eisenhower and his NSC members had become convinced that the Soviets were neck-deep in French Indochina. Therefore, the Eisenhower administration (following the Truman administration) continued to involve the United States incrementally more in Indochina over time. (In time, the People's Republic of China was likewise seen as a motive force in Vietnam but that is beyond the present scope.)

The increments were very much predicated on the United States desiring the French to become a solid member of the North Atlantic Treaty Organization (NATO) in 1949 onward and eventually to help create the European Defense Community (EDC)—as it turned out, something that never quite happened. The United States had helped pay the French expenses in Indochina during the Truman presidency and Eisenhower continued and increased these monies as well as U.S. involvement. (It is worth noting that the issue of Germany was at the heart of the EDC and neither the French nor others were eager to rearm Germany. Eisenhower, by contrast, believed a healthy and defensible Germany was necessary to rebuild war-torn Europe.)

The next increment was supporting Ngo Dinh Diem, a French-educated Catholic who had been part of the last Vietnamese emperor Bao Dai's tenure (the Bao Dai government). Bao Dai was unpopular and eventually the likewise unpopular Ngo Dinh Diem outmaneuvered Bao Dai and installed himself. President Eisenhower hosted Ngo Dinh Diem in the United States. Once Diem supplanted Bao Dai, the Eisenhower administration believed U.S. credibility would be enhanced because a popular sovereign would replace a monarchy. (The problem was Diem was only popular among the relatively insular Catholic community in Vietnam.) Nevertheless, Eisenhower can be seen in newspaper photos and newsreels in the mid-1950s standing next to President Diem at the airport in D.C. telling Americans what a great man Ngo Dinh Diem was. Eisenhower was the first of multiple presidents to attempt to sell Vietnamese dictators as the "savior" of Southeast Asia.

President Eisenhower had ostensibly supported the Geneva Accords on Laos and Vietnam (circa 1955) but instructed then secretary of state John Foster Dulles not to sign the document. The administration's position was that the United States had not been party to the accords and, while the United States would agree to act *as if* it was bound by the accords, it would not deign to sign something it had not negotiated.[16] (Before the United States finally withdrew from the Vietnam imbroglio, roughly equal numbers of Republican and Democratic presidents would incrementally involve America more in Indochina's affairs!) Vietnam was a proxy war and the real object of it was always the Soviet Union and/or the Chinese communists (Chicom in U.S. government argot).

This was the state of affairs President Kennedy inherited in January 1961. (In modern times, presidents are elected in November of even years and inaugurated in January of the next odd year. President Kennedy was elected in November 1960 and inaugurated in January 1961.) From the beginning of the Kennedy administration, Kennedy's NSC principals took a similar position—if not slightly more defiant—on what was happening in Indochina than the Eisenhower administration. Clearly, Kennedy and his NSC principals felt Nikita Khrushchev was testing the new administration and foisting wars of national liberation on otherwise happy people trying to effect Soviet's form of modern government. (Both Democrats and Republicans repeatedly underestimated the disfavor in which colonialism was held in the Third World.)

Indeed, it is worth quoting McNamara who came to dominate the NSC principals as few other members did.

The beginning of all things are small, and the story of my involvement in Vietnam is no different. When John F. Kennedy became president, we [the NSC members] faced a complex and growing crisis in Southeast Asia with sparse knowledge, scant experience, and simplistic assumptions. As time passed we came to recognize that the problems plaguing South Vietnam [The Republic of Vietnam or RVN] and its embattled leader, Ngo Dinh Diem, were far more complicated [sic] than we initially perceived.

Among the complications were two somewhat contradictory assumptions the NSC members held. The first was that the "fall" of the RVN to communism would threaten the security of the United States and the "Western world." The other was that only the South Vietnamese [RVN's army known as ARVN] could defend Vietnam and therefore America's role should be limited and in support of ARVN-RVN. There can be little doubt about which of the former assumptions ultimately drove policy: the fall of the RVN domino would challenge the United States and Western security.[17]

The Kennedy administration looked very much like its predecessor, the Eisenhower administration. Namely, they feared any sort of outright loss or setback and therefore became incrementally more involved over time. This, of course, meant supporting President Diem who with his brother and extended family became more tyrannical and imprisoned more political opponents, despite U.S. objections. It also meant that sham elections were held in which President Diem was repeatedly reelected with majorities in the 80 and 90 percent range. Catholic elites made a small minority in Vietnam and could never poll such numbers so everybody involved knew the elections were rigged.

Such contradictory elements of U.S. policy continued to build up in the early Kennedy administration until the spring and summer of 1963, when the contradictions proved so untenable they could no longer coexist.

It was 1963 (spring into the summer) when the Vietnam cauldron boiled over into such a mess that the Kennedy administration Americanized the war, eventually leading to the deaths of some 58,000 Americans and physical and mental injuries to many more. (President Johnson would soon continue Kennedy's policies but eventually Americanize the war substantially rather than merely incrementally.)

In the spring of 1963, in the historic capital of Hué, Catholics were allowed to celebrate their religious holidays. Contrary to the Catholic elites of Vietnam, the Buddhist majority was forbidden by the Ngo Dinh Diem government from celebrating Buddha's birthday. Protests resulted. The protests precipitated a series of "crises" in Vietnam, including Diem's government cracking down on Buddhists from Hué to Saigon. By summer, the protests had moved into Saigon where the arrests and crackdowns intensified. (Several Buddhists protested with the ultimate means of protest, self-immolation, which reverberated in the United States.)[18]

The question became how much longer could Diem stay in power with South Vietnam roiled by protests. The protests split some of Diem's military leadership where Catholics and Buddhists (mostly Hoa Hao) both served as officers. Moreover, the information flow between Vietnam and Washington was difficult. Therefore, the decision-making for what became the Diem coup varied between Vietnam (where the U.S. embassy and what became the military command in Vietnam existed) and Washington D.C. where the NSC principals met. The troubles began in summer of 1963 when the Kennedy NSC members got intimately involved in the decisions made in Hué and Saigon.

Before discussing the decisions made in Washington, it is important to note one other matter that would soon prove fatal to the policy. Somewhere along the line the CIA had begun planning for the possibility of a coup to remove President Diem from power. While the exact date is unimportant for present purposes, it is important to note who was involved and apparently directing the CIA in its contingency planning. The editor of the *Pentagon Papers* put it this way: "The operative question is not whether the Diem government as it was then moving could defeat the insurgency but whether it could save itself."[19] (That is, persons involved peripherally in the NSC involved themselves in deciding whether the Diem government could continue to exist!)

In fact, the volume of the *Pentagon Papers* dedicated to the Diem coup begins its narrative with the following.

The Diem coup was one of those critical events in the history of U.S. policy that could have altered [America's] commitment. The choices were: 1) continue to plod along in a limited fashion with Diem—despite his and [his brother Nhu's] growing unpopularity; 2) encourage or tacitly support the over throw of Diem, taking the risk that the [Government of Vietnam, or GVN] might crumble and/or accommodate to the [Viet Cong]; and 3) grasp the opportunity—with the obvious risks—of the political instability in South Vietnam to disengage.[20]

During the summer of 1963 (August), the NSC principals—or most of them—were out of town. (Anyone who has lived in D.C. understands that summers there are unbearable and the city largely closes in August and its denizens leave for more temperate environs. Such was the case in 1963 meaning many of the NSC principals in the Kennedy administration were out of town.) In addition, the previous ambassador to Vietnam had been recalled and his replacement, Ambassador Henry Cabot Lodge, had been instructed to head to Saigon in August, after some earlier meetings in Washington with the president and other NSC members. It appears that Ambassador Lodge and a fairly senior-level State Department official, Roger Hilsman, decided to have a try at making policy. (Hilsman had recently succeeded Averell Harriman as assistant secretary of state for Far Eastern Affairs.[21] Hilsman was therefore at best an NSC ad hoc member rather than an actual NSC member. That is, Roger Hilsman was not a statutory member of the NSC though evidence suggests he had attended some NSC meetings.)

Hilsman sent a telegram message to Lodge—the new ambassador—as Lodge was on his way to Vietnam in late August 1963. (Hilsman's expertise was low-intensity warfare or guerilla wars and his expertise was somewhat rare in those days.) In the telegram Hilsman noted that Diem's government had smashed Buddhist pagodas and had used the incident (protests in Hué) as a pretext for a general crackdown on his political enemies—not for the first time. Hilsman wrote Diem's brother Nhu had "tricked" Diem. He then rather boldly stated, "The U.S. Government cannot tolerate a situation in which power lies in Nhu's hands. Diem must be given a chance," wrote Hilsman, "to rid himself of Nhu" and Nhu's coterie and replace them with the "best military and political advisers" or else. The or else was made explicit: "If in spite of all your [Lodge's] efforts, Diem remains obdurate, then we must face the possibility that Diem himself may not be preserved."[22]

In his memoirs McNamara threw Hilsman under the bus, if indirectly. That is, McNamara says he and his deputy (Ros Gilpatric) believed a replacement for Diem could not easily be found but that planning was so far advanced that Gilpatric gave his approval for the coup after the fact. McNamara further wrote (decades after the fact) that he did not share General Maxwell Taylor's view (Kennedy's CJCS) that Hilsman's telegram was "an egregious end run" but he is careful about including such disparaging comments and calls Hilsman's actions the same in slightly different words.[23] (In fact, one of the odd things about McNamara's memoirs is that he dramatically says how wrong he and others were early on then spends the rest of the book demonstrating how wrong others were than McNamara.)

The problem with characterizations of rogue element or egregious end run is the fact that the coup neither occurred in August nor in September nor in October. Indeed, rumors of coups swirled around Saigon and Washington the entire summer until the coup took place in *November*! The

NSC principals were all back in town and aware of the Hilsman actions in August but did not move to put the kibosh on the coup. Indeed, Ambassador Lodge "shunned all contact" with Diem's government during October and no one from the NSC suggested he do otherwise. The NSC members were strangely inert once Hilsman's ultimatum was sent in August.

The *Pentagon Papers* asserted that differences of view existed among the NSC members in Washington as well as the ambassador's office and the military command in Vietnam (MACV). Lodge wanted it "clearly understood that they [Diem's government] must come to him prepared to adopt [Washington's] advice before [Lodge] would recommend to Washington a change in policy." The result was "friction" between MACV and the ambassador. (Anyone who has studied U.S. foreign policy knows that friction between the military and state department is anything but rare.)

In particular, Lodge's disagreements and disputes with General Harkins [MACV] during October when the coup plot was maturing and later were to be of considerable embarrassment to Washington when they leaked to the press.[24]

Vietnamese generals, broken into factions before the Kennedy administration, used the "friction" to again begin planning their coup operations. The NSC members were aware of the factions and that both the military and one or two CIA operators (especially, one named Lucien Conein) were talking to the generals, while they plotted against Diem. Yet the NSC effectively sat on its collective hands. If Hilsman's telegram had been such an end run, why did his superiors in the NSC do nothing to countermand the telegram for nearly three months?

It is worth quoting the *Pentagon Papers* in its ultimate conclusion on the coup plot against Diem and the indecision in Washington.

For the military coup d'état against Ngo Dinh Diem, the U.S. must accept its full share of responsibility. Beginning in August of 1963, [policymakers in the NSC and on the ground] variously authorized, sanctioned and encouraged the coup efforts of the Vietnamese generals and offered full support for a successor government. In October [Washington] cut off aid to Diem in a direct rebuff, giving a green light to the generals. [The U.S.] maintained clandestine contact with [the generals] throughout the planning and execution of the coup and sought to review [the generals'] operational plans and proposed new government. Thus, as the nine-year rule of Diem came to a bloody end, [America's] complicity in his overthrow heightened [America's] responsibilities and [its] commitment in an essentially leaderless Vietnam.[25]

One may search in vain for a direct or explicit mea culpa in McNamara's memoirs but he comes closest to it after saying, in effect, that Roger Hilsman was impetuous. "We all knew that Hilsmam went outside channels," wrote McNamara, clearly blaming Hilsman despite earlier softpedaling the same argument. However, the "fault lay as much with those who failed to rein him in as it did with Hilsman himself." McNamara admitted that the NSC members remained "deeply divided" over the action that led to the overthrow and that "no careful examination and evaluation of alternatives to Diem had been made" by McNamara or others in the NSC. The NSC members watched in apparent paralysis, while momentum carried things along. (However else one may characterize it, it cannot be characterized as a sterling example of the NSC functioning effectively. By contrast with the previous year's involvement in the Cuban Missile Crisis it is somewhat puzzling why the NSC was so dysfunctional?)

The Structured, Comparative Case Study Questions for Diem Coup

Question 1. Did the NSC function in a novel or new way? For present purposes, the question remains did the overthrow of Diem's government in Vietnam equal a novel use of the NSC, Defense or the IC? First, let us address the NSC. We have seen that Eisenhower likewise used the NSC (5412 subcommittee of the NSC) to plan and effect covert overthrows of governments the United States consider Soviet dupes or stooges. The cases of Iran and Guatemala both come to mind. So it was not novel in the sense of the United States using newly created institutions to overthrow governments.

However, in the Diem coup the NSC was used innovatively in that it was the first time, as far as I discovered, of the U.S. NSC being complicit in the overthrow of a government that the United States effectively created. Diem existed at America's behest and when Diem and his family proved embarrassing, the United States minimally acquiesced in the coup that resulted in his death. The United States did not desire Diem's murder, as far as could be determined, but the NSC sat on its collective hands from August to early November knowing that coups and rumors of coups swirled in Saigon. It did nothing to stop them and even encouraged them at various times.

Moreover, it was novel in the sense that an underling (an NSC deputy in this case) caused the coup to commence, while the principals were out of town avoiding the August heat of D.C. I hasten to add that between August and November when the coup actually took place, the NSC principals—anyone of them or as a group—could have easily called it off; instead, they behaved as if they were helpless and poor Hilsman's impetuosity was more than they could control. It proved a rather strange example of the NSC members simply watching the train wreck take place.

Question 2. Was the military used in a novel or new war? Also, the military was used somewhat uniquely in the case (in a novel way). Namely, what was becoming MACV (the military mission in Vietnam) was also involved in the intrigues. Military officers ran their own connections in the Diem government; and between CIA and the Pentagon, a sort of keystone cops routine unfolded in Vietnam. Though not the province of this study, with the elimination of Diem began a series of coups and countercoups that resulted in the United States utterly losing control of events in Vietnam. The amazing thing is that it continued for nearly 12 additional years like an uncontrolled train wreck unfolding over a decade plus.

Question 3. The intelligence community? Though the IC (in particular, the CIA) was involved in serious interference with other governments, in this case CIA operatives on the ground partially operated beyond what the NSC had authorized, at least as far as could be determined. It may not be a significant example of novel use but it is at least an arguable case.

Questions 4 and 5. Militarization of U.S. foreign policy? The Diem coup was another example of militarization of U.S. foreign policy. As noted earlier, the NSC had previously overthrown governments during the Eisenhower administration. But this was a government the United States had largely created. The subsequent escalation of the Vietnam War is prima facie evidence of militarization of foreign policy. Sources make it clear the Diem coup was the beginning of the end of the United States feigning support-only for the RVN and the beginning of direct U.S. involvement. As will be seen in the Johnson administration, more incremental steps were just around the corner.

LYNDON B. JOHNSON'S ADMINISTRATION AND HIS NSC PRINCIPALS

For the first couple of years, the Johnson administration was simply the Kennedy administration with a different president. When President Kennedy was assassinated—just weeks after Diem was overthrown and assassinated[26]—Vice President Johnson simply moved into the White House and kept the Kennedy administration's policies. (In fairness to President Johnson, it should be noted that as vice president Johnson was against the Diem coup. Thus, he inherited a mess he did not support.) As president, Johnson merely finished Kennedy's term, the NSC members remained essentially the same.

Johnson, of course, became the top of the NSC with Secretary of Defense McNamara and Secretary of State Dean Rusk, respectively. Likewise, McGeorge Bundy remained as the NSC adviser and became, arguably, even more influential in the new administration than he had been in its predecessor. (NSC adviser Bundy left the NSC in early 1966 for the Ford Foundation.) The vice president, obviously, changed but the vice president was not a factor in the NSC, despite being a statutory principal in the National Security Act of 1947. (In fact, the vice president did not become more than a nominal member of the NSC until well after the Cold War, as will be discussed in its proper place.) Secretary of State Dean Rusk stayed until the end; McNamara left only after the Tet Offensive (circa 1968) at which time he was replaced by Clark Clifford as Johnson's second secretary of defense. (The reader may recall Clark Clifford was part of the Truman administration. Both parties have "stables" of so-called experts who return in subsequent administrations.)

Robert Kennedy left the administration and the attorney general never regained its august status of NSC principal during Johnson's tenure. Maxwell Taylor (Kennedy's CJCS) remained through mid-1964 whereupon he was replaced by General Earl Wheeler (who served through much the Johnson tenure). In early 1966, McGeorge Bundy left—one of the first to bolt—for the Ford Foundation and a former deputy NSC adviser, Walt Rostow, became Johnson's second NSC adviser. Thus, little change occurred in the two administrations' NSC members.

That is not to say relationships did not change some. But McNamara remained a dominant force until late 1967 or, more likely, early 1968. In fact, if one is to believe McNamara's memoirs, written well after the fact (in 1995), the secretary of defense still did not know whether he resigned or was fired. "I do not know to this day whether I quit or was fired. Maybe it was both," wrote McNamara in 1995.[27] Once McGeorge Bundy left in 1966, Johnson relied on McNamara even more singularly than had President Kennedy. (It was during the Johnson years the Vietnam War became known as McNamara's War.) Dean Rusk, whom McNamara claims the Kennedy administration nearly fired, was somewhat rehabilitated in the Johnson administration and the military—from the chairman of the Joint Chiefs to the various service commanders figured even more prominently in debates in the Johnson NSC.

In what follows, two critically important cases from the Johnson administration are considered. The first is the Tonkin Gulf affair (August 1964) that resulted in the Gulf of Tonkin Resolution and, effectively, in a blank check for Johnson. (While not a formal declaration of war, it came as close to one as could exist without being one.) In consequence, Johnson was first able to retaliate with air strikes against Hanoi (North Vietnam or the DRV) for the Tonkin Gulf and eventually to land troops at Da Nang Vietnam, wholly Americanizing the war. After troops landed at Da Nang, the Vietnam War became America's war and there was no turning back until Americans turned on the war.

The second case is a lesser-known decision but nonetheless a critical one. In fall of 1964 into early 1965, a debate raged inside the White House (and the NSC) about what to do in Vietnam. Since the Diem coup (November 1963), things had gone from bad to worse and every few weeks, dire warnings swirled through the NSC about the fall of the RVN (South Vietnam) to communists. A particular decision—McNamara called it the "fork-in-the-road" memo in his memoirs—was incredibly important for it made the way for sending troops to Da Nang. It was debated and discussed in detail and though answers were not forthcoming, critical decisions flowed from the debates. It is an example of paralysis and dysfunction at the NSC level and helps explain the bureaucratic momentum that led to the Americanization of the Vietnam War.

(That is not to say the war would not have become Americanized under President Kennedy! Indeed, it had already to some extent. After all, other than the president the NSC members remained the same. Moreover, substantial dysfunction in Kennedy's NSC was already evident. Finally, one of the remarkable things about U.S. foreign policy during the Cold War— and even since—is the incredible continuity of goals and/or objectives of U.S. foreign policy. The said goals change very slowly, only incrementally, and create a continuity in U.S. foreign policy that is the rule rather than the exception, irrespective of who controls either end of Pennsylvania Avenue.)

These two cases will be used to illustrate increasing militarization of U.S. foreign policy (in the Vietnam War) as well as some novel uses of the NSC mechanisms of interest, and the NSC members. As was the case with the previous case study (Diem overthrow), the two main sources will be the *Pentagon Papers* and McNamara's *In Retrospect*. (With respect to the latter source, though McNamara wrote it some 20-plus years after he left the government, he nevertheless had access to notes and summaries from NSC meetings as well as meeting with certain members of the NSC principals committee. Clearly, McNamara indulges in the memoir writer's habit of putting his decisions in the best light but he also provides many verbatim records, well worth the reading.)

The Tonkin Gulf Affair

As just noted, after Diem's overthrow and assassination, the situation in South Vietnam (RVN) went from bad to worse. A revolving door of characters, of generals and other leaders, of coups and countercoups, and of juntas became so troublesome to President Johnson that he eventually demanded an end to this "coup shit."[28] The fact was, Vietnam was becoming an embarrassment for the president and for U.S. foreign policy. Johnson learned what his predecessors often learned: the United States has far less control over its clients than it supposed. Also, Vice President Johnson had been against the coup—that is, he belonged to one faction in the president's advisers, who had believed the United States must nurture Diem along a bit more. Now, he had inherited a foreign policy embarrassment with only bad options from which to choose.

On the one hand, President Johnson believed (as did his predecessors dating back to Truman) that Vietnam was critical to prevent Soviet expansionism elsewhere in the world. Thus, America could not walk away from Vietnam as the Cold War calculus of zero-sum game meant that if America withdrew the Soviets won. On the other hand, the South Vietnamese were corrupt, riven with factions, divided into elites and the masses, and as undemocratic as Ho Chi Minh's regime in the North. Johnson found himself on the horns of a dilemma.

In early 1964, President Johnson approved a series of covert operations (hatched from a subcommittee of the NSC then called the 303 committee) in Vietnam. The covert operations the 303 committee concocted for Vietnam came in two versions. The first was called DeSoto missions. The U.S. Navy (with the National Security Agency [NSA] platform on board, that is, the intelligence agency that conducts signals intelligence or SIGINT) would zigzag up and down Vietnam's coast. On occasion the ships would cross into North Vietnam's territorial waters (the 12-mile limit) and take a tack at North Vietnam. The ships would then tack back out to international waters using the onboard equipment to collect electronic signals (called telemetry) and other intelligence from North Vietnam's defenses.

The other version approved was OPLAN 34A operations, which included U.S. advisers along with South Vietnamese commandos landing on North Vietnamese islands or even the mainland, where they would detonate some targets to raise hell in Vietnam and sow confusion. There seems to have been little coordination between these two operations, implemented by different entities but all approved from the NSC subcommittee level. (McNamara says the NSC approved the missions in the 303 committee, named after the room in which it met in the Old Executive Office Building, adjacent to the White House).[29]

McGeorge Bundy (NSC adviser) chaired the 303 committee and it was constituted of the NSC members with a need to know about covert operations. (Recall, that was rather similar to how Eisenhower had conducted the 5412 subcommittee of the NSC to keep information tightly held.) On July 30, 1964, an apparently uncoordinated OPLAN 34 operation was conducted by Vietnamese commandos in North Vietnam's territory. The *USS Maddox* (conducting Desoto missions) was, the next day (July 1), likewise conducting its telemetry gathering along North Vietnam's coast (in and out of DRV territorial waters), when the North Vietnamese put the two things together and concluded that the United States was preparing to attack North Vietnam. The result was North Vietnamese launched small boats toward the *Maddox*, apparently firing on the ship on August 2, 1964.[30]

In Washington, Johnson held an NSC meeting to determine what to do about North Vietnam's "provocation." (McNamara notes he was not in attendance and had Cyrus Vance in his stead.) The advisers concluded that the provocation was not likely to have been from Hanoi. Rather, they concluded that some local commander may have taken events into hand and responded and, therefore, the U.S. response should be simply to register a complaint but not to retaliate against the DRV (North Vietnam). However, in order to show Hanoi that the United States would tolerate no curtailment of its freedom of navigation, a decision was also taken to send another destroyer into the area, the *USS Turner Joy*. All these decisions were made on August 2, Washington time.

Though McNamara does not say so directly, he implies that the NSC members had concluded that North Vietnam may have connected the two separate covert operations and reasonably concluded the United States acted provocatively (not *vice versa*). McNamara wrote that he and Dean Rusk briefed Congress the next day in executive session and explained that both OPLAN 34A and Desoto operations were in the same basic area. "We informed the senators that the DESOTO patrols, as well as the OPLAN 34A operations, would continue, and in fact another 34A raid occurred about this time against the coast of North Vietnam (it was then early morning August 4 Saigon time)."[31]

Roughly 12-hour later (Washington time) another incident occurred where the DRV sent boats to intercept *Maddox* and/or *Turner Joy*. The result was a short-lived confrontation during which the *Maddox* reported it was under fire from the enemy. Later, it was determined that the DRV had not fired on the *Maddox* and that strange atmospherics (and possibly nervous radar operators) mistakenly assumed they were under attack. (In fact, in the first edition of McNamara's *In Retrospect*, the author continued to feign ignorance of what happened and only corrected it in the subsequent edition where he confessed the second attack never occurred.)

For present purposes, it matters very little for the essential facts remain the same. All accounts jibe in terms of the fact that the incident (or incidents) was used by the NSC members as a *pretext* to hustle a resolution (drafted the previous spring by McGeorge Bundy's brother, William Bundy, from the State Department) through both chambers of Congress. The resolution became known as the Gulf of Tonkin Resolution and it was as close to a declaration of war as any president got in Vietnam. It was unanimously passed by the House, and only two senators spoke against it in the Senate. Of course, had the Gulf of Tonkin Resolution not been passed (irrespective of what actually happened in Vietnam), Johnson could not have put troops into Vietnam in spring 1965 (at least without another sort of incident to pass a similar resolution).

McNamara was likely being honest when he wrote the resolution grew out of Lyndon Johnson's belief that he needed political cover similar to what Eisenhower had been given in 1955 (the Formosa Straits situation, also known as the Taiwan Straits "crises"). He also notes that the language for the resolution originated in May from the State Department in response to Johnson's request. McNamara also wrote: "Of course, if the Gulf of Tonkin Resolution had not led to much more serious involvement in Vietnam, it likely would not remain so controversial. But it did serve to open the flood gates."[32]

The Structured, Comparative Case Study
Questions for the Tonkin Gulf Debacle

Question 1. Novel use of the NSC? The question here is whether the NSC, Defense, or the IC was used in a novel way? While the answer is a less resounding affirmative than previous cases, it is still an affirmative generally. However, the NSC itself was not used in a unique or novel way. The NSC had been used (be it the 5412 or the 303 committees) to approve covert operations conducted by the IC.

Question 2. Novel use of the military? Certainly, the Defense Department had used gunboat diplomacy well before the Vietnam War. Nevertheless, there was no evidence of the NSC approving disparate covert operations (perhaps intentionally though it is impossible to prove) whereby an incident was created that was then used as a subsequent pretext for war. It may be a matter of degree and shows the need to refine the comparative questions somewhat, but there is little doubt that what happened in Tonkin was novel—Johnson and his NSC members seized a pretext to get Congress to pass a resolution, drafted months before the incident that gave the president power to act subsequently if he deemed it necessary for U.S. national security. In other words, Congress passed a resolution at the behest of the NSC members that basically rendered congressional powers ineffectual in terms of Vietnam. Clearly, it was another step in the incremental militarization of U.S. foreign policy, whatever its intentions were. Evidence shows that the military had been agitating for some time for more direct involvement in Vietnam. Between the NSC and the military leadership, the Tonkin Gulf incident gave the Pentagon its wish.

Question 3. Novel use of the intelligence community? One might argue that having the NSA (part of the IC) place an electronic intelligence platform aboard U.S. Naval ships was novel but evidence suggest such may have been done earlier. The NSA was created in the 1950s so it had been around for some years by then. During the Vietnam War, the NSA was still a highly classified agency so discovering previous examples is somewhat tricky. For that reason, it is impossible to know whether it was novel or not.

Questions 4 and 5. Militarization of U.S. foreign policy? Also, the incident revealed another example of the militarization of U.S. foreign policy, irrespective of the NSC. Namely, the NSA and the Pentagon worked together to monitor and possibly provoke North Vietnam. To be clear, large parts of the IC are funded and controlled by the Pentagon including the NSA. With the Tonkin Gulf affair one sees a growing IC that began as relatively small entity in the National Security Act of 1947. NSA was secret then but it was not the only growth in the IC. The Defense Intelligence Agency (DIA) has also evolved since the act was passed.

What is clear is that the Tonkin Gulf incident opened the floodgates, as McNamara admitted, and things moved rapidly thereafter in terms of complete Americanization of the Vietnam War. The essence of Americanization was the militarization thereof. Rather than supporting the ARVN, the United States began replacing ARVN with American boys and the militarization continued until sometime in the Nixon administration when "Vietnamization" or ending the American militarization was arguably reversed.

THE FORK-IN-THE-ROAD MEMO AND ESCALATION

After the Tonkin Gulf affair, the Joint Chiefs (hitherto, somewhat reluctant to Americanize the Vietnam War) began to debate (supported by civilians such as Walt Rostow) a piecemeal escalation of U.S. involvement via sustained bombing of North Vietnam. (The Chiefs had earlier advocated more latitude in terms of what targets should be considered for American bombing and things like hot pursuit.) The United States had flown many bombing sorties in South Vietnam against the Viet Cong but the North had been largely spared—mostly for fear of causing more Soviet and/or Chinese intervention. (Some "interdiction" of the Ho Chi Minh trail in the North and in Cambodia and Laos had occurred by bombing, however.) Eventually, the chiefs recommended what they called Phase I followed by Phase II bombing sorties. Phase I was intended to bomb targets along the Ho Chi Minh trail and the DRV's communication lines to the Viet Cong in the South. If Phase I did not accomplish a humbling of communists in Hanoi, Phase II was intended to target key military sites in the DRV, ratcheting up the pressure. The chiefs reasoned that graduated escalation would eventually cause the DRV to sue for negotiations, once the brunt of U.S. power was felt by Hanoi.

Incidentally, an entire literature critical of the Vietnam War on the grounds of gradual escalation exists by both military historians and others. Often the blame is laid at President Johnson's footsteps, and he ultimately made the decisions as president and is therefore an appropriate target. But it should be clear that both uniformed military and civilians in the NSC— and elsewhere—supported gradual escalation. And the reason was sound: the threat of North Vietnam was never great enough to launch an all-out attack on North Vietnam. That is, few ever argued North Vietnam or its surrogates threatened the United States in any material way. The domino theory was an abstraction that never made much sense in terms of U.S. se- curity. The threat was the Soviets (or Chinese communists) gaining another beachhead. Therefore, to launch an all-out offensive against North Vietnam would have been difficult to explain to the American public. How could it be justified when the real enemy in Vietnam was the USSR (and secondarily the PRC). Thus, gradual escalation became the norm and not until Presi- dent Nixon decided to punish Hanoi for something South Vietnam did was there an offensive against the North worthy of the description of "punish- ment." Even then, President Nixon was doing it for perverse reasons.

During the last week of November 1964, the NSC members met to con- sider the chiefs' recommendation of Phase I and Phase II air strikes against North Vietnam (the DRV). The editor of the *Pentagon Papers*, Leslie Gelb, put it this way.

During the last week in November [1964] the NSC Principals met to consider the Working Group's proposal [the working group was created to present options to the NSC principals]. They were joined on November 27 by Ambassador Taylor [Taylor had replaced Lodge in Vietnam but was home for consultation]. Taylor's report on conditions in South Vietnam was extremely bleak. To improve South Viet- namese morale and confidence, and to "drive the DRV out of its reinforcing role and obtain its cooperation in bringing an end to the Viet Cong insurgency [in RVN]" he [Taylor] urged that military pressures against North Vietnam be adopted.[33]

(As noted in the previous chapter, the NSC principals and the NSC deputies committees were not formally established until the George H. W. Bush administration. However, as was also noted by the Kennedy administration's "ExComm" during the Cuban Missile Crisis, what became known by some as the NSC principals evolved far earlier.)

That is, Ambassador Taylor urged the NSC principals to accept the Phase I and if Phase I failed to produce results, then Phase II that the chiefs and the "working group" recommended. (Phase I was reprisal strikes against aggressive DRV acts. Phase II were strikes that involved some 90-plus targets in the DRV.) The NSC had assigned William Bundy—NSC adviser McGeorge Bundy's brother—to form a working group to enumerate options for the Johnson administration in Vietnam. The Bundy working group set about vetting recommendations—including Phases I and II—on November 2, 1964.[34] Interestingly, just weeks earlier George Ball (October 1964) sent Secretary McNamara and NSC adviser McGeorge Bundy an important memorandum. As undersecretary of state—the position subsequently became deputy secretary of state or the number two position—he was not an NSC principal per se. However, he was what today would be called an NSC deputy and had proved himself knowledgeable in both the Kennedy and Johnson administrations. Also, like Hilsman and others Ball attended some NSC principals meetings. Therefore, while not a principal, Ball's 60-plus page memorandum should have been circulated among NSC members. It apparently was not!

Undersecretary of State Ball did not recommend, in his memorandum, withdrawing from Vietnam (severing America's ties with South Vietnam) but he did note the contradictions in U.S. policy and tried to spell them out in his 60-plus page opus on how the United States was bungling deeper and deeper into the Vietnam quagmire. (It is hard to conceive he did so without clearing it with his superior, Secretary of State Dean Rusk.) Accordingly, Ball pointed out the risks inherent in the debate about escalation. He worried about the Kremlin's reaction, among other things.

Secretary McNamara, McGeorge Bundy, and Dean Rusk discussed Ball's memorandum on November 7, 1964 (three NSC principals). "I have been unable to locate notes of the meeting," wrote McNamara in his memoirs but he clearly implied that they should have taken Ball's arguments more seriously and at least debated Ball's memorandum. Secretary of Defense McMamara, NSC adviser McGeorge Bundy, and Secretary of State Rusk "seriously erred in not carrying out" Ball's exploration of other options, wrote McNamara 20-plus years later. McNamara then says the three (four if Ball is included) should have explored Ball's view with the president but they did not. McNamara says that Ball passed his memorandum to the president through Bill Moyers[35] which seems to suggest that neither of the three NSC members bothered to follow up on the memorandum. Indeed, it may suggest they buried it?

What happened next is somewhat extraordinary. First, it should be conceded that Thanksgiving and Christmas holidays fall quickly on one another each fall. Likewise, it is worth noting the president likely had many responsibilities over the holidays, not just meeting on Vietnam and determining the way forward there. Additionally, LBJ spent some time in December at his ranch in Texas. Finally, many other issues arose in the Cold War during the late 1964-early-1965 time frame. "Crises" were seemingly appearing regularly during those years of the Cold War. The Soviets were aggressive in their measures globally and the United States was aggressive in its responses to Soviet aggression and vice versa. In short, it is not intended to imply some sort of conspiracy to keep Ball's warnings from the NSC principals—after all, if McNamara is right, Ball got his memorandum to President Johnson eventually, though apparently not until February 1965.

All those things granted, what happened is still somewhat difficult to fathom. On November 19, 1964, the William Bundy working group reported to the president the group's thoughts to date. According to Secretary McNamara, Dean Rusk told the president on November 19 that the working group was focused on three ideas. First, a negotiated settlement on any terms obtainable (clearly, not intended to be palatable to President Johnson just recently elected in his own right). Second, a sharp increase of military pressure on the DRV (another unpalatable option given nearly universal concern among NSC members that a sharp increase by the United States would cause the Soviets and/or the Chinese to intervene). Third, an in-between course of graduated pressure.[36]

For anyone who has studied U.S. foreign policy, this will quickly be recognized for what it is: the Goldilocks approach to framing options. The group (in this case, the William Bundy working group meeting to discuss recommendations, as well as the way forward) frames three options, two of which by their very framing are intended to be throwaway options. One option is "Too Hot" while the other option is "Too Cold," leaving the in-between option as "Just Right." (The Goldilocks approach predates Vietnam and has been seen as recently as the Obama "surge" in Afghanistan announced on December 1, 2009. See Chapter 5.) Whatever else one might want to say about the decision-making in the critical period of fall 1964 through spring 1965, it must be said that President Johnson was poorly served by his NSC principals. Johnson bears some of the blame and only he was the constitutional commander in chief but his NSC principals served him very badly.

Of course, the working group eventually reported its views to the president and the NSC began debating the working group's proposals, as it were. While the final three recommendations appeared somewhat altered from the November 19 version, what it submitted was the following: (1) "Continuing the present course indefinitely with little hope of avoiding defeat." (2) "Undertaking a sharp, intensive increase against [DRV's] communication lines to the South and the ninety-four targets proposed by the chiefs (i.e., Phase II), with the object of forcing Hanoi to stop supporting the Vietcong and/or enter [sic] negotiations." And, (3) undertaking "the same bombing campaign in a graduated manner" that is the Chief's sequential recommendation.[37]

Thus, the debate returned to the NSC members. It was December 1964 when the NSC members and principals returned to debate the working group's recommendations. McNamara reports a distraught President Johnson asking all kind of questions about what to do and whether to support the RVN or not and whether *anything* would work. After contentious meetings Johnson decided, somewhat strangely, to give Ambassador Taylor one last chance to "'achieve political stability'" in South Vietnam but telling the NSC principals (and the CJCS present), "'if that doesn't work I'll be talking to you General Wheeler.'" He then provisionally approved the two-phase plan[38] (i.e., the Phase I-Phase II graduated escalation).

As noted, Saigon had become a revolving door. President Johnson had just been elected (his first and only term not as the replacement for Kennedy) and believed he had the political capital to make a tough decision on Vietnam. Also, as noted, Ambassador Maxwell Taylor (who replaced Lodge and was Kennedy's CJCS) had been in Washington to meet with the NSC members to facilitate a decision. Finally, as noted already, only George Ball had raised the specter of alternatives to continuing to maintain the rotten Saigon government. (Ball noted that once the United States assumed responsibility for the Saigon government—riding the tiger's back in Ball's metaphor—the United States might no longer control when to dismount the tiger.) Dean Rusk is strangely absent in some of these late 1964 debates again suggesting that he was not a regular member of NSC meetings then.

Ambassador Taylor returned to Vietnam (RVN) in early 1965 and the mess continued in Saigon. Indeed, the day before this momentous NSC meeting occurred another coup was attempted in Saigon. One final piece of the puzzle is required to understand the true dimensions of the soon-to-be-made decision to Americanize the war. That is, President Johnson pleaded with his NSC members (at least a few of them) expressing his frustration about Vietnam. President Johnson expressed "irritation with the" Joint Chiefs asserting that every time Johnson heard from the Chiefs, Johnson got "a military recommendation" that called for "large-scale bombing." But the president further asserted that he "never felt that this war [would] be won from the air." Rather, said the president, what was "much more needed and would be more effective" was "appropriate military strength on the ground," hinting he was prepared to do more than just bombing. According to McNamara, Johnson's musing was "out of the blue."[39]

Thus, in Johnson's inimitable way, he wedged himself—where, as president he belonged—squarely into the debate of whether Saigon needed more resources before it could reform democratically or whether Saigon must reform democratically in order to receive more resources. The date of Johnson's frustrations was December 30, 1964. The holidays were underway and Vietnam was causing the festive season to be anything but festive.

Ambassador Taylor responded to Johnson's "out of the blue" frustration with some caution. Taylor wrote that the United States faced a situation in Saigon that was deteriorating seriously. Taylor likewise asserted that the generals in Saigon "continued political turmoil, irresponsibility and division, . . . lethargy . . . and some anti-U.S. feeling which could grow" that the Viet Cong were capitalizing on; unless something changed soon the United States was "likely soon to face" a potentially "hostile government which will ask us to leave while it seeks accommodation with" the enemy (both Viet Cong and North Vietnam). "There is a comparatively short time fuse on this situation."[40] Taylor then launched into a seminar on guerilla warfare and the ratio necessary (ten to one) to win from America's perspective. In addition, it was with caution that Taylor informed the NSC principals and echoed Johnson's own view that the battle could not be won from the air—he challenged his former colleagues in the JCS.

There is little record of activity between the last day of 1964 and first month of 1965, possibly because Johnson spent time in Texas and others took some vacation time also. However, what came next is clear. It is so important and dramatic that it is worth quoting at length. LBJ's NSC adviser McGeorge Bundy is the author of the following memorandum to LBJ (and he is speaking for Secretary McNamara and himself).

McNamara and I have asked for the meeting with you [January 27, 1965 at 11:30] in order to have a very private discussion of the basic situation in Vietnam. In a way it is very unfortunate that we are meeting the morning after a minor coup, because that is not the present point. . . .

What we want to say to you is that both of us are pretty well convinced that our current policy can lead only to disastrous defeat. What we are doing now, essentially, is to wait and hope for a stable government. . . . [The authors' December discussions made clear] . . . that wider action against the Communists will not take place unless we can get such a government. In the last six weeks that effort has been unsuccessful, and Bob [McNamara] and I are persuaded that there is no real hope of success in this area *unless and until our own policies and priorities change.* (Emphasis added.)

The underlying difficulties in Saigon arise from the spreading conviction that the future is without hope for anti-Communists. More and more the good men are covering their flanks and avoiding executive responsibility for firm anti-Communist policy. Our best friends are somewhat discouraged by our own inactivity in the face of major attacks on our own facilities. The Vietnamese [GVN] know just as well as we do that the Viet Cong are gaining in the countryside. Meanwhile, they see the enormous power of the Unites States withheld, and they get little sense of firm and active U.S. policy. They feel that [the U.S. is] unwilling to take serious risks. . . .

The author(s) continue saying that the uncertainty is pervading America's own people in Saigon. In other words, it is not simply the case of America's South Vietnamese allies flagging motivation, but American military and embassy (state and intelligence) personnel too were discouraged. Policy, such as it had evolved, stated that the United States would go no further until there was a stable government in Saigon—left unstated but clearly germane was the government needed to have the patina of democracy when compared to the government in Hanoi.[41]

McGeorge Bundy and McNamara believed, said the memo, "the worst course of action" was to continue in "this essentially passive role," which could "only lead to eventual defeat and an invitation to get out in humiliating circumstances." The authors saw two alternatives. First, the United States could use its military power in the Far East to force a change of Communist policy. Second, they wrote, the United States could "deploy all our resources along a track of negotiation, aimed at salvaging what little" could "be preserved." They favored the first course but they believed "both should be carefully studied and that alternative programs should be argued" before Johnson.[42]

They added that the both understood the "grave questions" presented by any such decision as recommended. They both recognized the ultimate responsibility was Johnson's, they were just advisers. Both of them had supported Johnson's earlier decisions to move on a "middle" or incremental course. They both agreed that every effort should be made to improve U.S. operations on the ground and to prop up the authorities in South Vietnam as best they could. But they were both convinced that none of the aforementioned choices was enough and that the time had come for harder choices.

  You should know that Dean Rusk does not agree with us. He does not quarrel with our assessment that things [were] going very badly and that the situation [was] unraveling. He [did] not assert that this deterioration [could] be stopped. What [Rusk said was] that consequences of both escalation and withdrawal are so bad that we simply must find a way of making our present policy work. This would be good if it was possible. Bob and I do not think it is.[43]

The authors concluded with the observation that their memorandum raised questions that could only prompt deeper discussion. The two, however, had reached the point wherein their "obligations" to the president did not permit them to administer the present course "in silence," which would have the effect of allowing Johnson to think McNamara and Bundy saw "real hope" in the policy.

It should be clear why this memo proved so critical. Together, with the Gulf of Tonkin Resolution, the way was clear to Americanize the Vietnam War, something no one apparently thought would work! Rather, they thought something must be done—of sufficient gravity—to gain the DRV's attention. If they did not undertake something soon, the South would collapse. It was on the verge of collapse every few weeks. If Saigon collapsed,

America's "containment" policy would be severely undermined—so virtually all the NSC members believed.

Importantly, what none of them believed was that Americanizing the war would actually win the peace. They hoped by some good fortune, if they were able to keep Saigon from collapsing at some future date, Hanoi would eventually be exhausted. Virtually all the principals held it as axiomatic that U.S. power could prevail given enough time and given Saigon did not collapse. But no one thought victory was around the corner. Therefore, each subsequent step was seen by the NSC principals as the minimum necessary to forestall disaster. Disaster was defined as the president being at the helm of the ship of state when Saigon collapsed thereby losing America's first war (apparently, Korea was seen as a draw).

(Some have argued that Vietnam was a quagmire, which the principals did not see until too late, and to some extent that is accurate. Others argue that Vietnam was a slippery slope and the Johnson administration took one or two steps down the slope without seeing what was at the bottom clearly. Implied in either explanation is that, had the NSC principals only seen what was next—quagmire or slippery slope—they would not have committed the earlier steps. By contrast, this case shows that they saw clearly that only disaster awaited them at each step and that the NSC principals held onto forlorn hope that some good fortune would forestall disaster just long enough for American power to force a change in Hanoi's behavior. What is profoundly evident is dysfunctional NSC decision-making that dates back to America's earliest policies vis-à-vis South Vietnam and continued until the very end. Both Democratic and Republican presidents engaged in similar dysfunctional decision-making.)

What happened next was as predictable as tragic. The United States sent Marines ashore at Da Nang in March (just over a month after the fork-in-the-road memorandum). The initial impulse was to protect some of America's air assets at an airbase near Da Nang. Of course, once the Marines landed, it was a matter of weeks before someone decided so long as the Marines were there, they might just as well assume an aggressive posture, rather than sitting on their ditty boxes, as one commander put it. Once the Marines assumed a more aggressive posture, the United States began taking many casualties. Once the United States began taking serious casualties, the next incremental step was to send Marines out on search and destroy missions. By the end of the year, more than 200,000 Marines were in Vietnam. By the end of 1966, closer to 400,000 were stationed there. The rest of the story, alas, is history.

The Structured, Comparative Case Study Questions for Americanization of the Vietnam War

Question 1. Was the NSC used in novel way? It remains to ask the comparative case study questions of the fork-in-the-road memorandum and

associated NSC principals decision-making. Did this case study demonstrate a novel use of the Defense Department, the IC, or the NSC? The answer is neither simple nor straightforward.

To be clear, the process at the NSC—and that is the only place one can
even think of novel activities—is among the strangest decision processes
implemented by the NSC. But it is not "novel" or innovative in the ways
the question was intended. It was dysfunctional; it was almost surreal but
not novel except in its dysfunction.

It is useful to remember that mostly the same individuals had been meeting for four years, under two different presidents. The NSC principals in
the Kennedy and Johnson administrations—as pointed out earlier—were
essentially the same persons. Thinking over the entirety of Kennedy and
Johnson through early 1965 one would have to say the record is a mixed
bag in terms of outcomes (though outcomes are distinct from good or
sound process; sometimes, despite good process outcomes go poorly). But
the process was certainly odd and suggestive of small-group malady, not
unlike *groupthink* in the Bay of Pigs case study.

Two of the dominant NSC principals, the revered Bob McNamara (former "whiz kid" in the Pentagon during World War II and former president of Ford) along with a young, accomplished dean of Harvard College
(McGeorge Bundy) participated in a strange hijacking of the process. Nor
is it clear whether the president encouraged them to do so—there is at
least partial evidence that they were responding to the president's December suggestion to use American ground forces rather than air power?
In that case, they were getting strange signals from the president. In addition, while George Ball was not an NSC principal (at least not by statute),
he was an important NSC deputy. It appears that his *crise de coeur* was intentionally ignored, perhaps even buried. (Even granted as McNamara asserted the memo got to President Johnson, clearly there is no evidence the
memo was discussed.)

Forget for a moment that George Ball is the number two (what today is
called the deputy secretary of state). Thus, in today's argot, George Ball
would be considered a member of the NSC deputies and would likely be
heard through the deputies committee of the NSC. All one needs to know
is Ball's name comes up time and again. He is frequently heard as hand-
wringing in the early years of the Vietnam War. He took the time to write
a memorandum that was over 60-pages long. On record are Secretary
McNamara (Defense) and NSC adviser McGeorge Bundy having discussed the memorandum and McNamara asserts President Johnson got
his hands on it through communications guru Bill Moyers. Why was it
never discussed? Were the principals fundamentally averse to slowing
down decision-making vis-à-vis the Vietnam War? If so, why?

While the fork-in-the-road memorandum that so influenced the subsequent Americanization of the war is not novel in the sense intended in the
comparative questions, *it is novel in its degree of dysfunction*. McNamara
says little about it in his memoirs, justifying critics of McNamara who

said, "We waited nearly 30 years for this?" Interestingly, McNamara ends the chapter with the fork-in-the-road memorandum with a single sentence after it is presented. He wrote: "After months of uncertainty and indecision we had reached a fork in the road."[44] In likewise fashion he begins the next chapter with similarly noncommittal observation that the six months that followed "our fork-in-the-road" memo "marked the most crucial phase of America's thirty-year involvement in Indochina."[45] Indeed it did.

It bears repeating that Secretary of State Rusk was similarly dysfunctional, albeit in a different way. Rather than imposing himself on the process, if Bundy's representation is to be believed, Rusk covered his ears and refused to take any decision. Again, according to Bundy, Rusk neither disagreed with their assessment that things were deteriorating in Saigon nor said that deterioration could not be arrested. Rather, Rusk said the consequences of withdrawing or Americanizing the war were so bad as to insist that the NSC principals must find a way to make the policy—as it then existed—work? The policy to date was one of recurring failures.

In short, the NSC process was novel in terms of dereliction of duty. This was a president who had inherited a bad situation from Kennedy upon the latter's assassination. As soon as he inherited the mess in Vietnam it went from bad to worse, due to a coup that Johnson had not supported. That President Johnson counted on these three NSC principals is clear. It is hard to imagine a worse situation than inheriting the mess just described with two of the NSC principals suddenly telling President Johnson the United States *must* Americanize the war and a third one saying the United States must find a way to make current policy (which had failed time and again to date) work. It is more than mystifying!

Question 2. Was the military used in a novel way? Little evidence exists for concluding the military was used in a novel or new way. Containment was, by this time, in its second decade and the military had been used in multiple ways to enforce containment. Likewise, Joint Chiefs had long been represented in the NSC either on their own or through the chairman.

Question 3. Was the IC used in a novel way? Again, there is virtually no evidence to conclude so. The fork-in-the-road memorandum was an internal NSC process and largely took place in the White House and Old Executive Office Building next door.

Questions 4 and 5? Militarization of U.S. foreign policy? I chose this case study because it was such an interesting case of the NSC members blithely Americanizing and militarizing U.S. foreign policy. They seem oddly detached as if the decisions they were making were not going to result in massive numbers of U.S. troops being sent to Vietnam. In fact, the Vietnam War is full of strange examples of various NSCs (i.e., different administration) seemingly not realizing the full consequences of the decisions they made. Clearly, militarization was a direct consequence of this decision. Within two months the first Marine Battalions were sent to Da Nang, initially to guard U.S. air assets (so the ARVN could aggressively engage the

North Vietnamese) and soon to replace ARVN with Americans engaging the NVA (North Vietnamese Regulars) and the Viet Cong in the South.

PRESIDENT RICHARD M. NIXON AND HIS NSC PRINCIPALS

Perhaps more than any former president, president-elect Richard Nixon was ill-suited for the NSC process handed down to him from the National Security Act of 1947 and his predecessors. Nixon had distaste for direct, personal confrontation, the sort of give-and-take process that NSC principals regularly exchange. Nixon characterized himself as an introvert in an extrovert's job. He was secretive, often angry, and peevish and he believed his personal enemies existed throughout the federal government (the bureaucracy) from his days as senator and vice president.[46]

Nixon chose Henry Kissinger (then a Harvard professor) for his national security adviser (NSC adviser) who was much more facile in terms of face-to-face interpersonal skills and throwing bureaucratic elbows. Kissinger had been aligned with Rockefeller (a moderate Republican) though he had also worked as a staffer on nuclear arms earlier in the Kennedy and Johnson administrations. If Stephen Ambrose is correct, Kissinger approached the Nixon campaign through John Mitchell (eventually, Nixon's attorney general). Accordingly, Kissinger was willing to share his "inside" information from the Democrats he had served with Nixon so long as Kissinger's role could be kept quiet.[47] Kissinger was a critical member of Nixon's NSC for many reasons, among them the fact that he stayed with Nixon to the end (and indeed, stayed on after Ford took over after Nixon's resignation). Also, Kissinger was his first NSC adviser and would eventually become secretary of state, both roles significant in the NSC principals setting.

Nixon and Kissinger decided to make some changes in the NSC process by creating a series of new subcommittees, with Kissinger as the chair of each of the subcommittees. (Clearly, the creation of subcommittees was common but Nixon's model was, as will be seen, wholly different than previously seen.) This was done, apparently, to *ensure* that Nixon with Kissinger made policy and the other NSC principals were circumvented yet had the impression that they were helping form decisions. The idea was to isolate the secretary of defense and secretary of state—and others— such that they would be kept busy as virtual captives of their respective bureaucracies. The late presidential scholar Alex George wrote that Nixon's management style was "highly formalistic" with Nixon's peculiar personality making it imperative for the president to have a small group of staffers to serve as "buffers" from the "wear and tear of policymaking."[48] That is, buffers between Nixon and potentially powerful secretaries of defense and state and a few other important NSC members.

Kissinger was called Nixon's de facto secretary of state even when Nixon had Secretary of State William Rogers (a personal friend of Nixon's) serving at the State Department. Rogers apparently took his isolation all in stride. Melvin Laird was Nixon's secretary of defense, and though Nixon, apparently, intended Laird to play along with the new process too, Laird proved less pliant than Rogers. H. R. Haldeman (chief of staff), though not an NSC statutory member, often acted as one given his close relationship as Nixon's enforcer.

In the transition from Johnson to Nixon, Kissinger worked with Morton Halperin to reconfigure the NSC by creating the subcommittees: the make-over included dividing the NSC into six groups, each of which Kissinger chaired. The committees were (1) the Vietnam Special Studies Group, (2) a Special Actions Group ("crisis management"), (3) the Defense Programs and Review Group, (4) the Arms Verification (SALT) Group, (5) the Senior Review Group (an umbrella of sorts for other policy issues), and (6) the 40 Committee (covert actions).[49]

Note the rather interesting evolution from whence the 40 committee arrived. Recall, Eisenhower had created a 5412 committee (named after the NSC document that created it) and that subsequently evolved into the 303 committee in Kennedy and Johnson administrations (named after a room number in the OEOB). Nixon renamed it the 40 Committee and he intended to use it for covert operations the way Eisenhower and his successors had used it. The temptation to use covert measures had become powerfully irresistible to his predecessors and so it became with Nixon. In Nixon's case, those with a need to know included Nixon and Kissinger but also Richard Helms (by then the director of central intelligence, DCI). DCI was set up to be both the head of the CIA, the first permanent civilian intelligence agency, and the ostensible head of the entire IC in the National Security Act. (The DCI was supplanted by a new creation, the director of national intelligence, after 9/11 when the Intelligence Reform and Terrorism Prevention Act passed in 2004, as an amendment to the National Security Act of 1947).[50]

Before considering the case study (the secret bombing of Cambodia early in the Nixon administration's first term), it is worth noting that the reconfiguration of the NSC, centralized NSC decision-making in the duopoly of Nixon and Kissinger, is novel in itself. Every president since Truman has customized the NSC in some fashion.[51] To circumvent the NSC principals, however, is something beyond customizing the NSC. Nixon and Kissinger intended to make policy whereupon Kissinger would orchestrate discussions in the NSC subcommittee settings with different groups, compartmentalizing discrete groups of information so that the only two who had all the threads were Nixon and Kissinger. They effectively stymied the NSC process for long stretches during Nixon's tenure (January 1969 through August 1974).

To reiterate, the subcommittees held discussions but largely meaningless discussions that were orchestrated by the maestro Kissinger. The NSC subcommittees discussed their business (Vietnam or Arms Control, etc.)

but the discussion and decisions were made in the Oval Office between President Nixon and Dr. Henry Kissinger. In fact, often the NSC principals learned of this fact as they discovered ex post facto, once decisions were made and announced.

Secret Bombing of Cambodia (1969 and After)

Richard Nixon had supported close alliance with Diem (see the Diem coup in the Kennedy administration). But when Nixon inherited the war from Johnson, the country had begun to turn against the war in large numbers. Nixon was certain the Soviets were taking advantage of the protests in America and he had no compunction against making the Soviets pay a price for their perfidy. Nixon and Kissinger decided to expand the war into neutral Cambodia—next door to Vietnam—but decided to do so secretly, not to protect sources and methods (the traditional reason for secrecy) but to ensure the American public did not discover what they were doing.

Why? The public had turned against the war and in Congress there were calls for America to sue for peace on nearly any terms and even to withdraw unilaterally. Nixon had campaigned for "peace with honor," getting America out of Vietnam but on favorable terms. This made a furtive or covert expansion of the war an attractive option so long as it did not leak. (In fact, some readers may not realize that the Plumbers of Watergate fame were created to plug leaks, in particular, leaks of secret foreign policy.) Nixon decided on a high-risk gambit to bomb sites in Cambodia the Pentagon assured Nixon harbored Viet Cong and North Vietnamese supplies redoubts. Thus, in fewer than eight weeks from his inauguration, Nixon began a series of secret bombings using B-52s rerouted from Vietnam to Cambodia and he continued this well over a year.

Historian Stephen Ambrose wrote the following of Nixon's assumption of the Vietnam War:

It was Richard Nixon's fate that he had to preside over the retreat of American power. He hated it. Every instinct in him rebelled against it. For twenty years, in every crisis, at every turning point, his advice had been to take the offensive against the Communists. Attack, with more firepower, now—that was his policy.[52]

Nevertheless, when Nixon became president in 1969, the American people had largely turned against the war—it had dragged on far too long. Consequently, Congress has largely turned against the war. Thus, Nixon inherited a situation that he was temperamentally ill-suited to lead. It was simply not part of Nixon's DNA to retreat on anything. The "liberals" in the media and think tanks had abandoned Johnson and America's image had suffered severe setbacks in consequence. Nixon aimed to correct that problem by controlling information from the Oval Office, which left most of the NSC out of the loop. In short, Nixon planned to keep information on close hold so others could not criticize it. To do this he had to orchestrate the dog and pony show in the NSC subcommittees, noted earlier, that also saved Nixon from the personal confrontations he apparently loathed.

During the 1968 presidential campaign, Nixon gave a speech on Vietnam suggesting that the would-be president had an undisclosed way to get the communists in Hanoi to negotiate so that the United States could have peace with honor. The "secret plan" had been nothing more than Nixon imagining he could use American power the way Eisenhower had (when Nixon was vice president) to get the communists in Pyongyang (North Korea) to negotiate. It was not a plan, much less a secret plan. It was simply Nixon's faith that what President Eisenhower had done could be re-enacted by President Nixon. It assumed that the enemy in Hanoi could be threatened with massive American firepower and that they would thereby sue for peace. (The reader probably recognizes the faulty logic from Kennedy and Johnson administrations.) The problem was Hanoi only needed to hold on long enough to let the anti-war forces in the United States pressure the Nixon administration rather than vice versa.

Nixon also realized that the Pentagon's massive bombing campaign—the very campaign that was debated in early 1965 in the Johnson administration—had ultimately failed to bring Hanoi to the negotiating table. Rolling Thunder, as it was called once it became sustained bombing, had neither produced positive results in Hanoi nor in the United States (where protests had grown with each escalation of Rolling Thunder). Finally, Nixon realized too that the gamble General Westmoreland had made on fixing and killing the enemy after Hanoi's Tet Offensive had failed to destroy the North Vietnamese Regular Army (NVA), though it had killed thousands of Viet Cong (southern communists) in South Vietnam (RVN). The NVA had survived to fight another day.

Nixon had been aware of the debates in the Johnson administration and that Johnson grumbled about the constant demand of more and more bombing sorties from the Pentagon. The president therefore wished to try a more precise sort of bombing to interdict the Ho Chi Minh trail (though interdiction had proved a failure too). President Nixon had the mistaken idea that President Eisenhower produced results in North Korea by talking publicly about the possibility of using tactical nuclear weapons to end the Korean conflict. (Several things led to Pyongyang settling and Eisenhower had never seriously considered using tactical nuclear weapons.) Nixon had reimagined what Eisenhower had done and applied it to Nixon's presidency, calling it the "madman" theory. Nixon desired Hanoi to think he was desperate for peace and might be willing to do anything to achieve it.[53]

On January 8, 1969 (i.e., while still president-elect), Nixon tasked Kissinger with preparing a report on what the enemy (Hanoi) was doing in Cambodia. (Cambodia and Laos had both been debated in terms of "hot pursuit" and the Pentagon had asked President Johnson many times to allow bombing strikes in either country to interdict supplies). On February 18 (nearly a month after inauguration), Kissinger informed President Nixon that Hanoi was making effective use of Cambodia to move supplies southward. Apparently, Kissinger also informed Nixon that Cambodia was where COSVN (the central office for South Vietnam, a sort of communications hub between Hanoi and the Viet Cong) was located.[54] (There surely was such a hub of communications. However, to think of it as the Bamboo Pentagon, as some called it was unrealistic. It was likely small and moved frequently as did the Viet Cong and even the NVA regulars. Much of the Vietnam War was the enemy using guerrilla tactics against the overly heavy, mechanized American units that moved slowly.)

Just days later a communist offensive was launched in South Vietnam, apparently to welcome President Nixon to the Vietnam War.[55] President Nixon was on a hurried-trip to Europe to "consult" with NATO allies and was embarrassed by the offensive, though much smaller than the Tet Offensive in 1968. (In fact, the communists frequently launched offensives once the rainy season ended and materiel could again be moved along the Ho Chi Minh trail and Nixon might have easily learned of Hanoi's modus operandi had he checked with his secretary of defense or the Joint Chiefs.) En route home, President Nixon "suddenly ordered" the Pentagon to bomb Cambodia's "sanctuaries," something the Joint Chiefs had been agitating for since Nixon assumed the presidency a few weeks earlier. Before President Nixon's instructions could be effected, however, Secretary of Defense Melvin Laird "cabled his reservations from Washington."[56]

Laird rightly feared the bombing could not be kept a secret. He likewise feared that once public, bombing Cambodia (a neutral country) would create an unimaginable furor in the United States and that Congress would take it out on the new administration. Once Laird made his protests known, Secretary of State Rogers likewise added his thoughts, agreeing with Laird. Nixon was in Germany on his way back and he "rescinded" the order he had unilaterally given the Pentagon. Nixon returned home and brooded as only Nixon could do. Spineless "bureaucrats" had urged caution and in consequence Nixon was forced to back down, something Nixon loathed doing. What was more, Nixon's efforts to circumvent his secretary of defense and secretary of state had failed.

On March 4, 1969, Nixon gave a news conference. In response to a question about the communist offensive, Nixon said:

We have not moved in a precipitate fashion, but the fact that we have shown patience and forbearance should not be considered as a sign of weakness. We will not tolerate a continuation of a violation of an understanding. But more than that, we will not tolerate attacks which result in heavier casualties to our men at a time that we are honestly trying to seek peace at the conference table in Paris. An appropriate response to these attacks will be made if they continue.[57]

But in response to a subsequent question in the same news conference where Nixon was asked if he would resume bombing the DRV, President Nixon gave an answer that talked about deeds instead of words. He also said he would not threaten because making threats was ineffective.

Ten days later (March 14), President Nixon held another news conference where the previous comments and the offensive were brought up yet again. Nixon went out of his way to say that what he had previously said on March 4 had been "widely interpreted" as a warning. Further, President Nixon said it would be his policy (henceforth) to issue a warning only one time.

On March 15, President Richard M. Nixon phoned NSC adviser Henry Kissinger and ordered an "immediate" B-52 attack on COSVN. It is how Nixon ordered it and what he said that is of particular interest here. The president told his NSC adviser that the State Department (i.e., Secretary of State Rogers) was to be informed only *after* the point of no return. He further told Kissinger that the order was "not appealable." Interestingly, Dr. Kissinger argued that Nixon owed it to both Secretaries Rogers and Laird to hear their views of Nixon's decision. Thus, the order was appealable after all, or at least temporarily suspended. The next day (March 16), President Nixon held a meeting in the Oval Office (the NSC typically meets in the Situation Room), so it is unclear whether it was an NSC meeting. But he invited both Secretary Rogers and Laird to hear his plan and to respond.

After hearing their appeals (Rogers was against it but Laird eventually went along), Nixon ordered the attacks to begin the next day (March 17, 1969) so long as the weather was good. Thus began what became known as the Breakfast, then Menu bombings in Cambodia. Breakfast became an elaborate bombing campaign that was kept from Congress and other NSC members inside the Nixon administration. To do so, an elaborate accounting procedure was devised whereby the raids were documented as occurring in South Vietnam so the information would not leak to the media (and to keep meddlesome policy makers Nixon mistrusted and Congress in the dark).[58]

President Nixon had ordered sustained bombing of Cambodia without any consent (indeed, without any input whatsoever) from Congress. He ordered it to be kept a secret (thus, a complex accounting system was devised so that those in the Air Force implementing the secret bombings could keep the secret of where the bombs fell). Though the *New York Times* soon broke a story about the secret bombings (and about some other secrets with respect to North Korea, the so-called EC-121 incident), President Nixon got lucky in that other media ignored the *Times* story and the story disappeared soon thereafter. President Nixon had made a decision as commander in chief (arguably, within his powers) but had ordered it falsified so that he would not have to face either NSC members (and others) in Congress. And he ordered the information kept from the public for fear of protests. Both were contrary to the Constitution. Nor could he argue that it was to protect sources and methods (as subsequent presidents have done by signing a "Finding" notifying only the Gang of Eight in Congress); it was not to protect sources or methods but to protect the secrecy of the strange NSC system Nixon had created inside the administration.

Though the secret bombing of Cambodia continued until August 15, 1973 (about a year before President Nixon resigned), bombing Cambodia (a neutral country) would not be his last secret. Indeed, President Nixon and his NSC adviser Henry Kissinger cooked up several more secret schemes including secretly negotiating peace with Hanoi in Paris (while the State Department met with other Hanoi representatives across town in Paris, with no inkling that the real negotiations occurred between Kissinger and Le Duc Tho). President Nixon's plan to open China (recognized as the People's Republic of China in the UN and normalize relations with the PRC) likewise were kept largely a secret; so were certain aspects of arms control and the "linkage" of various diplomatic initiatives with the Soviets and the Chinese. It proved to be Nixon's favored way of doing business.

The Structured, Comparative Case Study Questions for Cambodia Bombing

Question 1. Was the NSC used in a novel way? President Nixon decided during the transition from Johnson to Nixon that he would reconfigure the NSC in way that suited his personality and his penchant to avoid direct, personal confrontations. He did so by centralizing policy making in the White House (typically, in the Oval Office) so that the NSC principals ceased to function as they were intended. The NSC principals were never intended to override a president's will but they were intended to advise the presidency. President Nixon ensured that in some cases they could not do so. In short, the principals committee was largely circumvented by Nixon's reconfiguration of the NSC.

It is supremely ironic that one of the results of President Nixon's novel uses of the NSC ultimately created such a backlash when discovered that one result was the War Power Act of 1971. The War Powers Act was an attempt by Congress to wrest back control it had yielded to the presidency in the National Security Act of 1947. Congress was angry at what it called the Nixon abuses and the imperial presidency. But Congress had deferred time and again to the presidency over time. Once the National Security Act became law, there was still a balance between Congress and the presidency in foreign policy. Over time, however, with each successive deferral to the presidency (and with each novel precedent we have thus far seen and others), the power began to shift from roughly coequal branches to an asymmetrical balance favoring the presidency. It is worth noting that

President Nixon's novels uses of the NSC produced the first real legal justification to wrest control back to a more symmetrical balance.

Question 2. Was the military used in a novel war? It is hard to know for certain if Nixon's double bookkeeping—accounting for bombs that were dropped in Cambodia as dropped in Vietnam—is novel. There is little evidence of any president or NSC doing so, but it is more of an issue of secrecy than of novel use. On the other hand, though not in this case, President Nixon and Kissinger (the two-man NSC) had spies in the Pentagon and, likewise, the Pentagon had spies in the White House! The question is whether to call this novel or simply oddly dysfunctional. It may be proper to say it was novel but with qualifications.

Question 3. Was IC used in a novel way? No. There was little discussion with the CIA or others in the intelligence community. (In retrospect, a much better case study for novel use of the IC in the Nixon administration might have been the Salvador Allende case in Chile wherein the CIA and the director of central intelligence were deeply involved.)

Questions 4 and 5. Militarization of U.S. foreign policy? Here the answer is straightforward. As Nixon became president, the Johnson administration was finally trying to wind down the Vietnam War, for any number of reasons, mostly exhaustion. In commencing the secret bombing of Cambodia, the Nixon administration expanded the Vietnam War into one or two additional nations: Cambodia and Laos. (Laos had seen a good deal of covert CIA operations, but Nixon arguably expanded the war there when in 1971 he backed an ARVN invasion.) Laos and Cambodia were pulled into the Vietnam War so that by the time Nixon left office and handed the mess over to President Gerald Ford, the United States was fighting major military operations in all three, thus militarizing foreign policy. Said militarization was directly linked to Nixon's decision to bomb Cambodia secretly. (The reader may know that in spring 1970—a year after beginning the secret bombing of Cambodia—Nixon announced a U.S. military "incursion," as he called it, into Cambodia. One result was a new round of protests on college campuses, including the tragedy and Kent State in Ohio.)

It is equally ironic that the War Powers Act resulted in making the presidency even more powerful, since the opposite was its desired effect. In negotiating between Congress and the White House and between Republicans and Democrats, the War Powers Act gave the presidency even more carte blanche. It gave the president 60 days (renewable for another 30) of super power to move troops into harm's way. In short, it gave the president even more power than before and it caused an additional militarization of U.S. foreign policy.

Arguably, in cases not considered here (the overthrow of Salvador Allende in Chile and perhaps the parts of the Phoenix Program in Vietnam), the IC was used in novel ways. Likewise, there may be cases (not here) that would illustrate President Nixon's novel use of the military. But as those were not cases considered, those observations must be left for

others. What there can be little doubt about, however, is that President
Nixon used the NSC in a novel way.

PRESIDENT RONALD REAGAN AND HIS NSC PRINCIPALS

President Ronald Reagan is known for various things, depending upon
whom one consults. By his admirers, President Reagan is known for telling
Mr. Gorbachev to tear down this wall (the Berlin Wall). To his critics, the
president is known as the aloof president who cared so little about the details of his NSC members—what they were doing, which ones, and when
that the principals were circumvented by *staffers* such as Oliver North and
Elliot Abrams. So little did President Reagan attend to his NSC members
that it is not entirely clear what the staffers were doing and at whose behest?

President Reagan served two full terms, and by many accounts he was
experiencing early dementia near the end of his second term.[59] Irrespective
of dementia claims, President Reagan is often beloved, even considered an
incredibly warm man by his critics. The issue of President Reagan's aloofness will be considered next. Nevertheless, it is fair to say that Ronald Reagan's aloofness in terms of his NSC is a matter of record that the president
agreed did not serve him well with respect to the NSC and what became
known as Iran-Contra scandal.

The President himself acknowledged promptly after release of the report of the
commission, headed by former Sen. John Tower (R-Tex.), that his penchant for del-
egating authority, which he said had served him well for two terms as California
governor and most of his presidency, was not effective in managing his National
Security Council. He pledged to correct the flaws.[60]

President Reagan's two terms were characterized by some degree of
turnover in terms of the NSC members. While Secretary of Defense Cas-
par Weinberger stayed until nearly the end of the two terms leaving just
14 months before the president's tenure concluded, Secretary of State
George Shultz began late (July 16, 1982) but served until the end of January 20, 1989. (Secretary of State Alexander Haig began the Reagan administration but lasted only 17½ months. The so-called troika in the White
House—consisting of Edwin Meese and Michael Deaver, along with chief
of staff James Baker—were disturbed by then secretary of state Haig's
performance, when President Reagan was shot and used Haig's antics
to push him out of the NSC.) In the case study that follows, Secretary
Weinberger and Secretary Shultz were both permanent NSC fixtures,
more or less, during President Reagan's tenure. However, the "troika" was
involved in NSC policy making by virtue of Reagan's aloofness.

The same cannot be said for the NSC adviser. During President Reagan's
two terms (eight years), six NSC advisers served. The first was Richard

Allen who began with the new administration but was gone before he finished a year (January 4, 1982). (President Reagan was inaugurated on January 21, 1981.) Allen was considered a weak NSC adviser—which is what candidate Reagan said he wanted as he planned to reemphasize the secretary of state over the Kissinger model of strong NSC advisers. The second NSC adviser was Robert "Bud" McFarlane, a Marine officer who served during much of Iran-Contra (October 17, 1983, through December 4, 1985). A Navy man, Admiral John Poindexter (retired) replaced McFarlane on December 4, 1985, and served until roughly Thanksgiving 1986. At that point, the Iran-Contra scandal had so blossomed that Frank Carlucci became Reagan's fifth NSC adviser. Finally, Colin Powell replaced Carlucci when the latter became Reagan's final secretary of defense making Powell Reagan's sixth NSC adviser. Neither Carlucci nor Powell is germane to the Iran-Contra scandal.

Someone who proved very important in the Reagan NSC (not so much as an NSC principal but outside the NSC setting) was director of central intelligence, William Casey. Casey worked with small groups of staffers and combinations of NSC advisers but appears to have been relatively out of his depth in the NSC principals' meetings. It appears that the White House troika along with strong secretaries of defense and state (Weinberger and Shultz during Iran-Contra) more or less paralyzed the NSC process.[61] Though in some administrations the DCI (now the DNI) is considered and NSC principal Casey was a bit of an outsider in the NSC principals but he still affected policy, as will be seen.

The Tower Commission's conclusions addressed Reagan's aloofness and management of the NSC as follows: "President Reagan's personal management style place[d] an especially heavy responsibility on his key advisers. Knowing his style, they should have been particularly mindful of the need for special attention to the measures in which this arms sales initiative [to Iran] developed and proceeded. On that score, neither the national security adviser Robert C. McFarland and Vice Adm. John M. Poindexter nor the other [NSC] principals deserve high marks."[62]

IRANAMOK[63]

At its heart, the Iran-Contra affair was the intermingling of two ostensibly discrete programs in the early Reagan administration. To ensure continuity of narrative, both will be briefly described. The first was President Reagan's frequently stated desire to be tough with the Contras in Nicaragua. Candidate Reagan campaigned against President Carter's weakness, generally, but specifically on Carter's handling of the revolution in Nicaragua that resulted in the overthrow of the Samosa government. Reagan believed America's allies, such as Samosa should be treated well since they had stuck with the United States during the Cold War against communism.[64]

The second element was the president's desire to get hostages released from Lebanon (held by what we today know as Hezbollah), which the president believed Iran interlocutors might be able to effect. As the Tower Commission Report states, Iran-Contra consisted of "the covert sell of arms to Iran at a time when official America policy called to continue the isolation of" Ayatollah Khomeini's Iran; and second, "the diversion of some of the profits of the [illegal sale to Iran] to the Nicaraguan rebels [called the Contras] at a time when Congress had ruled out direct or indirect American government aid."[65]

In taking a hard line on the Sandinistas (the government that had overthrown Samosa), President Reagan necessarily supported the Contras, some of Samosa's old colleagues from the former government (then out of power) who were scattered around Latin America. However, a number of important former government officials were located in South Florida where they plotted a return to power. President Reagan generally supported the Samosa government's return because he believed the Sandinistas were becoming a beachhead for communism in Central America. This he believed because the Sandinista government was relatively close to Fidel Castro's Cuba, a *bête noir* of Cold Warriors in both Republican and Democratic circles. (Incidentally, that is not to suggest Fidel Castro was a friend to America. Clearly, Fidel's Cuba worked to undermine various U.S. foreign policy objectives in the region. Even today, with the normalization of U.S.-Cuba relations underway, Fidel Castro continues to lament U.S. foreign policy and vice versa.)

With respect to Iran, it is worth recalling that Iran and Iraq were at war from 1980 until near the end of the decade. The U.S. foreign policy position was officially one of *realpolitik:* ensuring neither Iran nor Iraq won the war as much as possible. In other words, the official U.S. foreign policy position was helping Iran to bleed Iraq and helping Iraq to bleed Iran. However, the said *realpolitik* position in the Middle East presented certain challenges. One of the biggest was Lebanon. Lebanon, once known as the Riviera of the Middle East, had been in civil war since the 1970s. The status quo, if it could be called thus, was three religions living relatively peacefully without continued bloodshed. (Lebanon was created by France as a Christian enclave in the Middle East at the end of World War I as the Ottoman Empire dissolved.) The three religions were Lebanese Christians (Mennonite and a few others), Lebanon's Sunni population, and its Shi'ite population. (There was also a small sect of Islam called Druze Muslims confined mostly to the Chouf Mountains.)

One result was that a group of Shi'ite militants had formed during the civil war years. They eventually became a militia and political force in Lebanon, known as Hezbollah. Though they were Lebanese and therefore Arab, they shared religious beliefs with Iran's Shi'a (though Persians not Arabs) and also with the Alawite government in Syria (another sometime client of Iran's). Hezbollah has been supported in various ways by Iran's Revolutionary Guard and its Quds Force over the years. Hezbollah was a deadly enemy of Israel's and occupied mostly southern parts of Lebanon near the border with Israel (and Israeli-occupied Golan).

From the Reagan administration's perspective, as noted, the desire was for stability (lack of either Iraq or Iran winning outright). The administration did not have a "dog in the fight" as it were. At least it did not until someone started kidnapping Westerners, including Americans. One of the Americans eventually kidnapped was a CIA station chief William Buckley who was later tortured and killed. What became known as Hezbollah was implicated in his kidnapping as well as an attack on the U.S. embassy in Beirut (Lebanon). Unwittingly then, the administration's policy gave the United States a stake in Lebanon.

As readers may recall, the Reagan administration sent Marines (and the French sent French Paratroopers) to Lebanon in fall 1983 after cruising up and down the coast with warships that fired artillery into the mountains of southern Lebanon. Lebanon went from an area where the Reagan administration had few goals other than stability to a high-profile foreign policy mess in 1982-1983.

Eventually, the Israelis approached the administration about selling some armaments (TOW missiles to use against Iraq) in the Iran-Iraq War. The trouble was, America's laws forbade the sale of such materiel to "sponsors" of terrorism, as well as others considered enemies of the United States. The Israelis were asking for permission to transfer arms to Iranian "moderates" to prevent Saddam Hussein from gaining an upper hand in the war. Iran "badly wanted what the Israelis could provide" including TOW antitank and HAWK missiles.

Eventually, a go-between named Manucher Ghorbanifar, an Iranian with business contact in France and elsewhere in Europe, got involved with staffers in President Reagan's NSC. (While the book has mostly been concerned with the NSC principals, the NSC consists of principals—what were initially called members and advisers—what in modern times is called the deputies committee as well as the NSC staffers, who are all seconded from other bureaucracies such as State, Defense, the intelligence community, etc.) NSC staffer Michael Ledeen (without the knowledge of his boss, NSC adviser McFarlane) traveled to Israel where he met with Prime Minister Peres to involve the United States in this witches' brew of forces![66]

The idea that an NSC staffer could travel to Israel, meet with a high official of that country, and discuss replacing Israeli armaments sold to the Iranians—the Iranians were explicitly called a terrorist state during the period—seems stunning. But that is apparently what happened and it was just one of many examples of the inmates running the asylum (in the NSC). One wonders how Ledeen arranged travel, how the appointments were set, who created the agenda, and so on. Nevertheless, these problems were surmounted. Eventually, the Ledeen mission resulted in NSC staffers deciding to remove the middle man, the Israelis. Over time, the NSC staffers simply sold various weapons and other military hardware to Iranian "moderates" themselves, which led to a unique situation: the executive branch creating monies not appropriated by Congress.

Whether there were "moderates" in Iran remains a point of contention; and if there were, whether they could change any behavior of Iran's Hezbollah client in Lebanon was another contentious matter. But no value is served by rehashing those questions here. Suffice it to say, those and other questions remained unanswered. Instead, NSC staffers and others who believed they knew what President Reagan desired acted at his behest. (Reagan's aloofness was noted earlier.)

The way the two things became intermingled, of course, was through money (monies created in the executive branch rather than appropriated by Congress). First, the Israelis sold weapons to someone inside Iran and made money on the exchange. The United States eventually replaced those armaments in Israel. Before long, NSC staffers (apparently, more or less directed by director of central intelligence or DCI William Casey) determined that they could cut out the Israelis and create sources of money if the pesky oversight of Congress were absent. Their thinking included the notion that since Congress was being stingy with money for Reagan's pet projects—including the Contras—would it not be clever and ironic to take the monies from the arms transfers to Iran and use the same for the Contras? Since these same staffers (notably, Oliver North and Elliot Abrams) were working on the Sandinista-Contra portfolio, the two one-time discrete tracks became complexly intermingled. The question to determine is to what extent all of this was run from the NSC?

For the Iran-Contra affair, two main sources were used. The first is the Tower Report, a blue-ribbon panel created by Congress to investigate potential wrongdoing in the Reagan administration. It is the official record and an unimpeachable source of information. Former senator John Tower chaired it and Brent Scowcroft (formerly a deputy NSC adviser and later President George H. W. Bush's NSC adviser) cochaired the bipartisan panel. The second source is somewhat less critical but useful: Bob Woodward's *Veil*. Though Woodward has a solid reputation in terms of investigations into presidential maleficence, *Veil* remains somewhat controversial. But it also gives the case insights not found elsewhere, particularly about William Casey.[67]

For example, in Woodward's *Veil* the reader learns that DCI Casey, who was raised to cabinet rank in the Reagan administration, attended cabinet meetings and was made fun of by other NSC principals. DCI Casey didn't like cabinet meetings, wrote Woodward. He rarely spoke up at them and when he did he noticed others would trip over themselves to explain Casey's mumbling to the president. Casey noticed several times when this happened, James Baker (then the chief of staff) was laughing, cracking up: a big joke. Casey decided it didn't matter. "His direct channel to the president was more useful." Casey was used to going around Haig and others and Haig had been livid upon finding out about Casey's channel.[68] But DCI Casey apparently kept the channel open, though how much is unclear and subject to argument.

As noted, *Veil* proved a controversial book—certainly more so than other Woodward tell-all books of various U.S. presidential administrations. Nevertheless, Woodward has a good reputation for being a discrete operator among Washington's powerful and getting high officials (especially, NSC principals and staffers) to tell him what happened in given instances. Such was the case with *Veil*. Some of its more sensational charges about Casey talking to Woodward, however, were disputed by the Casey family after the former DCI's death. Still, Woodward confirms much of what the Tower Report concluded.

Woodward provides some unique insights into the relationship (the man behind the curtain in the Reagan NSC) of William Casey with others. For instance, in fall of 1983 (when parts of Iran-Contra were beginning), Woodward noted that William Clark (briefly President Reagan's second NSC adviser) was tired of the turf battles. Clark "was a beaten man, fed up with the bitter staff infighting at the White House. . . . He was barely on speaking terms with [Michael] Deaver, and he knew that [chief of staff James] Baker . . . provided an unending stream of vicious criticism, either to his face or behind his back."[69] Two-thirds of the White House troika had aligned against Webster and Webster was ready to leave. Later in October at a National Security Planning Group (NSPG) meeting, Casey was sitting there as Clark passed a note around the room. When Casey received it he read that the president had decided to appoint James Baker to be his third NSC adviser. "After the NSPG meeting, Casey joined Clark, Meese, and Weinberger" and the president where "Clark and Meese longest and most forcefully" argued that Baker would send the wrong signal to the Soviets. Baker was a moderate.[70]

The point is that Casey was an operator of some stature and while he tended to operate clandestinely (not a huge surprise given his role as DCI), he may well have been the principal orchestrator of the NSC staffers involved in the two seemingly disparate initiatives. Also, William Casey was in the OSS during World War II and he understood "compartmentalization" and "need to know," the tools of covert operations. The several NSC advisers Reagan appointed during his administration were weak actors without any real portfolio. They ran the NSC but its budget and number of employees were miniscule compared to the titans like Defense, State, and the intelligence community. With weak NSC advisers, President Reagan might make a comment, which the NSC principals would understand as just Reagan's rhetoric. But it is at least plausible that William Casey believed in the rhetoric and had the potential to operationalize rhetoric into policy and set NSC staffers out implementing it. In no other administration has such a thing occurred. But Woodward argued in *Veil* that Casey did so.

The Structured Case Study Questions for Iranamok

Question 1. Was the NSC used in a novel way? As with previous case studies, it remains to be answered whether Iranamok constituted a novel use of any of the three institutions created by the National Security Act of 1947. It seems self-evident that the NSC staff was used in ways never envisaged by the creators of the act. In fact, the staff was miniscule initially and although there are instances of staffers doing important tasks for presidents (Averell Harriman during Truman comes to mind), staffers have rarely been operational (what one author called foreign policy entrepreneurs).[71]

In fact, Iranamok is a wealth of novelties and innovations (provided one does not put a positive connotation on either word). That DCI Casey—who was an NSC principal in the Reagan NSC but had no authority over NSC staffers—operated said staffers as if they were CIA operatives was a stunning novelty. Why did he do it? Apparently, the Boland Amendments that were ratcheted up against the Reagan administration to prevent it from getting the United States involved in Nicaragua (President Reagan believed in involvement) had so proscribed what Casey's CIA could do that he may well have turned to the NSC staffers as the last persons available to operate in such a fashion.

It also appears clear that the NSC principals in the Reagan administration had become paralyzed with turf battles. In short, the NSC principals were dominated by Secretary of Defense Weinberger and Secretary of State Shultz and neither of them thought it prudent to get the United States involved in either the Nicaragua or the Iran imbroglios. Each secretary helped to block such activities at the NSC principals' level. It was apparently in this vacuum of leadership—or perhaps more correctly lack of a certain kind of leadership—that William Casey moved to make things happen.

The Tower Commission found no direct evidence that President Reagan knew what was being done at his behest, itself a novelty in presidential foreign policy and NSC activities. It did find notes and memoranda that President Reagan apparently read, but President Reagan was not a stickler for detail. It remains quite plausible (perhaps even likely) that President Reagan's mental fatigue allowed what staffers considered feigned "aloofness" to serve as approvals for their deeds. When they finally testified, North and others said as much.

Question 2. Was the military used in a novel way? Even Defense operated in novel ways. The Economy Act provided for departments, such as one branch of the U.S. military to sell goods and services to another branch as needed. William Casey was director of central intelligence, not a quartermaster officer in the Pentagon. But the CIA had no control over TOW missiles nor did CIA control other hardware the Iranians desired. Some fairly novel interpretations were made by the comptroller's office in which the Pentagon sold materiel to the CIA so it could be transferred to Iranian interlocutors.[72]

Question 3. Was the IC used in a novel way? Here the answer appears to be a solid yes. DCI William Casey appears to have been a key manager of NSC staffers, something that is almost unfathomable. It is difficult to judge precisely how much Casey handled Oliver North and others, but there is no doubt that he helped to create an off-the-shelf capability for the White House (NSC or other) to implement and pay for its foreign policy initiatives that were intended to be secret. The reader likely realizes that the executive branch has no money except monies appropriated through Congress and the appropriations process. This was truly novel and somewhat frightening.

Questions 4 and 5. Militarization of U.S. foreign policy? Again, Iran-Contra or Iranamok represented another gradation of the militarization of U.S. foreign policy. President Reagan—or the troika more likely—might have been able to get congressional approval with more patience but patience was not one of their virtue. NSC staffers became operational and in doing so they became foreign policy entrepreneurs who simply ignored congressional oversight and appropriations in order to serve the goals they believed President Reagan held. Whether Reagan held them or not, it is difficult to tell, mostly because of his aloof management style but also, sadly, due to the diminution of his mental faculties as time passed. There is no question foreign policy was militarized.

SUMMARY

In the previous chapter, a steep increase in the militarization of U.S. foreign policy associated with the early Cold War and fears—recall, it was bipartisan fear and bipartisan consensus that drove the said fear—of Soviet aggression globally was seen. The steep increase in militarization was driven by the aforementioned fears. But it was also affected by the end of World War II, the fact that America had necessarily built a massive military power to invade Normandy and drive back fascism in Europe. When the war ended, the will to dismantle the machinery proved illusory and much of it was kept in place. A justification for America's new role as world power was needed and the fear of Soviet expansion proved an expedient justification. (That is not to say the fear was not reasonable. Only in retrospect do some of the fears seem exaggerated.)

Thereafter, we saw the proliferation of covert operations in the two terms of Eisenhower. Part of it was left over from Truman's last few years. Recall, for instance, that NSC-68 was a document created in late 1949 and early 1950 with the knowledge that the Soviets had finally detonated an atomic weapon in late 1949. NSC-68 was created to determine how close the Soviets were; in turn, the document recommended covert and paramilitary means to thwart the Soviets as well as deficit spending, if necessary, to ensure the United States eventually bested the Soviets in that awful conflict, the Cold War. By 1949 (if not earlier), consensus existed that the United States could not charm Stalin and his successors. The Soviets were determined to dominate and therefore the United States would meet the challenge and thwart them in their designs.

In this chapter, we have seen a proliferation of both overt and covert military means of thwarting the Soviets and their clients (e.g., Cuba's Castro brothers). From East Asia (Vietnam, Laos, Cambodia) to Latin America to the Middle East, overt proxy wars developed between the United States and its allies and the Soviets and theirs. Arms races of various kinds were joined. Direct and indirect conflicts, both of overt and covert varieties, proliferated. Congress increasingly deferred to the presidency and indeed, if one but looks at the course of the Cold War, one will invariably see that equal numbers of Republican and Democratic presidents filled the White House. (Truman, Kennedy, Johnson, and Carter were the Democrats. Eisenhower, Nixon, Ford, and Reagan were the Republicans.) It mattered little which party controlled foreign policy from the executive or which party was in control of Capitol Hill.

If America's early isolationist impulses were shattered by World War II, then the Cold War shattered America's naivete about how the world worked. European colonial empires were the original version of hegemonic power. Pax Americana supplanted European domination. One result was Americans—meaning a majority of policy-making elites, the attentive public (shapers of public opinion), and the masses—became comfortable with something that had once been unpalatable to them: the indispensability of American power to a healthy international system. If America would ever return to the halcyon days of introversion and deferral to Europe, it would have to come later in the Cold War or after the Cold War concluded. We will look toward the post-Cold War period next to see if any retreat is evident.

CHAPTER 5

The Transition from the Cold War to the Post-Cold War Period

The December 1989 Panama invasion, and more importantly the Gulf crisis, changed all that. The military was not going to play a smaller role in the new world, as some had expected. It was moving to center stage.

—Bob Woodward, *The Commanders* (New York: Simon and Schuster, 1991), 32

This will not stand, this aggression against Kuwait.

—George H. W. Bush, August 6, 1990

... Would the United States return to the 1920s and once again turn its back on the world's troubles? Or more plausibly, would it return to the 1940s, when World War II ended and the country edged toward new international commitments? If the United States was the only remaining superpower, how should it use its power? Should it reorder the world in its own image? Was America bound to lead, as many argued? Or should the country veer more toward the old isolationist slogan of America First? Some foreign observers, perhaps too mindful of American history, leaped to the erroneous conclusion that isolationism would sweep the country. The London *Economist* (September 28, 1991) speculated that by the mid-1990s one of the two political parties, probably the Democrats, would be as "committed to isolationism as American parties can be."

—William G. Hyland, *Clinton's World: Remaking American Foreign Policy* (Kindle Locations 41–46)

INTRODUCTION

In this chapter, the focus is on cases in the post-Cold War period. However, before looking at the post-Cold War it is useful to consider the George

H. W. Bush administration, the administration in power as the Cold War ended and the transition to the post-Cold War began. The end of the Cold War gets variously dated as 1989 (when the Berlin Wall came down), 1990, and 1991. By the 1991 failed coup attempt to stop Gorbachev's reforms, clearly the Cold War was finished. Nevertheless, evidence that Cold War was ending—if not quite over—includes the Berlin Wall falling, which also signaled the old Soviet Red Army would no longer enforce the Soviet sphere of influence. Whichever date one accepts, as the Cold War concluded Russia and its former Soviet Republics, many of which began asserting independence immediately, ceased to exist as such.

The George H. W. Bush administration lasted only one term. Given its brevity, I have included just two case studies: one from the transitional end of the Cold War (1989), America's invasion of Panama to remove Manuel Noriega in addition to the 1991 Gulf War. President George H. W. Bush was a transitional president in important ways: he and his NSC headed U.S. foreign policy during the transition from the Cold War to post-Cold War period. Notwithstanding the Panama case study occurring in late 1989, the two case studies together belong in this chapter with other post-Cold War administrations for comparative purposes.

Following the Bush 41 presidency, a case from the Clinton administration during the 1990s is presented. The 1990s were the post-Cold War decade and the decade was full of interesting changes in world politics. First, the USSR, America's foe for four-plus decades, imploded leaving the United States a unilateral power (arguably, a hegemonic power) in the world political system. Second, early in this book it was mentioned that some—including President George H. W. Bush—thought that the United States might be able to temper decades of empire building (even return to its former, restrained self, prior to World War II and the Cold War). That is, some thought with the Cold War over, the United States might return to a status wherein the United States did not dominate the world political system (some even thought quasi-isolationism). (Whether or not the U.S. was ever truly isolationist is another issue, altogether—mythology in U.S. foreign policy held that the United States was formerly an isolationist power.) Of course, in retrospect, we know the United States continued to dominate the system; and with the absence of the USSR to check its aspirations, the U.S. became even more dominant. So the 1990s are an important decade for these reasons. Third, during the 1990s, as the United States was becoming Pax Americana, al Qaeda and other transnational actors were on the rise. Thus, again the 1990s are an interesting decade and quite distinct from the Cold War decades.

As the Cold War came to an unexpected conclusion—at least the timing was unexpected—the question was once again: "What was America's appropriate role in world politics?" The Bush administration presided over the reunification of Germany, the end of the USSR, and the beginning of the New World disorder that became evident as the 1990s proceeded.[1] As concluded in the last chapter, if ever the United States was going to return to its previous role in world politics of secondary power, deferring to Europe or others, it would have come in the wake of the Cold War. For a couple of years, President Bush decreased defense spending and there was a fair amount of talk about peace dividends and reinvesting in America.

The United States did not, of course, return to its former role as minor power deferring to others. Nor did those of us who study foreign policy think any such thing was likely. The United States had become far too vested in maintaining the *status quo* of the international system (in terms of the remnants of the old Bretton Woods regime as well as the UN system and, ultimately, the system in which the United States was a hegemonic power). Nevertheless, the talk about peace dividends circulated and there were at least some discussions about decreasing the U.S. role (and consequent defense spending) during the early 1990s. In the absence of having the USSR to focus the nation's attention (and its policy makers' attention) each day allowed people to begin thinking about a post-Cold War period where defense savings could be used to prepare the United States for globalization and other looming forces. In retrospect, it seems a bit of a shame the United States did not make serious attempts to reprogram some fraction (say 20%) of the roughly $300 billion it spent yearly during the Cold War.[2]

To be sure, the end of the USSR did not mean an end of threats or security interests for the United States. Instead of one big thing (containing the Soviets), the George H. W. Bush administration learned that the United States would need to watch multiple smaller things. This chapter looks at two of them that occurred during President Bush's tenure. The two are the Noriega threat that prompted the Panama invasion (1989) and what became Desert Shield and Desert Storm in 1990 and 1991, respectively. Both cases were handled by the same NSC principals whom President George H. W. Bush assembled, when he replaced the Reagan administration (January 1989).

PRESIDENT GEORGE H. W. BUSH'S NSC PRINCIPALS

As is commonly known, President H. W. Bush was the vice president for the entire eight years of the Reagan administration. His resume was much more extensive than Reagan's (in terms of foreign policy); and yet by virtually all accounts, the vice president was kept outside "the loop" during Reagan's two terms. (This likely had to do with the nature of President Reagan's aloof management style and the "troika" that filled that void of Reagan's management style. President Reagan's style and the troika have been discussed in a previous chapter.) When President Bush was inaugurated, he intended to draw sharp distinctions between his approach to foreign policy and his predecessors' including President Reagan's.

One way to do so was by selecting Brent Scowcroft (a sometime critic of President Reagan's foreign policy and one of the vice chairs of the Tower Commission that examined the dysfunction of Reagan's NSC during the Iran-Contra affair). By selecting Brent Scowcroft, the president was sending a signal (albeit a tempered one) that the Bush 41 team would return to America's school of *realpolitik*—both Republican and Democratic Parties have factions that are steeped in *realpolitik*. President George H.W. Bush was going to be his own man and his presidency would differ substantially from others, particularly in terms of foreign policy. President Bush's foreign policy credentials were such that featuring his foreign policy made intuitive sense during the campaign, even if it worried some of the Reaganites.

In addition to Scowcroft, President Bush selected his Texas friend James Baker to be secretary of state. Baker had held multiple positions in government and within GOP circles and would serve as President Bush's secretary of state until the president imposed on Secretary Baker to become his campaign chairmen for his reelection campaign (circa 1992). During the two case studies he was secretary of state, and an activist one at that.[3]

Richard "Dick" Cheney (before joining the Bush 41 team was serving as a House member from Wyoming) would be President Bush's secretary of defense. Interestingly, Cheney was not Bush's first choice. Rather, Bush originally selected Senator John Tower (Republican from Texas and of Tower Commission notoriety) as his secretary of defense. However, Senator Tower encountered serious troubles on Capitol Hill (particularly, in Senator Sam Nunn's Armed Services Committee). On March 9, 1989, the Senate voted to return the nomination to the Armed Services Committee and Tower's bid to be secretary of defense ended.[4] (It serves no possible interest to re-litigate the charges or their merit but Tower was a drinker of some repute and was accused of philandering too and the argument was made that the secretary of defense, the man charged with the nuclear codes of the United States, must be a sober person, in all the meanings of the word.) The point is that after the Tower nomination went down, President Bush selected Dick Cheney who became his secretary of defense (and despite whatever he did later in the W. Bush administration), the record demonstrates that he was an active secretary of defense and an integral part of the H.W. Bush NSC principals. (Likewise, many considered Cheney an excellent secretary of defense.)

For the director of CIA, Bush chose William Webster. In some administrations, the director of central intelligence (DCI) is an NSC principal. And as demonstrated in an earlier chapter, the statute made the DCI a statutory adviser to the NSC (today, the DNI has supplanted the DCI). However, in President Bush's one term in office, Webster was invited to NSC meetings only when the issue considered the intelligence community (IC) directly. Webster did not play an integral role in the NSC principals in the H.W. Bush administration. The reader may recall that President Bush had previously served as DCI late in the Ford administration and the president had a pretty good handle on CIA and IC activities in any case. President Bush therefore included Webster only when matters specifically involved U.S. intelligence.[5]

Another adviser to the NSC is the chairman of the Joint Chiefs of Staff (CJC), who is by statute the military adviser to the president and to the NSC (in the H. W. Bush administration, military adviser to the NSC principals). In the case of the H. W. Bush administration, the CJCS was originally Admiral Crowe. However, by the fall of Bush's first year in office, Crowe's term expired and President Bush eventually selected General Colin Powell to replace Admiral Crowe. Without doubt, CJCS Powell played an important role in the Bush NSC principals committee.[6] Together with his immediate boss, Secretary Cheney, the two exercised important influence on decisions made during President Bush's tenure.

As was mentioned previously, the vice president—though identified in the National Security Act of 1947 as a statutory member—never played an important role in actual NSC deliberations until rather recently. (This began, at least to some extent, during Clinton's tenure and beginning with Vice President Cheney in George W. Bush's two terms, the vice president began playing an influential part in the NSC. President Obama has continued the W. Bush precedent and it is likely that future vice presidents will be de facto as well as de jure members of the principals committee going forward.) Nevertheless, President Bush's vice president, Dan Quayle, played virtually no role in either of the case studies considered in this chapter.

PANAMA, TRANSNATIONAL DRUGS, AND GENERAL NORIEGA

The "war on drugs" dates back to the Reagan administration. Whatever one thinks about it, the war on drugs became part of U.S. domestic policy and as global cartels began to be prosecuted, in time, it became a foreign policy issue as well. By the time president-elect George H. W. Bush was inaugurated in January 1989, Noriega and Panama were on the radar in terms of U.S. foreign policy. Somehow, General Manuel Noriega had gone from being on the CIA's payroll as an informant to becoming one of the main pariahs in the war on drugs. By the time Colin Powell took over the chairmanship of the JCS (October 1, 1989), Noriega was threatening U.S. civilians and troops in the Canal Zone in Panama and becoming a particular foreign policy problem for the Bush NSC.

President Jimmy Carter signed a treaty in 1976 that provided for the Panama Canal to revert to Panamanian control and sovereignty, with a few exceptions in the Canal Zone. The date for turnover was December 1999 and by 1989 an increasing numbers of incidents occurred having to do with the Canal Zone. Panama's General Noriega and his forces were testing the United States vis-à-vis the Canal Zone. (Some were a result of the United States asserting its sovereign rights under the treaty. Others were a result of Panama attempting to test the United States to see just how far the Panamanian dictator could go without getting slapped down. It was a tense situation throughout the year 1989.)

During 1989, Panama held elections and the hope in the United States was that a democratic alternative to Noriega might be elected. In May, after the elections, Panama failed to elect Noriega's handpicked candidates, something that delighted the Bush administration. However, Noriega decided to suspend the outcome. Worse, when a "democracy" movement began to spread in Panama, pro-democracy protestors took to the streets to jeer at the "pineapple," as Noriega was derisively called by some of the protestors. Noriega's "dignity brigades" (called "digbats" by the Pentagon) were really a Noriega goon squad and they descended on the protestors and bludgeoned them with iron bars and other crude weapons. The pictures flashed all over CNN (in those days, the only cable network) and went "viral" (spread rapidly as today's YouTube videos sometimes spread).

As a result of the "optics" of the video coming from Panama, an NSC principals meeting was held (including, then chairman of the CJCS Admiral Crowe). The resolution from the NSC meeting was to send some additional Special Forces to Panama so that the commander of SOUTHCOM (then, a man named General Woerner) would have additional flexibility. (Apparently, Admiral Crowe and others believed Woerner too deferential to Noriega and they arranged to replace him with General Max Thurman that fall. Thurman, known by some of his admirers as Mad Max or Maxatollah, was thought to be the sort of commander the Pentagon brass considered vital to SOUTHCOM operations.[7]) The Pentagon rose to Noriega's test of U.S. resolve.

There was another factor that probably pushed Panama from a minor annoyance to a major NSC focus. A CIA operative had been captured earlier by Panamanian forces and President Bush was concerned about the operative's treatment. (Among George H.W. Bush's accomplishments was his one-year tenure as director of CIA, also known as the director of central intelligence or DCI.)[8] Noriega's forces were holding the CIA operative in confinement and the United States was having little luck getting the Panamanian leader to allow the appropriate visits to ensure the operative was well. Later, the man's wife was roughed up as well, really creating consternation in the White House. According to Bob Woodward's account, back in spring:

Crowe saw that the president—former CIA Director Bush—was very worried about the agency's captured operative. Bush also had made it clear that he wanted the military to be able to seize Noriega and bring him back to the United States for trial. The implications of going into a sovereign country and seizing its leader could be immense; Crowe saw no sign that the consequences were being fully considered.[9]

This was before the days when "extraordinary renditions" were common and the United States was rather more careful and abashed about exercising its own power inside a sovereign nation.

Also, earlier in 1989, President Bush's Justice Department issued an update on a ruling made during the Carter administration on whether the FBI (under Justice) could arrest fugitives for justice outside the sovereign territory of the United States. President Carter's Justice had decided no. President Bush's Justice Department said yes! (Later, this same ruling was used for what became known as extraordinary renditions in the Clinton and especially the W. Bush administrations. Extraordinary renditions remain controversial to this day.) The ruling was limited to the FBI at the time.

Meanwhile, Colin Powell prepared for his hearing before the Senate Armed Services Committee in order to replace Admiral Crowe. Powell testified in September 1989. By October, CJCS Powell had assumed his new position inside the Bush administration just as word of a coup in Panama crossed the wires. Although arguably incidental, it may have had a bearing on subsequent actions so it deserves brief mention. When the Bush administration decided not to intervene in the coup—and to be clear, it was an on-again, off-again coup—congressional criticism mounted on Bush and his indecisiveness and others suggested the Bush NSC had acted amateurish.

The Bush administration began paying close attention to events in Panama in October 1989. Now CJCS Powell and Secretary of Defense Cheney began watching events carefully from the Pentagon, as did the Joint Chiefs. Contingency plans were updated, then updated again, and then refined some more. At Justice, yet another ruling was issued. In November, the Justice Department expanded its spring interpretation. Justice asserted that *posse comitatus* (which forbade U.S. military forces to arrest in the United States) did not apply abroad. Therefore, the military could be used to arrest drug traffickers and other fugitives overseas.[10]

Around the same time, President George H.W. Bush signed an intelligence finding. (An intelligence finding allows the president to do something without seeking consultation with Congress, provided the president cited a clear and present danger to U.S. security interests. Accordingly, President H.W. Bush was compelled to notify the Gang of Eight on Capitol Hill. The eight are the Speaker and the Minority Leader in Congress, the Majority and Minority Leaders in the Senate as well as the chair and vice chair [again, majority and minority respectively] of the House and Senate Oversight Committees on Intelligence, the House Permanent Select Intelligence Committee, and the Senate Select Intelligence Committee).[11]

In this case, the finding President Bush signed authorized $3 million for the CIA to begin to disrupt events in Panama, with a view toward augmenting if the first tranche failed to prompt another coup attempt.

In effect, President Bush was asking for the CIA to rid him of the meddlesome Noriega (not unlike Henry II's reported plea for someone, anyone to rid Henry II of the turbulent Thomas Becket). All the pieces were in place for what became the Panama intervention.

On December 16, a pretext for another round occurred. A shooting in the Canal Zone triggered a series of Pentagon contingency plans that had been put in place since early October so the United States would not be caught flat-footed in Panama. (The Bush administration had been criticized earlier for not responding to Noriega's antics.) On Sunday, December 17, the NSC principals met with President Bush at the White House and discussed what to do next. They discussed using military force to overthrow Noriega; they discussed the earlier Pentagon contingency that had been approved, and a "snatch" operation to spirit Noriega out of Panama. Bush approved all the former and the clock began ticking to December 20, when all the contingency plans would be executed.[12]

Of course, the contingency plans did not work to perfection. The "snatch" of Noriega did not happen until the New Year. Arguably, the military response was overwrought for a simple snatch—the use of stealth bombers in Panama?—but the process had been building for months. The administration was not prepared to look amateurish again and the NSC had decided to use the various issues in Panama as a pretext to get rid of Noriega and render him to the United States where he would be subjected to a court trial. Despite the controversies surrounding the Panama intervention, Noriega ceased being a problem for the United States.

In Woodward's *The Commanders*, the comparison of the two cases (Panama and the First Gulf War) was stark. Whereas the Panama case was largely run from the Pentagon (with Pentagon contingency plans dominating), the 1991 Gulf War was quarterbacked from the NSC principals committee. While the NSC principals met in the case of Panama, the meetings were relatively few and seemingly desultory. In the case of Iraq (as will be seen shortly), nearly every aspect of Pentagon contingency plans were considered and debated at the NSC level. Part of the reason, surely, had to do with the newness of the Bush administration (its first year in office), but it is also true that U.S. military action in Panama was to rid Panama of Noriega not to defeat the state.

Structured Case Study Questions for
U.S. Intervention in Panama

The question is whether Panama represented a novel use of the intelligence community, the Defense Department, or the NSC?

Question 1. Novel use of the NSC? There is little to suggest the NSC was used in a novel way. (It is true that the Bush administration formally created both an NSC principals and NSC deputies committees. But as we have seen elsewhere, what amounted to the NSC principals dates back to the Kennedy administration.) The only novelty was the way president George H.W. Bush worked with his NSC adviser (Scowcroft) along with the other principals in such a systematic way. But as suggested much earlier in this book, each president brings stylistic and management differences to the NSC. These differences in themselves do not constitute novel uses but management styles.

Question 2. The military used in novel way? We have seen, arguably, novel use of the CJCS with the secretary of defense in the NSC but not the Pentagon per se. The Pentagon takes orders from the president, the commander in chief, and that has not changed since 1947 (or 1847, for that matter). There is some novelty in the fact that the "war on drugs" was turned into a foreign policy matter. But that could well stem from an activist president simply looking at his charge differently than previous presidents (in effect, idiosyncratic differences in personality and/or management style as noted with the NSC).

Question 3. Novel use of the intelligence community? Again, the answer seems to be no. There was little evidence that the IC was used in a novel way with respect to Panama. There may be evidence that is still classified but unless and until it is declassified the answer must remain a negative.

In short, there is little evidence in the case of Panama to suggest novel uses of any of the three institutions created by the National Security Act of 1947. On the other hand, the case seems to provide evidence of the *militarization* of U.S. foreign policy. A series of rulings by the Justice Department of two different administrations made the way clear for the militarization of the "war on drugs" in ways not seen before (namely, literal war on narco states).

Questions 4 and 5. Militarization of U.S. foreign policy? On the issue of militarization of U.S. foreign policy, clearly the Panama invasion is evidence of militarization of U.S. foreign policy. This was the first post-Cold War case study and rather than using a small, covert operation to snatch Noriega, President Bush decided to launch a military invasion of a former ally. That is not to say the decision was wrong. Clearly, as commander in chief, President Bush authorized the military to launch its invasion including stealth bombers. The administration had been somewhat embarrassed by earlier criticism of its policy vis-à-vis Panama and it decided to ensure Noriega was not going to continue being a persistent thorn in the administration's side.

SADDAM HUSSEIN AND THE
PERSIAN GULF WAR, 1991

By the time Saddam Hussein became a major issue for the H.W. Bush presidency, the Iran-Iraq War of the 1980s was over. The United States had followed a strategy of *realpolitik* in the war: if one side seemed to be winning, U.S. policy was to help the other side in order to reestablish stalemate and keep the warring states warring (and hope that prevented either Iraq or Iran from creating mischief elsewhere). Whether that was the intent of the Reagan administration or simply the way it worked is more difficult to judge. However, by spring 1990, the Iraq-Iran War had ended and Iraq began to present more problems for the United States in the short term than Iran had.

Before presenting the case study narrative, it is useful to remind the reader that Saddam's Iraq had issues with Israel. (It goes without saying that Arab states like Iraq have issues with Israel. But in this case, Israel had launched a preventive attack on Iraq's nuclear reactor at Osirak in 1981, while Iraq was at war with Iran.) Thus, Saddam had extra reason to worry about the Israelis and, perhaps even, for making some wild accusations about Israel? Besides, in that neighborhood nursing a grudge against Israel is clever politics and nobody doubted Saddam had a certain cunning that allowed him to stay in power for so long.

During the spring of 1990, Saddam gave a speech to the Iraqis in which he mentioned Israel (creating great roars of opprobrium as intended) and warned Israel that should it attack Iraq again (it had not since 1981 so why threaten?), the Iraqi military would create a holocaust in Israel (rain down fire on half of Israel). This speech and additional intelligence caused the Bush team to worry about Iraq's efforts to build an atomic weapon (one that could be used against Israel and others). On April 3, 1990, Saddam sought to deflect charges the United States and United Kingdom made about Iraq's pursuit of nuclear weapons.

In an escalating war of words with the West, the truculent Iraqi leader rejected American and British charges that his government [was] attempting to make a nuclear weapon, adding menacingly: "We don't need an atomic bomb, because we have the double chemical," a clear reference to binary chemical warheads or nerve gas.

"I swear to God that if Israel dares to hit even one piece of steel on any industrial site, we will make the fire eat half of Israel," Hussein warned in a midafternoon address broadcast over state radio.[13]

Somewhat lost in translation was the qualification that "if Israel dares to hit" any industrial site in Iraq, Saddam would retaliate with chemical weapons.

There are likely many reasons the qualification was overlooked in the West. First, Saddam was given to inflammatory rhetoric that leaders in the West seldom use. Second, Saddam had been hinting of his displeasure of the other Sunni regimes (Saudis, Kuwaitis, others) in the region who had not helped defray the costs, sufficiently, Iraq incurred against Iran (a common foe to Arabs, especially Sunni Arabs, which Iraq had battled during much of the 1980s). Finally, when the issue of weapons of mass destruction (WMDs) is raised, it is easy enough to miss the fine details. When Saddam threatened—or hinted a threat—of chemical weapons, he shocked Western leaders including some inside the Bush NSC.

In any case, the speech got the attention of the Bush 41 White House and President George H. W. Bush. Over the course of the spring and summer, Prince Bandar (former Saudi ambassador to the United States) made multiple trips back and forth from the Saudi Arabia to Iraq to the United States, where the message Bandar gave the Bush administration was Saddam was just being Saddam. (It never hurts to threaten Israel in the Arab world to rally crowds and Saddam was somewhat paranoid of another Israeli attack on him—what with all these charges of Iraq seeking nuclear weapons—than Israel had reason to fear him.) Bandar told NSC adviser Scowcroft and President Bush (as well as Powell) that Saddam was paranoid. Bandar also told his contacts in the Bush NSC that it was an Arab matter and the Arabs could handle it. (It is unclear whether it was the entire NSC principals committee or simply a group of three principals?)

However, by the end of July, an intelligence officer at the defense intelligence agency (DIA) thought there might be more to the threat than some inside the Bush NSC were thinking. Pat Lang (fluent in Arabic and an officer at DIA with access to the top) looked at satellite pictures of two and then three divisions of Iraq's elite Republican Guard units deploying near the border with Kuwait. (Kuwait was formerly a province in Iraq and made a sovereign state under British colonialism in 1961. Also, Kuwait was one of the targets Saddam had lambasted for failing to help Iraq pay the costs of keeping Iran at bay.) Lang worried that it may be a bluff but it may be real too. The same steps would be taken in either case and there was no practical way to distinguish between a bluff and the real thing until it happened or failed to happen.[14]

On the evening of August 1, 1990, it became clear it was no bluff. Saddam's armored columns were racing toward Kuwait City and NSC adviser Brent Scowcroft visited the president (at his residence) to inform him Iraq had begun invading Kuwait. (At this point it was still unclear what he intended because, among other reasons, America's Arab Allies did not believe Saddam would go so far and because the NSC principals thought it unlikely.) In any event, on the evening of August 1, the president was informed that some kind of military engagement was underway by Saddam's Iraq against the Kuwaitis.[15]

Woodward notes that the NSC deputies had not had a meeting on the emerging problems in the Middle East because Robert Gates (then deputy NSC adviser was out of town).[16] The deputies did meet on July 27 but the meeting seems largely inconsequential. The entire NSC met on August 2, 1990, and the policy making for what became the Gulf War then began in earnest. (Bob Woodward is one of the few journalists who has written about the centrality of the NSC in U.S. foreign policy.)

On August 2, the principals met about Saddam's invasion but were unable to come to any conclusion about how to respond. No resolution was found and the president seems to have become somewhat sidetracked by the effect the invasion was likely to have on the global oil market (an important issue in the United States to be sure). "Scowcroft worried that the debate was wandering and unfocused. The United States could not respond [to Saddam's invasion of Kuwait] by bombing the world's oil supply" (an option that was kicked around by the principals).[17]

Eventually, the discussion focused on a two-tier solution (reminiscent of Phase I and II in Vietnam in an earlier chapter). CJCS Powell insisted that two "tiers" of options were available to the NSC principals. Tier 1 would be a single retaliatory response only, with what assets the United States had available to demonstrate to Saddam that the United States took the invasion deadly seriously. In short, Tier 1 constituted an initial response while the United States monitored events on the ground, allowing it to escalate as warranted by events.

The second tier would be predicated on the Pentagon's Plan 90–1002 (the Pentagon's contingency plan) and would unfold over a month or more. CENTCINC, General Norman Schwarzkopf (who had been ordered to return to Washington from the command's U.S. headquarters in Florida) explained that plan 90–1002 was a defense of the Saudi Peninsula and would involve between 100,000 and 200,000 troops over weeks.[18] Tier 2 might take longer to effect but if necessary the United States might reverse Saddam's invasion.

Again, the meeting drifted into the problems and difficulties involved in responding to something that was already done (how to react to a *fait accompli*?). President Bush insisted, "But we can't just accept what has happened in Kuwait just because it's too hard to do anything about."[19] The president felt the United States could not simply accept the invasion as a *fait accompli*. To do so risked additional redrawing of borders by ambitious leaders such as Saddam. Again the meeting ended inconclusively.

Scowcroft was "alarmed." Accordingly, the NSC adviser thought "Iraq was a major threat to the vital interests of the United States." Scowcroft believed that the vital interest threat dated back to President Carter's enunciation of the Carter Doctrine that said the United States would consider an attempt to control Persian Gulf oil by an outside source (read, the Soviets), a threat that would be repelled by the United States by whatever means necessary, including military means.[20] (The role of the presidency is a powerful force that promotes continuity from administration to administration.)

Therefore, after the meeting, the NSC adviser Brent Scowcroft returned to the West Wing and sought to speak with President Bush. "Mr. President," Scowcroft said, "I think you and I are the only ones who really are exercised about this." But President Bush had to run off to Colorado.[21] So while Saddam's invasion was hanging fire, policy making was on temporary hold.

Scowcroft was wrong about he and Bush being the only ones who were exercised. Evidently, Secretary of Defense Cheney was too. He had been scheduled to go with the president to Colorado but instead begged off to return to the Pentagon and push his uniformed and civilian leaders to give him military plans. In fact, if Woodward is correct, Secretary Cheney and CJCS Powell had their most tensed exchange ever over Cheney pushing for better plans.[22]

Later that day, the president and Brent Scowcroft returned to Washington (from Colorado) where they resumed their discussion about Iraq and Kuwait. Apparently, Scowcroft worked out a good cop, bad cop role-play scenario between himself and President Bush for the NSC meeting they planned for the next day (August 3, 1990).

On August 3, the NSC met again in the situation room. With notes, Scowcroft began the meeting with the assertion that the NSC needed to begin the discussion with America's long-term interests. He argued the United States could not allow Iraq to effect an invasion of Kuwait and present it to the world as a *fait accompli*. The United States must do something in response to ensure the *fait accompli* does not become a precedent. Next, the president indicated that he "agreed" with his NSC adviser, thus resetting the tone of the debate. Scowcroft again took the baton and argued, "there had to be two tracks." First, the United States must use force to stop Saddam's land grab and had to make that clear to the world. Second, Scowcroft believed Saddam had to be toppled and accomplishing that must be done covertly.[23]

Bush immediately ordered the CIA to begin planning specific contingencies in order to destabilize Saddam's regime. The president wanted to "strangle" Iraq economically and to begin supporting anti-Saddam forces within the country (presumably, the Kurds in the north and the Shi'a in the south, since that is what happened subsequently).[24]

President Bush wanted Secretary of Defense Cheney and CJCS Powell to go to Camp David with the president over the weekend, where they were to brief President Bush and NSC adviser Scowcroft on specific military options to repel Saddam's armed forces from Kuwait.[25] (The NSC meeting just described was on a Friday so President Bush was signaling he wished to meet with his NSC principals on the weekend at Camp David.)

Subsequent NSC meetings were held at Camp David and back in Washington. But for present purposes we have seen enough to make some conclusions. Desert Shield, the first part of the process whereby Saddam would be given an ultimatum to remove his troops from Kuwait or face grave consequences, began almost immediately. It allowed the military time to tweak contingency plan 90–1002 and move vast numbers of troops and materiel into Saudi Arabia and nearby to prepare for Desert Storm. Desert Storm would begin in February (1991) if and after Saddam failed to heed the ultimatum.

In the meantime, President Bush directed a diplomatic offensive to get China (the PRC) and Russia to go along with (the administration's push veto) in the United Nations. A coalition of Arab and other states was assembled giving the United States legitimacy in its subsequent actions. Secretary Baker traveled to Russia where he successfully enlisted the Russians in behalf of America's cause to end Saddam's seizure of Kuwait. (Incidentally, that President Bush got Russia to go along and China to abstain from vetoing was a remarkable achievement.) During the Cold War, the UN Security Council was almost always stalemated and this was the first time since the Korean War when the UNSC worked as intended.

The rest is history. Desert Shield became Desert Storm in February 1991 and the U.S. military effort to push Iraq's army out of Kuwait back to Iraq turned into a rout. So successful was it that President Bush (and his NSC principals) decided to call it off and not go to Baghdad. The pictures of miles of Iraqi army carnage with charred bodies created a macabre tableau and while President Bush considered going all the way to Baghdad to topple Saddam, he also realized the UN mandate and the coalition mandate—part and parcel of the same thing—did not give him the flexibility to overthrow Saddam.

Structured Case Study Questions for the First Persian Gulf War

The question is, was Desert Shield, Desert Storm a novel use of any of the three main creations of the National Security Act of 1947? The reader must remember the times: Panama and Iraq were the first post-Cold War uses of the military. The Cold War was over and whatever pattern had been established during it, the president was free to establish a new pattern in its wake. And indeed, he spoke of a New World Order rather optimistically at times.

Question 1. Novel use of the NSC? With Iraq, a modern NSC with active participation of all the military representation, as well as the full complement of civilian representation would actively enforce U.S. values and objectives in the post-Cold War world, including a politically savvy CJCS, something that has more or less stuck since. In short, President Bush's action were significant for what would become post-Cold War U.S. foreign policy, as activist if not more than during the Cold War.

(While a somewhat different issue, it is worth mentioning that President George H. W. Bush set the model of the modern, post-Cold War NSC. The previous model had been constructed and assembled to contain the USSR wherever it might try to break out of the perimeter George Kennan argued for in 1946.)

Question 2. Novel use of the military? Yes, even more than the NSC the military was featured as a leading tool, the antithesis of the old War Department of earlier eras. Then, the president and his secretary of state made decisions and if war was declared (by Congress), a military was raised to respond. Now the military was being used to enforce U.S. foreign policy objectives around the world, and not just against the USSR.

Therefore, while it was not novel compared to the Cold War pattern, Iraq was most certainly novel in the post-Cold War. As the country was speaking of peace dividends and changing the trajectory of U.S. foreign policy, the Gulf War (as it became known) established a new post-Cold War trajectory that was, surprisingly to some, rather more forward leaning and militarized than many expected. Talk of peace dividends soon died away. President Bush's decisions to intervene in Panama and, even more, in Iraq set the standard of the United States intervening militarily for regime change in the post-Cold War world. In short, America became the single global power that would thereafter keep the world stable by using its military power to enforce its values (its unique sense of democracy and liberty) in global politics.

Question 3. Novel use of the intelligence community? There was no evidence that the IC was used in a novel way. The evolution of the IC is something that occurred over years of the Cold War. By the time the United States enacted Desert Storm, that evolution was long completed.

Questions 4 and 5. Militarization of U.S. foreign policy? Clearly, what became the First Gulf War represented the militarization of U.S. foreign policy in the post-Cold War world. The United States was the new sheriff in town. President Bush said it himself, notwithstanding awkward syntax. This will not stand; this aggression against Kuwait. The United States was henceforth responsible (at least partly) for ridding the world of unwarranted aggression.

PRESIDENT WILLIAM J. CLINTON: THE FIRST, FULL POSTWAR PRESIDENT

President William Jefferson Clinton was America's first, fully post-Cold War president and he inherited a world in which the United States played a central role in maintaining the system's status quo. The Cold War was over; the Soviet Bear had been slain or at least made quiescent. (As of this writing, one might reasonably ask about a reinvigorated Russia. However, when President Clinton inherited the presidency, few foresaw the reemergence of the Russia of today.) However, the fact that the Cold War ended did not make the world a stable, benign place where the United States simply ruled by fiat. In fact, the post-Cold War world proved to be rather less predictable than the Cold War. Instead of one big thing (the USSR), the United States involved itself with many smaller things. President Bill Clinton was the first president to conduct foreign policy in what had emerged from the Cold War and the unification of Germany—in short, the relatively stable milieu he inherited from President George H.W. Bush. It would not be stable for long.

PRESIDENT BILL CLINTON'S NSC PRINCIPALS

Both Republicans and Democrats have stables of foreign policy "experts" who work in think tanks and the private sector when their party is out of office. Sooner or later their party returns to power and they are called on to return to the ranks of government, capitalizing on their previous experience to move upward in the bureaucracy (whether State, Defense, the NSC, or others).

The Clinton team, unsurprisingly, selected foreign policy people from the Democratic stable (previous Carter people largely). Clinton chose Warren Christopher to be his first secretary of state—Christopher had been deputy secretary of state under Jimmy Carter. Clinton's first secretary of defense was Les Aspin (D-WI), long-time chair of the House Armed Services Committee. President Clinton decided to upgrade the U.S. ambassador to the UN to cabinet rank (and to the principals committee) and he chose Madeleine Albright (who would eventually become his secretary of state). Two Clinton friends from college, Strobe Talbott (journalist but also Russia expert) and Winston Lord, were given prominent positions that made them sometime NSC principals. Strobe Talbott was "special" ambassador to Russia and Winston Lord was undersecretary for Far East Affairs inside State. As noted in an earlier chapter, the National Security Act of 1947 makes no limits as to whom the president includes; it merely identifies advisers and members, which has evolved over time into the NSC principals committee. When presidents include others not mentioned in the National Security Act, they are called ad hoc members (to make a distinction between statutory members and others).

Winston Lord had served previously with Kissinger and in choosing his first NSC adviser, Anthony Lake, Clinton likewise selected a person who had once worked for Kissinger (in fact, he resigned over the Cambodia invasion in spring 1970, angering Kissinger). CJCS Colin Powell was scheduled to finish his second term in the Clinton administration and he constituted the single high-level NSC principal holdover in the new administration.[26] For director of central intelligence (DCI), Clinton chose James Woolsey, years later associated with neoconservatives on the issue of Iraq. Neither Anthony Lake nor Les Aspin would survive Clinton's two terms. Secretary of Defense Aspin was replaced by William Perry just after the Somalia debacle—one year and a week into

Clinton's first term—and Lake's deputy Sandy Berger replaced Lake as NSC adviser in spring 1997.

The Clinton Administration's Intervention in Former Yugoslavia

The late William Hyland (himself a former NSC deputy and intelligence official in former administrations) noted that one of the new administration's NSC documents—in the Clinton years, they were called Presidential Review Directives and Presidential Decision Directives respectively—was on Bosnia. NSC adviser Anthony Lake drafted it and sent it to the secretaries of defense and state, DCI Woolsey, and CJCS Powell. In it, NSC adviser Lake wrote that he and President Clinton were scheduling an NSC principals meeting for Wednesday, January 27, 1993, whose objective was (somewhat redundantly) to "develop broad strategic goals and strategies" that would "guide [the Clinton administration's] policies toward former Yugoslavia."[27] The document and the NSC meeting were within Clinton's first week as president.

Clearly, the administration had begun deliberations on Bosnia (its first major foreign policy initiative) with a view that it was Serbia that was the aggressor causing problems in the former parts of Yugoslavia that had begun to break into separate nation-states in summer 1991. (It was a common perception in the mainstream media that Serbia was the aggressor. Serbia may have been. But it was also clear that Serbia's Milosevic had become the bogeyman for the media and a more objective analysis showed that Serbia and its various enemies, whether Bosnia or Croatia or otherwise, were both committing heinous acts.) The NSC document clearly stated that the kinds of policies being considered were "humanitarian relief" for Bosnia and "stopping further Serbian aggression," as well as "rolling back Serbian conquest" to date.[28] (The reader may realize "rolling back aggression" was undertaken by President George H. W. Bush in the Iraq case study.)

Irrespective of who the aggressor was, the former Bush administration had begun its own work on the former Yugoslavia's unraveling that began in the summer of 1991. President Bush, for instance, had sent Secretary of State Baker to Belgrade (June 1991) to try to reduce tensions. The day after Secretary Baker left Serbia, Serbia and Slovenia went to war (Slovenia was the first to declare independence from former Yugoslavia, which was controlled largely by today's Serbia). It was brief and soon Serbia and Croatia, the next to declare independence, were at daggers drawn. A ceasefire was arranged and under it Serbia continued to hold some 20–25 percent of Croatia. The Bush administration had been opposed to military intervention in former Yugoslavia because, while it supported democratic change, it did not wish to rub Russia's nose it its misfortunes (Yugoslavia had been part of the Soviet Bloc, albeit a troublesome part). Even with Yugoslavia under Tito, it had been considered part of the Soviet empire and therefore was, arguably, part of Russia's sphere of influence.

The Clinton team believed explicitly in democratic change globally and spoke of a policy of "enlargement" (of NATO's umbrella and America's protection). As the new administration got underway, it faced some complex relationships and a problematic status quo in former Yugoslavia. CJCS Powell (and, indeed, others in the military) was against involvement, arguing there were no clear military objectives (versus political ones). There the matter remained for the first month of the Clinton administration.

(Though it is not this book's purpose to apologize for Russia, the Bush 41 administration promised Russia that NATO would not expand into the former Soviet sphere, namely, the old satellites of the USSR. Enlargement was likely seen by the Soviets as a potential breach of the former president's promise. In fact, enlargement was containment by another name. Whom was NATO (i.e., the United States and its partners) interested in containing? While Russia was relatively weak, the Clinton team likely did not think directly of Russia; but once foreign policy objectives are enumerated, they tend to die very slowly and they show up in multiple administrations irrespective of which party is in office. If one looks at NATO today it has, in fact, expanded into Poland as well as the Baltic States. While Russia's motives are more complicated than simply responding to NATO's expansion, that which it was once told would not occur has created friction between the United States and NATO versus Russia. Of that there can be little doubt.)

"Clinton confronted a confusing alignment of political forces. A humanitarian disaster loomed, and there were increasing reports of atrocities by Serbs. Washington could try to persuade the parties involved to stop fighting, but diplomacy would have to be backed by some threat of force. Given the skeptical state of congressional and public opinion, such a threat was unlikely. Public opinion polls indicated strong opposition to American involvement (60–70 percent against)."[29] President Clinton faced a touchy situation. (Not unlike President Reagan's in Nicaragua during the early 1980s.) On the one hand, he had articulated support for democratic change—what appeared to be underway in former Yugoslavia—but on the other hand, he faced a public that opposed intervention. Moreover, President Clinton was sensitive—recall he chided the Democratic Party for allowing itself to be outflanked by the GOP on national defense—to talk that he was "soft" on national security issues.

If there was an internal consensus in the Clinton NSC principals, it was for what was called "lift and strike." When Yugoslavia had begun to unravel, embargos were put on all the parts of former Yugoslavia to keep armaments from making matters worse in the region. If Clinton lifted the embargoes selectively, then the Bosnians could receive assistance. That accomplished, perhaps the United States (with NATO support) could assist with air power. Though not an NSC principal, the late Richard Holbrooke had been ambassador to Germany in the early 1990s and was a forceful voice for involvement in Europe. (He would later be considered to replace Warren Christopher in 1997 but was ultimately passed over.)

Apparently, Anthony Lake was the most "hawkish" of the NSC principals on Bosnia. Hyland says Lake "was the most hawkish, probably more as a devil's advocate than a genuine convert; in one exchange, for example, he compared Bosnia to Vietnam." But along with Secretary of Defense Aspin and CJCS Powell, Secretary of State Warren Christopher were "opposed to intervention, but rather than rejecting it outright [Christopher] posed a series of prior conditions that made it inconceivable."[30]

On February 9, 1993, President Clinton announced and Secretary Christopher elaborated on a new plan. It would consist of the following. First, a U.S. envoy would be appointed to facilitate peace talks between Bosnia and Serbia. Second, the United States would press for stronger sanctions and enforcement of a no-fly zone. Third, a new international war crimes tribunal would be established. But the United States would not use airpower to punish Serbian "aggression."[31] The challenge was to get America's European allies to go along with the new plan and Warren Christopher headed out to secure Britain's and France's agreement. Trouble was, the allies did not agree. Secretary Christopher returned home empty-handed and licking his wounds. His alternative plan was a dead letter at that point.

In fact, the Serbia-Bosnia problems languished from spring 1993 until 1995 and the Clinton administration took tremendous criticism over its feckless policy and its impotence. A common complaint about the administration's foreign policy was that it was a do-nothing policy, or that the president talked and talked but never took any real initiatives and the few he did take were poorly conceived and even more poorly executed.[32]

Bosnia was a black eye to the Clinton administration's foreign policy. The process had been chaotic. Clinton had demanded that he has consensus on the NSC to act but consensus was nearly impossible given the lack of specific objectives and given the military's position on getting the United States involved in "peacekeeping missions." (While peacekeeping has become more accepted among many in the military in the 1990s, it was then considered a four-letter word.) Moreover, critics of Clinton began taking to the airwaves (C-SPAN) where they would give impassioned speeches denouncing Clinton's foreign policy and reminding viewers that Clinton had been a draft dodger—what do you expect? (House member Bob Dornan, specifically denounced Clinton in some of the most vehement language ever heard on the chamber floor, in modern times.)

By early 1995, however, Bosnia had become a symbol of Clinton's failed foreign policy. There was increasingly serious talk of a complete UN withdrawal, in which case American combat troops might have to intervene to protect the UN forces as they withdrew. Several new factors, however, began to change the situation in a way that made a peace settlement feasible.[33]

Also in February 1995, President Clinton signed a Presidential Decision Directive (PDD-NSC 34) that permitted some substantial changes in how and to whom the United States could send conventional arms transfers. Whether it was prompted by the experience in Bosnia or not remains unclear, but it allowed new flexibility for the United States to arm the Bosnians and others provided the criteria were met. (The conventional wisdom at the time was that Serbia was being armed by Russia thus arming Bosnia was simply leveling the playing field.[34])

What is clear is that something had to happen to act as the precipitant to end what critics called the free fall of U.S. foreign policy in the Clinton administration. Somalia and now Bosnia—the United States had rarely looked more impotent in terms of foreign policy. Milosevic's forces helpfully complied. Serbia began a siege of Srebrenica, a city in Bosnia that the Serbs shelled mercilessly. CNN and the print media covered the siege endlessly. Bosnian prisoners held by Serbs were featured and likened to the Nazi death camps of World War II. Clinton reportedly yelled at his NSC people using profanity in tirades in which Clinton claimed he was being pilloried by the media, and his NSC was to blame.[35]

Public opinion began turning and Americans began supporting the use of military force (in conjunction with NATO) to end Milosevic's tyranny. Finally, the Europeans began to fall into line. Richard Holbrooke (then assistant secretary of state for European Affairs) was sent to negotiate with Bosnia, Croatia, and Serbia. "Under the guidance of National Security Advisor Anthony Lake, a significant reversal of policy was instituted."[36] A new policy directive was issued. Clinton approved a covert plan for Bosnia to import Iranian arms to level the playing field.[37] (Bosnia had a substantial Muslim population and Iran, among others, sought to help Muslims in the former Byzantium battleground between Christianity and Islam.)

President Clinton was reported to be frantically working on a peace plan for Bosnia in which the United States was to take the lead (from Europe). Accordingly, the president convened three NSC meetings in August 1995. The result was that NSC adviser Anthony Lake produced a plan that revolved around bringing the three warring parties together and lifting the sanctions on former Yugoslavia. Lake (and an NSC staffer) went to Russia where they talked to Yeltsin's advisers directly to get them to buy into the U.S. plan.[38]

Richard Holbrooke proved an able negotiator and the Dayton Accords proved a remarkable settlement. Announced on September 8, 1995, the accords were premised on three principles. First, Bosnia (and Herzegovina) would continue as a nation-state, Serbia would no longer contest its existence. Second, the territory would be split based on a 51/49 division of the land between them. Both Bosnian entities (Bosnia and Herzegovina) would retain the right to sign treaties of recognition with neighboring countries.

Structured Case Study Questions for Former Yugoslavia

Was the Clinton administration solution in Bosnia (woefully slow initially) a novel use of the military, the intelligence community, or the NSC? In terms of either the military or the intelligence community, the answer appears to be no. (I hasten to add many of the documents from the period are still classified and it is certainly possible that CIA or others facilitated the Iranian armaments to Bosnia in novel ways. In the absence of the documentary evidence, however, I have to conclude in the negative.)

Question 1. Was the NSC used in a novel way? It would seem that the NSC was used somewhat in novel ways. Initially, Clinton attempted to operate on the principal of consensus among his NSC principals. The NSC is an interagency process fundamentally and it seems unlikely that holding the process hostage to consensus makes much sense. The result was two years—at least—of the NSC process appearing to be broken. But ultimately, NSC adviser Anthony Lake seized the initiative and changed Clinton's consensus-based process back to one in which the NSC adviser held pretty exceptional power. However, it seems more dysfunctional than novel. Thus, the conclusion is the NSC was not used in a new or novel way.

In retrospect, a better case study than the Serbia-Bosnia one could be selected. For instance, a cursory look at how President Clinton responded to Serbia-Kosovo troubles a few years later seems to suggest some novel uses of the military and possibly the NSC principals. The cases were selected before the case studies were completed, however, and in the current case little evidence suggests a novel use of the NSC.

Question 2. Was the U.S. military used in a novel way? Again, the answer seems to be no. The military had been reluctant to get involved in Vietnam, initially, and it was likewise reluctant to get involved in former Yugoslavia. (Again, it may have been more useful to select the Serbia-Kosovo conflict some years later.)

Question 3. Was the intelligence community used in a novel way? Again, the answer is no. Many documents from the period are still classified so it is impossible to say definitively. But no evidence was found in this case.

Questions 4 and 5. Militarization of U.S. foreign policy? Here, the answer is a qualified yes. Ultimately, the United States sent troops and U.S. bombers to the region. That the United States would place the military in a former sphere of the USSR was novel. The reader may recall that eventually bombers did bomb Belgrade (Serbia) though that was more associated with a subsequent round of Serbia-Kosovo. Nevertheless, placing and keeping thousands of troops and military personnel in the former Soviet sphere represented a new iteration of militarization of U.S. foreign policy.

PRESIDENT CLINTON'S RESPONSE TO THE GROWING TRANSNATIONAL THREATS (AL QAEDA)

While George H.W. Bush was president when the first, arguably, Jihadist terrorist attack occurred in the United States (when El-Sayyid Nosair killed Meir Kahane in New York), al Qaeda (the Sunni-Salafi Jihadist group created by Osama bin Laden) were appearing on America's radar screen.[39] Within days and weeks of the Clinton inauguration, additional attacks occurred that began to capture the attention of policy makers in the Clinton administration. First, on January 25 (just days after Clinton's inauguration), Mir Qazi (sometimes spelled Kasi) shot up the entrance to the CIA in Langley, Virginia. Just a few short weeks later, the first World Trade Center attacks occurred (February 26, 1993). From its first few weeks in office, the new administration began to sense the post-Cold War world might include some threats that challenged America's imagination and its traditional instruments of statecraft.

Before discussing the Clinton NSC's response, it is worth mentioning some of the reasons the United States was slow to respond to this looming, transnational threat. One reason is that the U.S. Constitution protects individual's civil liberties with respect to religion. Not only does the Constitution preclude the United States respecting one religion over another, the tradition has evolved over time that a wall should exist between religious and secular matters (government). The United States tends to be pretty sensitive about violating civil liberties enumerated in the Bill of Rights, and rightly so. Thus, while zealous Sunni Muslim clerics denounced the United States, while attending conferences in the United States was considered something the United States should tolerate. (Obviously, such occurrences would be less tolerated today.)

Also, of America's intelligence entities (first assembled under civilian leadership in the National Security Act of 1947), only the FBI is a domestic intelligence agency. (At least in theory, the CIA and groups like the NSA are precluded by law from collecting intelligence inside the USA.) The FBI is allowed to collect intelligence inside the United States; but as it is also a law enforcement agency (a peculiarity of the FBI), it is instructed by federal law to separate intelligence collection from law enforcement. Thus, the United States had no intelligence entity (apart from municipal and state law enforcement) that collected intelligence on foreign nationals who came to the United States to study or work and who agitated in behalf of reestablishing the Islamic Caliphate under Islamic law (sharia).

Finally, the Cold War made the United States ill prepared for Jihadist terrorism. Since the Cold War (and before), the United States had simply never worried about non-state actors. Nation-states were the only unit of analysis worthy of national security attention. Nation-states like the USSR or the People's Republic of China had militaries and might attack the United States or its allies around the globe. During the four-plus decades of the Cold War, the bureaucracies that implement foreign policy (State, Defense, intelligence community, NSC, and others) got into the habit of belittling non-state or substate actors as national security threats to the United States. (Some readers may recall when the Air Force finally responded to the bombings of New York on 9/11, the jets scrambled flew out over the ocean waiting for Russian missiles or jets to appear on their radar.)

During the 1970s, for instance, the Palestine Liberation Organization (PLO) conducted terrorist attacks on Israel and others. Those attacks, typically, consisted of hijacking an airplane in order to hold its passengers and crew hostage long enough to publicize the PLO's political demands. People had died in terrorist attacks during the Cold War, but they were few and far between. (Even in 1983 when President Reagan sent Marines to Lebanon, Hezbollah who was ultimately blamed for the attack was a creature of Iran's. Thus, even when non-state actors did something worth noting, the United States associated the action with some nation-state.)

During the 1990s, an accretion of evidence slowly built that suggested the United States might need to pay attention to non-state actors, whether they be criminal syndicates (in Russian and in Latin America) or Jihadist terrorists or others. It was during the Clinton administration's first and second terms, though not at the NSC principals committee level, at least initially, where those changes began to take place. (Multiple authors mention what the Clinton NSC principals called the "brown blobs" meaning messy situations that were not neatly contained within a single nation-state's borders.) The Clinton administration responded at the NSC level, as two of Clinton's NSC staffers made clear in their memoirs of their time in the Clinton NSC.

The NSC is that rare thing in Washington, a flat organization. Under the national security adviser [what I have called the NSC adviser] and his one or two deputies, it averages between eighty and a hundred professionals—roughly twenty senior directors and the rests directors—during the second half of the 1990s. In the final three years of the Clinton administration, the Transnational Threats Directorate was unusual in being run by a bureaucrat with an additional title: "national coordinator for counterterrorism, infrastructure protection, and security." The man who held that position was Richard A. Clarke.[40]

The Transnational Threats Directorate (TNT) was a subgroup of the Counterterrorism Security Group (CSG) inside the Clinton NSC, created in 1997. PDD-39 memorialized Clarke as the lead for the group and instead of Clarke attending State Department meetings PDD-39 (according to the authors, a result of Clarke's bureaucratic acumen), thereafter instructed State and others to attend Clarke's meetings.

On May 22, 1998, President Clinton signed Presidential Decision Directive 62 (PDD-62), the work product of the NSC. "It was probably the first major policy document to address head-on the threat of 'asymmetric warfare,' in which an opponent who recognized American military superiority tries to attack the nation by targeting civilians with unconventional means." It created the lines of authority for government agencies inside the United States for such attacks, called "consequence management."[41]

Together, these two PDDs and Richard Clarke nearly alone (Daniel Benjamin and Steven Simon being his only two staffers in TNT) carved out an entirely new function in the NSC: to track and prepare for al Qaeda or like-minded organization to attack the United States Moreover, the TNT was extremely successful preventing the Y2K-Millenial attack and others. So critical did Richard Clarke become that he became an NSC principal by the time Anthony Lake yielded to Sandy Berger the NSC adviser's position.

It was not just these factors (others included ridding the administration of Louis Free, the FBI director and diminishing AG Janet Reno's role) that made the TNT so successful. The two staffers were incredibly hard workers and well versed in terrorism (Islam and other religious variants). They both left the Clinton administration in its last stages to write the book that so well chronicled the progress made in the late Clinton second term to prepare the United States for what would eventually be 9/11.

Alas, during the transition from Clinton to George W. Bush, the TNT progress got lost in the shuffle as did the focus on al Qaeda so recently developed in the NSC and the CIA. (Director George Tenet declared "war" on al Qaeda in 1998, following the U.S. embassy twin bombings in Kenya and Tanzania but little came of it.) Clarke, who had made enemies in the Clinton administration made new ones in the W. Bush administration including his boss, Condi Rice, the new NSC adviser. He was demoted to a lower-level staffer and not part of the principals committee in the Bush administration.[42]

The NSC deputies finally approved a draft presidential directive (the work product of the NSC during the Clinton administration) on September 4, 2001. On September 10, deputy NSC adviser (during President George W. Bush's first term but the NSC adviser during his second term) gathered the deputies to discuss a three-year strategy including al Qaeda and the Taliban (Afghanistan and Pakistan).[43] But as the 9/11 Commission makes clear, time ran out. According to George Tenet (DCI in the Clinton administration's second term), the light "was blinking red" and, while Bush "officials were alerted" and "many were doing everything they possibly could to respond," no one was working on the various leads that had been accumulating for three or four years.[44] 9/11 overtook the transition.

Structured Case Study Questions for the Rise of al Qaeda

For present purposes, the question is whether any of the three main entities created by the National Security Act of 1947 were used in novel ways?

Question 1. In the second Clinton term, the NSC (though largely the staff rather than the principals or deputies committees) was clearly used in a novel way. President Clinton issued two PDDs directing the larger bureaucracy (bureaucracies, really) to devote more resources to transnational terrorism (Islamic Jihadist and others), as will be discussed later. The first NSC document put FEMA in charge of disaster relief should some sort of unconventional weapon be loosed on the United States and the second created a wholly new entity inside the NSC to monitor and thwart al Qaeda-like groups. That the small group was unable to force the larger bureaucracy to move faster does not belie the fact that Richard Clarke created the new entity.

Moreover, Clarke—who was not an NSC principal by statute—eventually moved his way into the NSC principals committee (as an ad hoc member). The last couple of years of the Clinton administration, Clark (as made clear by Simon and Benjamin) became a force to be reckoned with in the NSC principals committee. He probably would have become a powerful voice in the new George W. Bush administration (and may have even better prepared the new team for 9/11) had he not so alienated Condi Rice, his boss in the new administration. Instead, he was demoted and eventually moved laterally into another job then left the administration entirely.

When President Clinton created, inside the NSC, the special group for transnational threats (subsequently called the counterterrorism security group, or CSG) and put Clarke in charge, that was a novel creation. Later, of course, Richard Clarke had access to intelligence reports, as was later revealed in the 9/11 Commission report.[45] That Clarke eventually made his way into the NSC principals committee as a staffer is not especially novel since presidents have often included ad hoc members. Nevertheless, the CSG was a novel creation. To be clear, it was created in the NSC staff not at the same level as the principals committee or even what President Clinton created early on, the National Economic Council (NEC).

Question 2. Was the U.S. military used in a novel way? Again, in this case study, there was no evidence of novel use of the military. The NSC is the apex of policy making and it can instruct the bureaucracy to do any number of things. Whether a given bureaucracy does as it was instructed is another matter. As noted earlier, bureaucracy changes very slowly even while threats are changing around it. In the case of the military, there is probably little one could expect to change, if for no other reason U.S. laws and precedents. The military could have done very little to prevent attacks like 9/11 which originated outside the United States but were launched from within the United States.

Though not discussed before, the Pentagon and the CIA both paid for what became the unmanned aerial vehicle (UAV) program during the Clinton administration and one might argue it was novel. However, technology is constantly updated and the UAVs or drone simply happened to come along during this time. The same UAVs have evolved tremendously since the Clinton administration and it is difficult to make a case that said evolution represent novel use of the Pentagon or CIA, the two entities that use them.

Question 3. Was the intelligence community used in a novel way? While it was only briefly mentioned, DCI George Tenet declared war on al Qaeda in late 1998. Inside the CIA, specifically, a unit was created to work the al Qaeda problem. It was called the bin Laden group. Arguably, DCI Tenet's declaration of war was novel as it seemed to jar other parts of the bureaucracy into taking the transnational threat seriously. In fairness to the Clinton administration, the bureaucracy did respond to the Y2K threat and others transnational matters but ultimately the response to what became 9/11 was not robust, however novel it may have been.

Questions 4 and 5. Militarization of U.S. foreign policy? Of course, the actual attacks of 9/11 did not occur until the George W. Bush administration had been in office some nearly nine months. Nevertheless, the response to 9/11 was a clear and unmistakable militarization of U.S. foreign policy during the Clinton administration. The reader will recall that in somewhat less than a month, U.S. forces (mostly Air Force and Special Forces) were in Afghanistan chasing al Qaeda from its redoubts in that country. The 9/11 Commission noted multiple instances wherein the military was instructed to use drones to kill what sources believed might be bin Laden during Clinton's tenure. That they never actually got him does not change the fact that a new militarization of foreign policy occurred. It has continued through the George W. Bush two terms and both terms of President Obama, who actually ordered the drones to kill the American citizen Anwar al-Awlaki in September 2011 (he was killed in Yemen).

Of course, it was not until early 2003 that the United States invaded Iraq to remove Saddam Hussein from power (and Saddam had nothing to do with 9/11). Still, that additional iteration of militarization was justified by the George W. Bush administration based on 9/11.

THE BARACK OBAMA ADMINISTRATION
AND OBAMA'S NSC PRINCIPALS

The chapter will conclude with a case study from the Obama administration. Together, the chapter's cases help to make the case of continuity in

U.S. foreign policy between Clinton and George W. Bush, a Democratic administration and a Republican one respectively. As will be seen, President Clinton started the process of preparing the United States for transnational threats. George W. Bush continued that process in spades with his response to 9/11 and, arguably, his decision to expand the "war on terror" to Iraq.

Barack H. Obama was elected in November 2008 and became the 44th president of the United States in January 2009. Candidate Obama was elected on a platform of ending partisan politics as usual. Interestingly, Obama's election was somewhat reminiscent of the Clinton administration with its economic focus. (Of course, the economy was in worse shape than when Clinton became president. The United States suffered the worst economic recession—borderline depression—that began in August-September 2008 and continued through the first couple of years of his administration.)

President Obama inherited two wars from the George W. Bush administration. The Iraq War began in 2003 but by the time Obama inherited the previous administration's policies, the "surge" in Iraq was essentially completed and a status of forces agreement (SOFA) that President Bush signed in 2008 was in place. The SOFA determined that U.S. troops, unless supplanted by a new agreement, would withdraw at the end of December 2011. Of course, Obama also inherited the Afghanistan war, which at that point was, arguably, under-resourced due to the movement of troops from Afghanistan to Iraq during President Bush's tenure.

Candidate Obama's rhetoric about change, notwithstanding, President Obama followed his predecessors' precedent of nominating former officials from the stable of foreign policy "expertise," though in this case the Democratic stable. Obama's first secretary of state was, somewhat surprising (given the animosity during the campaign), Hillary Clinton who served the entire first term. President-elect Obama asked Robert Gates (George W. Bush's second secretary of defense) to stay on as secretary of defense, which Gates did for some two-plus years. Obama's first NSC adviser—and for present purposes, the only one on which we need focus—was General (retired) James Jones, former commandant of the Marines. NSC adviser Jones served as NSC adviser until October 2010.

Other members of Obama's NSC principals included director of national intelligence (DNI)[46] and Obama's first vice admiral (retired) Denis Blair who was replaced by General James Clapper (formerly, of the NSA) in May 2010. Obama's first chairman of the Joint Chiefs (Admiral Mullen) served through the Afghanistan decisions and was active in the NSC principals committee. Tom Donilon served as President Obama's deputy NSC adviser and he would eventually replace James Jones. Another NSC adviser worth noting was John O. Brennan (counterterrorism and homeland security adviser inside the NSC). Leon Panetta served as the director of the CIA—what was the DCI before the law changed in 2004—and attended several NSC meetings also. Finally, as has happened with other presidents on occasion, Obama's chief of staff (i.e., his first chief of staff) Rahm Emanuel, though not an NSC principal attended many NSC meetings and was involved in policy making, especially as it pertained to the decision to "surge" troops in Afghanistan.

(At this point, the reader may wonder why George H. W. Bush cases were followed by a case from the Obama administration? Obviously, the George W. Bush administration—which lasted two terms—was wedged in between. President George W. Bush's foreign policy has been well covered by others. For instance, Bob Woodward wrote a trilogy of books about the foreign policy of the Bush 43 administration. That President Bush's foreign policy represented a militarization of U.S. foreign policy is self-evident to virtually any analyst of U.S. foreign policy, whatever else one wishes to think of President George W. Bush.)[47]

The present author has no quarrel with President Bush or his decision to respond to the 9/11 attacks as he did. But his decision to send troops to topple Saddam Hussein in Iraq (arguably, residual business from his father's own administration) was nearly universally seen as conflating two distinct threats into one. In fact, as will be seen soon, Obama's "surge" in Afghanistan—announced on December 1, 2009, was very much modeled after President George W. Bush's decision to "surge" troops in Iraq earlier. The fact is, Obama (a new kind of president) behaved rather like previous administrations featured in this book, whether Republican or Democrat. (Recall a secondary thesis of this book is that tremendous continuity exists from presidency to presidency. Obama very much fits the pattern. Campaign rhetoric is one thing. What a president does once in office is very much a different matter.)

It is also important to note that President Obama made two distinct decisions on Afghanistan in 2009. The first was made almost *pro forma*, with very little activity from the NSC involved. It was announced in February and again in March 2009, in the first two months of the administration. A decision at the end of the Bush presidency to send roughly 30,000 additional troops to Afghanistan was held in abeyance so the new administration could take its own measurement of the situation in Afghanistan. (President Bush told his NSC principals that the decision would have no roll out with Bush in his last couple of months as president.) Thus, President Obama addressed that boost in troops, already requested nearly immediately and without a substantial NSC process involved. Obama ran on the assertion that Bush's war in Iraq was one of choice whereas the war in Afghanistan was one of necessity, thus making the boost in troops early in 2009 relatively desultory in terms of the NSC.

THE OBAMA DECISION TO "SURGE" TROOPS TO AFGHANISTAN, 2009

However, matters conspired to force Obama to make a second decision on Afghanistan just a few months after he had determined to send some

25,000 troops in the spring and early summer. First, from the previous decision regarding Afghanistan, a decision was made in the NSC to develop a strategy to go along with the troops announced in spring 2009. Second, an outsider was brought into the NSC principals committee, Mr. Bruce Riedel (a former intelligence analyst with expertise on Afghanistan and Pakistan) who developed the main ideas regarding the Taliban along with al Qaeda. Riedel developed a plan to disrupt and dismantle hard-core al Qaeda (and Taliban), as well as reconcile with less hard-core members of the "insurgency," which was remarkably similar to what had happened in Iraq under Bush. (In Iraq under the Bush "surge," the United States planned to seek reconciliation with Sunni tribal elements in Iraq; likewise, under Obama in Afghanistan, the thinking was the United States could not kill its way out of Afghanistan and therefore would need to reconcile with those who could be co-opted.[48])

Additionally, Secretary of Defense Robert Gates (along with CJCS Mullen and others) convinced President Obama that Obama needed to make a change in Afghanistan where General McKiernan commanded U.S. (and allied) troops. The change put Stanley McChrystal (who had run Joint Operation and Special Forces in Iraq during the Bush "surge") in Kabul to replace McKiernan. (In fact, Robert Gates wrote in his memoirs that he did not realize he was the first to relieve a "wartime commander" since Truman fired McArthur.[49]) By replacing McKiernan with McChrystal, a 60-day review began by the new commander of the situation in Afghanistan. It was the said review that resulted in McChrystal's recommendation to the NSC for an additional 40,000 troops that led to the "surge" in Afghanistan. That is, in addition to the nearly 25,000 Obama had already approved in spring, General McChrystal eventually recommended an additional 40,000 troops be sent to Afghanistan, which Obama's NSC debated (as will be seen presently).[50]

The McChrystal review began a clock ticking that would lead through July and into August 2009. Since Washington closes down during August, it effectively meant that what would become the "surge" decision in Afghanistan would not begin until September 2009. Thereafter, President Obama held a series of NSC meetings (nine in all) during which time various options were presented to Obama of how to proceed in Afghanistan. The options were for what was called a counterterrorism-plus options (some 20,000 troops and mostly covert operations), a fully resourced counterinsurgency option (some 90,000 troops over the next 5 years) and the "just-right" option of 40,000 troops "surged" as quickly as could be managed and given "off ramps" as an exit strategy.[51]

It is an interesting story with most of the Pentagon aligning behind the McChrystal recommendation in September; the president pushing back on the process and demanding real options rather than three options, two of which were framed so as not to be palatable and a give-and-take process of negotiated policy making that often takes place at the NSC principals level. Secretary of State Clinton fell into line much with the McChrystal proposal—somewhat surprisingly—as did General Petraeus (then the head of CENTCOM or CINCCENT). On the other side of the decision were NSC deputy adviser Donilon, NSC adviser Jones, and the vice president (Joe Biden) pushing for something less that 40,000 (it was framed as a counterterrorism rather than counterinsurgency strategy). President Obama eventually decided to send around 34,000–35,000 troops instead of the 40,000 recommended. The decision was not made until the Thanksgiving Holiday and was, as noted earlier, announced on December 1, 2009.

Therefore, the "surge" decision in Afghanistan announced on December 1, 2009, turned out to be remarkably similar to the Bush "surge" in Iraq made in 2006–2007. Both decisions represented militarization of U.S. foreign policy. In the former case, Bush embraced militarization as a solution. In the latter case, Obama seemed reluctant to embrace militarization but the NSC process eventually forced him to do so. For purposes of foreign policy, it matters little whether the president was eager or reluctant but whether the result was militarization.

Structured Case Study Questions for the Afghanistan "Surge"

Again, we must consider whether any of the three entities created by the National Security Act of 1947 were used in novel ways?

Question 1. Novel use of NSC (any of its parts)? The answer is not as clear-cut as was hoped when the case was selected. Surely, the use of multiple NSC principals' meetings was not novel for an important decision, especially one deploying large numbers of troops. However, as noted earlier, it was novel compared to Obama's own NSC process used earlier in the years to increase troops in Afghanistan. That is, the first decision was without much ceremony and with a relatively few NSC meetings—of course, partly the reason was the administration was new and partly the reason was candidate Obama had campaigned for more troops in Afghanistan.

Still, it was a process that was new to the Obama administration. It involved a good deal of give and take between the participants (the NSC principals of the Obama administration). Secretary of Defense Gates related in his memoirs that he nearly resigned over some of the "politics" and language that bothered him in the Obama administration. (However, he also wrote that the previous Bush administration had been incredibly political implying that politics has worked its way into the NSC process over time.)[52] Politics aside, the NSC was not used in a particularly novel or unique way.

Question 2. Novel use of the military? Certainly, neither the Defense Department nor the military (nor the secretary of defense, unless one accepts Secretary Gates's thoughts on resignation) were novel. As noted earlier, the "surge" in Iraq was a similar process. One must likewise conclude no novel use of the military.

Question 3. Novel use of the intelligence community (IC)? There was no evidence found that the IC was used in a novel way during the "surge" in Afghanistan in 2009. After 9/11, a good deal of innovation and improvisation—as well as reformation—of the IC occurred. But it had mostly occurred before Obama became president. That Obama continued to follow the precedents of the W. Bush administration was hardly surprising here, where continuity has been the rule rather than exception.

Questions 4 and 5. Militarization of U.S. foreign policy? But the case does establish, clearly, the continued militarization of U.S. foreign policy since the Cold War. The U.S. military is used for traditional set-piece battles as it always has been. But it is also used for counterinsurgency operations (COIN) as both "surges" in Iraq and Afghanistan have demonstrated. Even COIN is not novel, though the name has changed over time. During World War II, the Pacific Theater was two militaries—the Army supplemented by the Navy—under General MacArthur's command and the island-to-island fighting done by the Marines. But World War II (and indeed, one might argue the Cold War) were wars that were foisted on the United States. In Afghanistan, certainly the attacks of 9/11 were without major provocations (at least so most Americans think). But since 1991 and the end of the Cold War, and without any generalized threat such as the USSR provided during the Cold War, the military has been increasingly deployed over time and the military budget has been increased over most of that time.

While one cannot conclude the NSC or other entities created by the National Security Act of 1947 led to the militarization of U.S. foreign policy, what is clear is that U.S. foreign policy has continued to become militarized over the two time periods considered in these case studies: the transition from the Cold War and post-Cold War eras. The so-called peace dividend never materialized. Rather, under both Republicans and Democrats, America has continued to grow as a military, hegemonic power.

SUMMARY

In this chapter, cases were presented from two post-Cold War administrations (Clinton's and Obama's) as well as the Bush 41 administration (which included a late Cold War case as well as the Gulf War, arguably the first post-Cold War case study). While U.S. foreign policy history may be divided into any number of phases, in this book the Cold War was divided into the 1950s and the main years of the Cold War (1960s through 1980s) and the post-Cold War era. Before World War II, U.S. foreign policy matched America's status as a secondary or tertiary power in the world and very little depended on America's buy in. For this book, the interest was from the beginning of the Cold War through its conclusion and then the post-Cold War era.

Herein the assertion was made that something changed with the onset of the Cold War—the militarization of U.S. foreign policy and that it stemmed from the National Security Act of 1947—during the 1950s and it continued and increased during the subsequent decades of the Cold War. Once the Cold War ended, however, U.S. foreign policy continued to militarize and may have increased in the rate of change.

Recall that once the Cold War ended, "pundits" and others (including President George H. W. Bush) thought U.S. foreign policy might mellow, that the United States might spend less on defense and reprogram those savings into domestic needs that were sacrificed during the Cold War. As this chapter demonstrated, that did not happen (nor was it ever likely despite talk of a New World Order). Rather, the United States (formerly, one of two superpowers responsible for the international system) found itself alone atop of the system it had helped fashion. It included the UN system and what it represents and it included the Bretton Woods system. In short, America found itself trying to protect the status quo that it helped create.

This George H. W. Bush cases demonstrated how critical the George H. W. Bush administration was to transitioning the United States (and U.S. foreign policy) from the old Cold War system to the new post-Cold War system. Even though President Bush decreased defense spending for his first couple of years, that began to change and returned to climbing defense appropriations following Panama and the Gulf War. Thereafter, Presidents Clinton and Obama—others have made the case for President George W. Bush—both continued the militarization, making it a bipartisan effort.

The Clinton administration ran on domestic issues, not a foreign policy resume. But relatively early on President Clinton realized that, while the United States might have ridded itself of one major headache (the former USSR), it was discovering new, smaller headaches and finding them in almost every corner of the globe, including in Russia's historic sphere of influence.

President Clinton soon learned how to conduct foreign policy and his template was the former Bush 41 administration. Many reasons exist for President Clinton to follow President Bush's lead so closely. Presidents ultimately are a pretty exclusive club and they tend to do what was being done in the previous administration unless they campaigned against it and that is not necessarily a deal breaker. Additionally, the bureaucracy created by the National Security Act is massive and it shares an interest with U.S. presidents in maintaining the status quo. It is not just Defense and the uniformed military, though Defense accounts for millions of personnel. Likewise, State and the massive intelligence community must justify their annual appropriations to other agencies that get involved in U.S. foreign policy from time to time (Agriculture, Commerce, Justice, and others).

In fact, if one thinks it through just a little it is not so unusual that the United States would be slow to change or that a trend—say militarization—continues in increments year after year. The movement to militarize U.S. foreign policy began because the United States had spent its first century seeking to maintain the American experience in self-government and republicanism. By the 20th century, the United States could no longer safely ignore nationalism or fascism or other issues that might eventually affect U.S. interests. Pearl Harbor taught policy makers that the United States had spent too much time turned inward and had not prepared for threats from abroad.

Thus, the National Security Act was the memorialization of this new thinking. Its creations were intended to make it very difficult for the United States to return to its former introverted posture, to ensure isolationism could never again become the policy of the United States. Over the 40-plus years of the Cold War, Americans—mass public, attentive public, and policy-making elites—had become used to the status quo in which America was an important and, arguably, the most important nation in the world, a hegemonic power that shaped its environment without the need for permission from anyone. America and Americans had formed new habits and the new habits included a substantial say in how the world worked.

Momentum already meant the United States would keep doing what it had been doing for decades, leading the world as a superpower. After the USSR disappeared, the United States was simply the sole superpower and that meant it did not even have to worry about how the Soviets might react. Thus, the die was cast.

During the Cold War, nearly equal numbers of Republican and Democratic presidents led the White House (and thus U.S. foreign policy). Since the Cold War ended, there has been the H. W. Bush administration (Republican), two terms of William Clinton (Democratic), then two terms of W. Bush (Republican), and two terms of the Obama (Democratic) administrations. Each president has found it much easier—much simpler—to continue doing what the United States has been doing rather than upset the status quo and accept the risks of doing so.

Previously, we saw that President H. W. Bush (who may initially have been inclined to change the status quo) learned things worked better when he continued to use the U.S. military for virtually any problem the United States might have. After Bush, President Clinton learned the same thing. After Clinton's two terms, President W. Bush and President Barack Obama have learned what their predecessors learned: why rock the boat?

This chapter has demonstrated two of those administrations continued what H. W. Bush started. The case studies collectively demonstrate that it scarcely matters whether a Democrat or a Republic is in the White House. The militarization of U.S. foreign policy continues irrespective of who controls the White House, or for that matter who controls the opposite end of Pennsylvania Avenue.

PART III

The Rise of the American Security State

In Part III of *The Rise of the American Security State*, the evidence gathered in each of the 14 case studies used in Part II is tabulated and considered in more detail. What inferences may be made from the case studies? What generalizations about U.S. foreign policy become evident? What can we deduce about the future of U.S. foreign policy given the trends over the three chronological periods? And what challenges to America's democracy might be perceived from the evidence presented in the case studies?

While working on the case studies yet another presidential election occurred in the United States. In 2016, Donald Trump (formerly a moderate Republican with many Democratic friends) appeared almost out of nowhere. Pundits told America that Mr. Trump did not stand a chance against the Republican field. The odds were too stacked against him. Likewise, when Mr. Trump outmaneuvered his GOP peers in the Republican primaries, pundits told America Mr. Trump could not possibly compete against Hillary Clinton. In both the GOP primaries and the fall presidential elections, pundits said Mr. Trump's temperament was altogether unfit for the presidency. He was too bombastic. He was not presidential.

As of this writing, Mr. Trump has become President Trump. Given the trends evident in the case studies in Part II, what might one reasonably infer about U.S. foreign policy under the Trump administration? These are the questions raised in Part III.

CHAPTER 6

What the National Security Act Has Meant for U.S. Foreign Policy

INTRODUCTION

In this chapter, an effort to assess and tabulate the evidence from the three chapters of case studies is presented. The incredible metamorphosis that U.S. foreign policy underwent during the Cold War and since would not have been possible without the National Security Act of 1947. In a matter of a few short years (1941–1947), the United States changed trajectory from a somewhat introverted, internally focused nation to an *extroverted* world power. Indeed, one might reasonably argue that in those short years, the United States morphed into an interventionist power, something it has remained ever since.

Few Americans who lived then realized that the United States was undergoing dramatic change. America's long association (perhaps flirtation) with isolationism had so deeply affected America's worldview (its *ethos*) that it was inconceivable that the United States could become an empire before the 1950s. Empire was wholly anathema with America's early republican inclinations. Nevertheless, the United States became a world power or empire—absent the colonization that was so prevalent with Europe's empires—around which global politics pivoted. After the Cold War, U.S. imperium grew into hegemony.

It is important to present the reader with some sense of what these changes meant for the United States and for U.S. foreign policy. The United States changed from a regional (Northwestern Hemisphere, albeit with interests in the Pacific) power to a global power in an incredibly short period of time. Saying the change could not have happened absent the National Security Act does not mean that the act created the American Security State (Pax Americana) alone. Rather, it means without the act the metamorphosis would have been impossible. In creating a unified Defense Department that was permanent (hitherto, defense spending was ad hoc), defense spending began to increase steadily. America changed from a second-rate military power to one of two superpowers.

In creating the CIA (an intelligence community or IC that too was permanent), likewise, the United States began collecting and analyzing intelligence in a massive way that increased steadily over the course of the Cold War. Indeed, CIA was intended as a civilian chain of command over intelligence—recall, prior to CIA, Navy and other tactical intelligence existed. CIA led to a permanent IC that has blossomed into 17 distinct intelligence collection and intelligence analysis entities. In 2004, the office of the director of national intelligence (the ODNI and the DNI respectively) was created to avoid another 9/11 just as CIA was created to avoid another Pearl Harbor.[1]

Both in terms of military and the IC a dramatic growth in institutions (and the number of employees each needed) was realized. Indeed, Congress intentionally spread aspects of military and intelligence out into as many congressional districts as possible in order to preclude a return to America's past history of relative isolationism. With manifold congressional districts having a stake in perpetuation of the military- and the intelligence-community-industrial complexes that service either, those who created the National Security Act of 1947 fully realized it would be difficult to undo what they created. To be clear, the evidence suggests that there was anything sinister about it. Rather, those who wrote and passed the National Security Act believed American had to assume an active role in preventing Soviet expansionism and if that meant large military and IC institutions, then that was the price to be paid. (It appears no one believed these institutions were to last in perpetuity. In fact, there seems to have been a vague belief initially that the hegemonic powers of Europe would likely return and relieve the United States of at least some of the burden. Until that happened, however, the United States was going to need to fill the breach.)

In creating the National Security Council, inside the executive office of the presidency rather than elsewhere, Congress gave the presidency new foreign policy responsibilities and prerogatives that each successive president has seized and multiplied over time. The said seizure has been truly bipartisan. (In a sense, the main role of the presidency has grown to become to protect presidential prerogatives.) As foreign policy authority has increased in the presidency, Congress inevitably yielded to the presidency the prerogatives vested in the legislative branch by the founders vis-à-vis the Constitution. After the Vietnam War—or near the end of it—there was an attempt to wrest power back from the executive with such legislation as the War Powers Act, but Congress was too fractured to reclaim the power the Constitution gave it once the presidency had become so powerful. That both major parties were complicit made it all the more difficult for Congress to regain its Constitutional prerogatives.[2]

In sum, the creation of these three institutions set the foundation on which the rise of the American Security State would invariably grow and evolve over time. It should not surprise the reader that the security state grew and as new bureaucracy was created to manage the Cold War (and eventually its aftermath), the American Security State continued to grow. Bureaucracy did what bureaucracy has invariably done: made itself seem invaluable to policy makers and therefore protected future growth. In both uniformed and civilian leadership of the military, in the intelligence community, and in the National Security Council bureaucracy has continued to grow and assume new responsibilities and powers. It is worth restating the author's position that he makes no value assessment on rise of the American Security State. Others will have to decide whether it has grown too big, too unwieldy, and too unresponsive to its "masters," the American people. The task that was undertaken here was to explain the basis of the growth—what made it possible? It was an empirical question rather than a normative one.

Thus, beyond the chronology of each case study, it was my intention to use the case studies to pose the same set of questions of each study. The case studies provide the data for the analysis. The analysis is a qualitative approach because the data are not easily quantified (or at least in a systematic way that is meaningful). Nevertheless, when the data are quantifiable the same growth has been seen.

The United States began a herculean military buildup as the Cold War began (unsurprisingly). In the late 1940s, the United States began spending enormous sums on national security—protecting the American homeland from external threat—and it continued to spend large sums steadily from around 1950 through the end of the Cold War in 1991.[3] The growth of military spending and of the military—initially, to defend the United States but over time defense included projecting U.S. power globally—is a literal manifestation of U.S. foreign policy becoming militarized.[4] The story, however, is more than a story of defense spending.

Rather, as the United States changed from a regional power to one of two superpowers to the sole hegemonic power it became after the Cold War, change inevitably occurred in terms of how Americans viewed themselves and their Republic. When a nation-state changes from a small-time military power to a world power, changes in the way its peoples see themselves and their state are inevitable. In this chapter, I desire to consider those changes in more detail.

The reader will recall that in the Introduction to Part II (the case study chapters), the method used herein was discussed. The method employed was a structured, focused case study analysis in which the same questions were asked of each of the 14 case studies under consideration.[5] The method is similar to other qualitative approaches such as process tracing.[6] Because so few quantifiable indicators of U.S. foreign policy exist, the analyst is forced to attempt to tease out empirical observations from often unsystematic, fundamentally qualitative data. By using a structured, focused case study approach, case studies became the data source and it is the analyst's job to make the observations generalizable, systematic, and clear to the reader.

A principal hypothesis herein is that U.S. foreign policy has become *militarized* over time. To even a casual observer of U.S foreign policy, that statement should seem almost axiomatic. Prior to World War II, the United States was not a major player in world politics (the United States had a smaller Navy than Italy, for instance). As World War II engulfed Europe and Asia, the United States was pulled into the vortex and one result was the United States emerged as a world power—not unlike what happened to the United Kingdom during the 18th and 19th centuries—and was compelled to protect its interests though military means. (Cold War and containment of the USSR was the principal military means.) So militarization of U.S. foreign policy began with World War II and its aftermath rather unsurprisingly. The Cold War followed as did the contest between the United States and the then USSR over which two superpowers would prevail. Therefore, from around 1947 (in fact, increase in defense spending lags and does not show until 1950) through the end of the Cold War (at least 1990), the United States continued to increase defense spending year after year through the late 1980s.[7]

There is nothing especially controversial about the proposition that the United States spent increasing sums of money on defense from 1947 through 1990. So long as the reader attaches no negative or pejorative meaning to "militarized"; likewise, saying that U.S. foreign policy became militarized over these decades should prove uncontroversial. Again, it is a simple empirical observation and no normative evaluation is intended by it.

The book's principal thesis was that the National Security Act of 1947 has quite naturally led to the militarization of U.S. foreign policy and the creation of the American Security State. It therefore becomes useful to organize the data in some way that the reader may easily consider the findings. In each case study I applied the same structured, comparative case study questions as a method of organizing the data presented itself. Let us recall the structured questions applied to each case study.

Of each case studies, it was asked, first, whether the administration used any of the three entities created by the National Security Act of 1947 in a novel or an unusual (extraordinary) way (e.g., created a new precedent)? As with the other entities created by the National Security Act of 1947, the NSC consisted of the NSC principals and the NSC staff (both the NSC principals and deputies committees emerged by 1989 or so). But even much earlier, from President Kennedy forward something we might reasonably call the NSC principals existed along with NSC staffers. The same was asked of the Defense Department and the intelligence community (in their vast complexities). The second comparative question was: Is there evidence, in the answers to the previous three questions or elsewhere of the militarization of U.S. foreign policy? Finally, was there evidence of an expansion of presidential powers?

THE WEIGHT OF THE EVIDENCE

In Table 6.1, I have arranged the cases in the table's first column (let us call it column zero). The cases are arranged chronologically and by chapter. Then, Column 1 includes three sub-columns that represent binary—either yes, or if uncertain or no left blank—answer to the corresponding structure, comparative case study questions. So that Column 1 (A, B, C) all relate to the question of whether any of the three main parts of the NSC demonstrated novelty. Column 2 is likewise subdivided into (A, B, C)

Table 6.1
Presentation of the answers to the structured, comparative case study questions.

| Chapter | Case | 1. NSC | | | 2. DoD | | | 3. IC | | |
		1.a	1.b	1.c	2.a	2.b	2.c	3	4.	5.
3	Truman (Korea)	Yes						Yes	Yes	
	Ike (Shah of Iran)	Yes						Yes	Yes	
	Ike (Guatemala)	Yes			Yes			Yes	Yes	
4	JFK (Bay of Pigs)	Yes			Yes			Yes	Yes	
	JFK (Diem Coup)	Yes			Yes			Yes	Yes	
	LBJ (Tonkin)	Yes			Yes			Yes	Yes	
	LBJ (Escalation, '65)	Yes							Yes	
	Nixon (Cambodia)	Yes			Yes				Yes	
	Reagan (Iranamok)		Yes	Yes		Yes			Yes	
5	H. W. Bush (Panama)				Yes				Yes	
	H. W. Bush (Gulf War)	Yes			Yes				Yes	
	Clinton (Bosnia)	Yes			Yes				Yes	
	Clinton (Transnational)		Yes	Yes				Yes	Yes	
	Obama (Afghanistan Surge)								Yes	

The first column names chapter in which the case study appears. Following the chapter and case study abbreviation, Columns 1.a through 1.c are columns representing the three main parts of the National Security Council, created by the *act*. Columns 2.a through 2.c present the Armed Forces (A), the Uniformed Military Leadership (B), and the Civilian Leadership (C). Finally, Columns 4 and 5 are as follows: four represents the question whether the case study itself made the case for militarization and 5 whether any other information indicated militarization of foreign policy as defined above.

representing A (armed forces), B (civilian leadership of defense), and C (uniformed leadership of defense). Finally, Columns 4 and 5 represent the questions: Did the case study demonstrate militarization, and was there evidence elsewhere of militarization of U.S. foreign policy?

Now, let us recall the conclusions in each case study in sequence. The Truman administration's decision to respond to the invasion of South Korea (ROK) by North Korea (DPRK) was clearly a novel use of the NSC. Until the Korean War, President Truman allowed the executive secretary (a position that eventually morphed into the NSC adviser) to preside over NSC meetings. The NSC, as was intended, was a sort of think tank inside the presidency (then located in the Old Executive Office Building [OEOB] adjacent to the White House). It worked up recommendations—many, as it turned out, to use military power—but President Truman rightly reserved the decision to employ military power for himself.

However, with the onset of the Korean War, the NSC changed and it began its trajectory to what it has become in modern times: the NSC principals, NSC deputies, and NSC staff as the apex of foreign policy and national security decisions. Truman used it for the first time as a body that would help him to make decisions (rather than simply churn out papers). He canvassed his NSC members on how to respond to Korea and the consensus was that North Korea would not have launched the Korean War had Stalin's USSR not blessed the aggression. The Korean War represented the change of trajectory of the modern NSC from an advisory committee that met without the president then presented him its positions, to an active advisory committee over which the president presided to come to decisions on U.S. national security.

The next two cases were quite similar but also with some distinctions. Both the overthrow of the Mossadegh government in Iran (Operation Ajax) and the subsequent overthrow of the "leftist" Arbenz government in Guatemala were covert, paramilitary operations for the purpose of regime change. (Regime change became part of American foreign policy argot after 9/11, particularly with respect to George W. Bush's decision to invade and overthrow Saddam Hussein. But the phrase perfectly describes what the Eisenhower administration did in Iran and Guatemala in 1953 and 1954 respectively). It was the beginning of the use of covert, paramilitary activities to change governments Eisenhower considered hostile to the United States and its interests (or friendly to the USSR, which amounted to the same). After Eisenhower, several presidents used similar covert programs for everything from regime change to affecting elections to assassinating foreign leaders deemed unsatisfactory to the president and NSC.

As for the differences, the case of Iran was not originated in the United States. It was the United Kingdom and its intelligence services that approached the United States with a decision to overthrow Mossadegh. That the United States went along with it and participated made the subsequent decision to overthrow Arbenz simpler. President Eisenhower was the first modern president to see the utility of regime change. Subsequently, when the Arbenz government created trouble, the 5412 committee (an NSC subcommittee) met and decided to do in Guatemala what the British teamed with the Americans accomplished in Iran.

One could argue that the 5412 committee of the NSC was used in both cases, and it was. But in going along with the British whose petroleum interests were significant in Iran, the Eisenhower administration was, effectively, trying to restore the British to their prominence (including England's colonial prominence despite the fact that most Americans loathed colonialism). When President Eisenhower's NSC (5412 committee) decided to overthrow Arbenz, it was asserting America's self-interests quite apart from British interests. (In fact, it is striking how quickly Pax Americana supplanted Pax Britannica after World War II.) And it was doing so in America's hemisphere, a hemisphere held sacrosanct in U.S. foreign policy since the Monroe Doctrine (1821). Earlier it was concluded that it marked a new, more assertive U.S. foreign policy that had originated in the NSC.

Next came the Bay of Pigs debacle in Cuba early on in the Kennedy administration. Recall, the Eisenhower administration met with the incoming president twice (once after the fall 1960 election and again on the day of the inauguration). In both meetings, President Eisenhower made known to the incoming president that his new team would need to watch carefully events in Indochina (then Laos but soon Vietnam) as well as in Cuba (where Castro had already nationalized the means of production). President Kennedy's NSC principals may have served him poorly by not thinking through the scheme already concocted by the CIA (particularly, Allen Dulles and Ted Bissell). But in any case, the Kennedy NSC members decided to move ahead with what the Eisenhower administration had begun.

Then what happened was the new administration took the template left them by Eisenhower (and it was probably inevitable given Allen Dulles staying on as DCI) and then tweaked a few details whereupon the administration launched the operation. There were NSC meetings wherein the principals discussed Cuba but what became known as the 303 committee (Kennedy's version of the 5412) adjusted the plan, which had the result of bungling it even more. For instance, President Eisenhower had always asserted that the United States could not support the plan without an alternative Cuban government ready to assume the powers of governing once the operation occurred. Ultimately, President Kennedy made the decision to approve the operation knowing full well that no such alternative government existed. (Whether it would have changed the outcome is unknowable.)

In moving ahead on Cuba, President Kennedy had changed the way the NSC operated. Both the principals and more secretive 303 committee meetings worked in tandem creating the perfect disaster that was the Bay of Pigs debacle.[8] Now, two consecutive presidents had come to rely on that most addictive of drugs, covert operations for regime change. (It is addictive because it allows presidents to act with little to no consultation with Congress. Before the Church Committee hearings in the mid-1970s, the president was able to launch covert operations with virtually no consultations. After, the House and Senate Select Committees on Intelligence were created, allowing president to effect covert operations with "timely" notification of the chairs and vice chairs of the two committees along with the leaders and vice leaders of the two chambers, the so-called Gang of Eight.)

It is not difficult to understand why these covert operations became so addictive to presidents and NSC members. By their nature—only those with a "need to know" received the information thereby circumventing Congress—the president alone (with select NSC principals) was making foreign policy and worrying about the details ex post facto. As it turned out, the devil was indeed in the details. Eventually, the two intelligence oversight committees were created as a result of the addiction but there is evidence in the post-9/11 world that presidents continue to keep members of Congress in the dark about certain covert programs.

Next, let us recall the decision to overthrow President Ngo Dinh Diem in Vietnam (the Republic of Vietnam). It was an odd case indeed. In that case, the president and his NSC members were grappling with what to do in Vietnam. Virtually everyone around the president believed that the Soviets were testing the new president in Indochina. (In fact, the Soviets and "Communist China" were testing the United States, according to virtually all Kennedy administration NSC principals.) The president inherited much of the mess from Eisenhower but now it was his mess and the question was what to do about it?

The answer was to delay making difficult decisions. Throughout 1963 events continued to deteriorate in Vietnam. The local Viet Cong were making inroads against the Republic of Vietnam. The Diem government was not taking hold. (It was always too exclusive, too Catholic and French to satisfy broad-based support in Vietnam.) As the United States continued to muddle through, fateful events occurred. First, Diem's government cracked down on a Buddhist celebration in the central city of Hué in May 1963. Non-Catholic Vietnamese protested massively, including possibly some provocateurs. But what the Kennedy NSC did next was almost unfathomable.

One relatively high-level official from the State Department colluded with a new ambassador just replacing the old one in Vietnam to co-opt U.S. foreign policy on a weekend in August 1963, while the NSC principals were out of town. While the top NSC members were vacationing, Roger Hilsman sent a fateful telegram that effectively put on notice the government in Saigon (the embassy, and the intelligence presence there) to green light a coup that had been bumbling along on and off for weeks (if not months). That was extraordinary.

But that was not all. From August until the coup occurred in early November 1963, the NSC principals met time and again. State Department personnel and those in Defense met multiple times. The NSC continued to wrestle with what to do about Diem (and his brother Nhu) and how to get Vietnam back under the control of U.S. foreign policy. In short, they continued to muddle along without countermanding the Hilsman ultimatum. In sitting on its collective hand, the NSC principals allowed the Hilsman *fait accompli* to become U.S. foreign policy. They watched; they agonized; but they allowed the coup plotters to continue plotting without withdrawing the telegram or staying it. They wanted to have it both ways: if the coup occurred they could wash their hands of it in Washington and pretend it was not a conscious decision. It was policy by inertia, by indecision.

Whatever one chooses to call it—and it is difficult to think of a positive characterizations—it was a ratcheting up of the militarization of U.S. foreign policy during the Cold War. It was, also, a refinement of the war by proxy that had begun in Korea (and elsewhere) but was becoming more and more militarized over time. (Though not the scope of the present narrative, it is worth noting that the Soviets too were active and militarizing their foreign policy. The United States did none of this in a vacuum.) Now the United States had caused a coup in Vietnam that removed from power a client the United States had earlier helped put in power! And U.S. foreign policy was once more militarized beyond earlier examples.

Next came the two cases in the Johnson administration, the administration that was thrown into office by the assassination of President Kennedy some three weeks after the Diem coup (and assassination). President Johnson, it will be recalled, kept the Kennedy NSC principals in place. Indeed, he kept the Kennedy foreign policy in place virtually intact. There was an NSC document (NSAM 273) that memorialized Johnson's adoption of Kennedy's rather pitiful path in Vietnam. And that remained the case until roughly a year later when President Kennedy would have been running for reelection (had he lived) but in which Johnson was elected president in his own right (November 1964).

In the case study, the story was picked up there. In spring 1964, William Bundy (not to be confused with his brother McGeorge Bundy, the NSC adviser for Kennedy and Johnson) began working on a draft of a resolution that would become the Tonkin Gulf Resolution later in the year. The reasoning was straightforward: President Eisenhower had managed to get a similar blank check (a resolution in which Congress abdicated its right to declare war and instead gave the president permission to do what the president thought best) having to do with the so-called Taiwan Straits crises during the mid-1950s. President Johnson thought it might be wise to have something similar. After all, conventional wisdom held that the communists were testing the United States time and again and at multiple places around the globe. Thus, William Bundy was working on the language for the said blank check from the State Department.

When the events of the Tonkin Gulf occurred, that draft resolution was pulled off the shelf and submitted to Congress. What precipitated it? Recall the two somewhat separate covert operations approved by Johnson's 303 committee of the NSC. One was for asserting U.S. rights to navigate international waters near North Vietnam (DRV). Of course, the real reason for it was to collect telemetry and other signals intelligence from DRV's defense infrastructure. It was called the DeSoto missions and the reader will recall that in late July and early August 1964, DeSoto ships were weaving a path in and out of North Vietnam's (the DRV) territorial waters back into international waters collecting the said telemetry.

The second covert operation was called OPLAN 34A and it was basically South Vietnamese commandos launching sabotage attacks on DRV (both on the mainland and on islands). Of course, the United States helped fund the commando raids. However, the OPLAN raids were not coordinated by the NSC's 303 committee, at least as far as I could determine. Once they were approved, the two operations were turned over to their respective agencies (CIA, NSA, and defense) to implement. However, the two operations came together in early August when OPLAN raids very likely caused the DRV to think the two distinct operations were connected.

The result was the DRV sent small military boats to challenge the *USS Turner Joy* and eventually the *USS Maddox*. Recall, it was not asserted that anything untoward was intended. That is, the case study made no attempt to discover whether the Johnson administration (the NSC principals or the 303 committee) consciously used the challenge as a pretext to launch reprisals raids (called Flaming Dart) but it matters little for present purposes. The point is the case represented a clear militarization of U.S. foreign policy and a potentially novel use of the NSC and intelligence assets.

The next case study was the fork-in-the-road memorandum that NSC adviser McGeorge Bundy and Secretary of Defense Bob McNamara sent to President Johnson in early 1965. The memorandum, it will be recalled, summed up months—if not years dating back to Kennedy—of frustration with America's ally in South Vietnam (the RVN). An underlying assumption of U.S. foreign policy in Vietnam had been the Vietnamese had to lead the effort against the Viet Cong insurgency in the South. (Even then some North Vietnamese Regular—called NVA regulars by American policy makers—forces were in the South but the Viet Cong were the principal enemy.) The U.S. position since the Truman administration was that the United States could help against communist infiltration but Vietnamese had to do the basic fighting against their communist brethren.

As far back as the Diem coup an argument within the U.S. government, first in the Kennedy administration (in which Johnson was vice president) and then in the Johnson era, turned around sequencing. The question was: must the United States provide the Republic of Vietnam (RVN) with resources sufficient to the task before the government of Vietnam (South Vietnam) could enact some democratic reforms? Or did the South Vietnamese have to demonstrate evidence of reform before the United States provided resources sufficient to defeat the communist insurgency. Different factions in the different U.S. administrations took opposing positions on the sequencing question. The NSC principals—at least, Secretary of Defense McNamara and NSC adviser McGeorge Bundy—believed communist insurgency must be defeated in South Vietnam lest communism score a victory in the zero-sum conflict of the Cold War.

Suddenly, in early 1965—and the reader may recall that Undersecretary George Ball wrote a 60-plus page memorandum, relaying his concerns that the United States was getting itself deeper within the Vietnam quagmire from which, at some point soon, it may not be able to extricate itself—to the two most important advisers to President Johnson. Ball's memorandum disappeared for two months only to surface later. In the meantime, Johnson's inherited NSC adviser and secretary of defense wrote their own memorandum telling the president that they had concluded that the United States must jettison its previous reluctance and begin doing the heavy lifting in South Vietnam. *The memorandum suggested nothing less than the Americanization of the war*, in contrast to the previous three administration's positions of assistance only.

The question is, then, did this constitute novel use of the NSC (principals, deputies, staff)? The answer is unequivocally yes. Two members seemingly circumvented the NSC principals setting and sent a special recommendation to President Johnson who had just been elected in his own right a few months earlier. Without explaining why the previous sequencing debate no longer mattered, they simply presented a new alarming case: if the United States did not show the patient (the South Vietnamese), the doctor (the United States) was willing to go all out to save the former, disaster lay ahead. Disaster certainly lay ahead.

The military was not used in a particularly novel way in Vietnam per se. The United States had fought proxy wars before (e.g., Korea). While the Joint Chiefs frequently recommended more bombing at that point, that too was not a novelty. Therefore, the question about using the military in a novel way was answered in the negative. (One might argue that air mobility was novel in Vietnam but this book is interested in militarization of foreign policy.)

But the case study provided clear evidence of militarization of U.S. foreign policy. The fact is that the United States gradually, incrementally militarized the Vietnam War and the previous victories (many covert) led to a sense of false confidence in what the United States might accomplish in South Vietnam. Within weeks, Marines landed at Da Nang and began guarding air bases there. Within a few more weeks, guarding air bases was seen as too cautious and what became known as search and destroy missions were launched around Da Nang. By Secretary McNamara's own calculations, the number of U.S. troops between late 1964 and early 1965 was 23,000 (with 225 killed in action). By July 1965, the number was 81,400 U.S. troops (with 509 KIA). By December 1965, the number was 184,300 U.S. (1,594 KIA) and by December 1967, the number was 485,600 (with nearly 16,000 KIA).[9] It would be difficult to conclude otherwise that the Johnson Americanization of the Vietnam War was a direct example of the militarization of U.S. foreign policy.

Next was the Nixon administration case study. President-elect Nixon campaigned for "peace with honor" in the Vietnam War. He also allowed or acquiesced to an apocryphal story about him having a "secret plan" to end the Vietnam War. In fact, he had no secret plan or any plan in particular. Rather, former vice president Nixon believed Eisenhower's hawkish talk about ending Korea had scared North Korea into suing for peace. (Why he thought so is unclear, as the evidence did not suggest it. Indeed, only an armistice was signed. The North Koreans dragged their collective feet on a peace treaty.) Nixon believed that when Eisenhower campaigned against Truman in the 1952 election, Eisenhower made a point of saying if elected president he would go to Korea and do what was necessary to end the war. This of course took time and multiple increments before a ceasefire agreement was finally signed in 1953. (After the armistice, Eisenhower thereafter withdrew most of its military presence but kept between 30,000 and 40,000 troops there over the next eight years. Each president after Eisenhower continued the trip-wire deterrence of between 30,000 and 40,000 U.S. troops through the Cold War. Even today some 20,000-plus U.S. troops are stationed in South Korea.)

President Nixon concluded that Eisenhower's firmness made all the difference in Korea. Therefore, President Nixon wanted to accomplish a similar feat in Vietnam. Nixon remarked to multiple persons, including H. R. Haldeman, that he would do something similar to what Eisenhower had done. He called it his "madman theory." If only the North Vietnamese could be made to believe that Nixon was nuts, so obsessed with communists that he might use nuclear weapons to achieve peace, the North Vietnamese would cave like the Koreans had.[10]

Nowhere in any of this was Cambodia mentioned. However, when the North Vietnamese proved tenacious and pugnacious early on in Nixon's tenure, the president and his NSC adviser Dr. Henry Kissinger decided to launch a series of secret bombings against what they believed were North Vietnamese sanctuaries inside of neutral Cambodia.[11] What became the Menu Bombings of Cambodia and eventually led to an overt military invasion of that country (spring 1970) began on March 18, 1969, not quite two months into the Nixon administration.

Did the secret bombing of Cambodia that began in March 1969 and continued until May 1970 constitute a novel use of the NSC. Again the answer is a pretty straightforward yes. President Nixon effectively circumvented the NSC principals committee. (That is not against the law. It is simply unusual and novel. No president is compelled to use his NSC principals.) In doing so, President Nixon rendered his NSC members obsolete. In having NSC adviser Kissinger preside over the multiple NSC subcommittees, President Nixon maintained the charade that the NSC principals were still doing their jobs. Again, whether it was illegal or not is another matter entirely. It was a novel use of the NSC principals and staff.

Likewise, it would be difficult to conclude anything other than Nixon's odd bombing of Cambodia constituted a militarization of U.S. foreign policy. It was a covert militarization—intentionally kept secret from Congress and it eventually became part of President Nixon's impeachment hearings—but it was a militarization. The secret bombing did not produce a more pliant North Vietnam. So President Nixon eventually invaded Cambodia and finally shared his contention of communist sanctuaries (he and military leaders called it the Central Office of South Vietnam [COSVN] of the communist insurgency in the south) with the American public openly. As noted, one of the articles of impeachment brought against Nixon concerned the secret bombing of Cambodia.[12]

Next came the Reagan administration during the 1980s, a renewed period of the Cold War after a slight relaxation called détente. President Reagan openly talked of aiding the Contras in Central America against the Sandinistas government that had seized power in Nicaragua. That the administration could never do much more than talk about it—and of course, take several covert actions—was a function of the American public's fatigue with war. (The Vietnam War had ended only a few short years earlier, with finality in late April 1975.) The Vietnam War had a profound negative effect on public opinion and that effect was such that the public believed (polling data showed the majority position throughout much of the 1980s) America needed to get its act together domestically and not be so focused on compelling behavior in other countries, whether Central America or Cuba or elsewhere.

Time and again President Reagan called for more action but the Boland Amendments continually constrained the administration. As was demonstrated in the Iran-Contra case study, a very interesting and peculiar thing happened in consequence. And it is quite the opposite of what we saw in the Nixon case study of Cambodia. Namely, a "troika" within the administration made policy, both foreign and domestic, based on its notion of what the president believed. The troika resulted in a vacuum inside the NSC where normally the NSC principals discuss and debate various policy options, particularly what the media and public think of as "crises." But with a president whose management style was "aloof" in the extreme, the vacuum was filled by NSC *staffers* largely in the OEOB adjacent to the White House.

Thus, contrary to the centralization that one saw in Nixon's foreign policy, an utter decentralization down to the NSC staff level occurred and the result was the Iran-Contra affair in Reagan's. NSC staffers (along with the two different NSC advisers out of the six NSC advisers who served President Reagan in eight years) cooked up the Contra assistance program with a view of circumventing Boland Amendments. That constituted the Contra part of Iran-Contra.

Likewise, when Western hostages were kidnapped in Lebanon, NSC staffers and two NSC advisers (and importantly, then director of central intelligence William Casey) formed a sort of foreign policy troika inside the NSC. It was novel and it was quite different from anything envisioned in the National Security Act of 1947, which created a small, rather inert staff and no NSC adviser (only an executive secretary). When President Reagan made comments at NSC meetings (and others) about his desire to get hostages released from Lebanon, the same group initiated the Iran leg of the Iran-Contra debacle. If the president said he wanted something, surely he wanted it. It was therefore the responsibility of the foreign policy troika to make the president's desires occur in fact.

When proceeds from the sales of military armaments to Iranian "moderates" produced monies that Congress had not appropriated, those monies were intermingled and the two legs of the Iran-Contra affair became one. Once that occurred, laws were broken (possibly earlier too), including arms export and licensing laws. As the Tower Commission Report stated: "The Iran initiative was handled almost casually and through informal channels, always apparently, with an expectation that the process would end with the next arms-for-hostages exchange . . . It was subjected neither to the inter-agency review process [the NSC] nor the process for covert operations inside the government." Similarly, "Interagency consideration of the initiative was limited to cabinet level, and inadequate at that. . . ." Finally, "Insufficient attention was given to the implications of the N.S.C. staff having operational control of the initiative rather than the C.I.A."[13]

What may one conclude about the NSC staff and two NSC advisers, Bud McFarlane and John Poindexter? Whatever else, one may certainly conclude that what happened constituted a novel use of the NSC machinery. It cannot be argued that it was the NSC principals, since the principals were largely circumvented. But the NSC staffers and two NSC principals—the NSC adviser and Bill Casey of CIA—both conducted foreign policy on their own hook, as it were. It was a stunning circumvention of the interagency process that the National Security Act of 1947 created.

As for militarization of foreign policy, again it is straightforward. Congress attempted to limit the Reagan administration from involving the United States in war in Central America. The administration—at least a group of individuals including two NSC advisers and multiple staffers along with the CIA director—was disinclined to heed Congress' prerogatives. Therefore, a strange rogue operation was launched that endangered hostages—once it became clear the United States was willing to barter hostages for armaments, Iran kept coming back for more and Iran's allies in Lebanon continued kidnapping more hostages. One presumes an interagency process might have seen the inherent contradictions, but it is impossible to know for certain. Nevertheless, the administration militarized foreign policy both in terms of the Iran-Iraq war (insinuating U.S. policy) and in Central America (supporting the Contras and covert acts to hurt the Sandinistas).

In Chapter 5, case studies from the end of the Cold War and the post-Cold War era were presented. For analytic reasons, the book used a Cold War typology that divided the Cold War into two periods making three periods when the post-Cold War era is included. The early Cold War—Presidents Truman and Eisenhower—was characterized by novelty in almost everything done by the NSC and with the military. These first two presidents after the National Security Act of 1947 pushed the boundaries of the act. Then, the heart of the Cold War came next with Presidents Kennedy, Johnson, Nixon, and even Reagan (after a brief détente). The last phase was the post-Cold War era after the USSR had imploded; and if ever the United States was going to return to its pre-World War II posture of isolationism (which it was not going to do), it would have happened as the USSR was imploding. Also included was a case study from the transitional period, 1989, for comparative purposes.

President George H. W. Bush was an important president, notwithstanding his tenure of one term only. The Bush 41 NSC processes and patterns have shaped every post-Cold War presidency and the NSC since. In the case of President Bush (41), I presented two case studies: the first was the Panama invasion (premised on rescuing a CIA agent) and the second was the war in the Gulf (First Gulf War) to oust Saddam from Kuwait. Recall, as the Cold War was ending and in the post-Cold War period, world politics seemed somewhat chaotic. The world seemed a mass of confusion and the president had to discern what threats mattered to the United States in a world where the USSR no longer challenged the United States for supremacy. Germany was unified (reunified), the Soviets went away, rendering NATO somewhat obsolete (at least as constituted to prevent a Soviet invasion of Western Europe), and nationalism was reemerging as a potent force in the world.

In that context was the Panama operation in 1989. President Bush (41) believed Manuel Noriega challenged U.S. sovereignty and treaty rights in the Canal Zone. (Whether his analysis was right is beside the point.) Coupled with some relatively minor military provocations and the capture of an intelligence agent (CIA), the early H. W. Bush NSC met and decided to act. The Panama invasion (rescue and overthrow of the Noriega regime) was therefore accomplished. The novelty comes in the rationale. Of course, protecting U.S. personnel and military movement was not novel. But the H. W. Bush administration used the military to effect democratic change in Panama.

There is no evidence of novelty in the way the NSC worked at any of the three levels, unless one accepts that a new pattern of NSC was born. The way the modern NSC works evolved from two main sources: Kennedy's NSC principals (such as ExComm in the missile crisis) and from George H. W. Bush's configurations during his four years. No suggestion was made that it was novel, simply that the NSC has evolved incrementally over time and the modern NSC has therefore emerged from all previous presidencies.

However, Panama did constitute a new militarization of U.S. foreign policy in the emerging post-Cold War period. Using the military to foist democratic change in the New World Order was novel. Subsequent presidents have used it including, notably, President George W. Bush in Iraq. Thus, no longer was the military simply used to prevent Soviet gains in the Cold War. It was now openly used to effect democratic change. I will leave it to others to decide whether the precedent was prudent or not? Given U.S. treaty obligations in Panama, President George H. W. Bush's decision was a new phase of U.S. foreign policy.

Next came the case of Saddam Hussein after he sent the Iraqi military into Kuwait, sacked that government, and proceeded to loot the country. President Bush's (41) response was to call several NSC principals meetings wherein the principals agreed on a twofold approach: the first would be to give Saddam the opportunity to exit Kuwait peacefully and return his troops to Iraqi soil whereby the old government of Kuwait might be reestablished (Desert Shield). Part two was a military intervention to move Saddam out of Kuwait by force.

Again, no claims of novelty were asserted in terms of the NSC process. Rather, the NSC principals committee functioned as it was intended. It convened, the interagency process occurred, the president heard the views of his principals, and then made his decisions. However, sending hundreds of thousands of U.S. troops to the Gulf to force the Iraqi military out of Kuwait in the post-Cold War era clearly constituted the militarization of U.S. foreign policy. Whether that was good or bad is another matter.

Next came the Clinton administration, the first wholly post-Cold War presidency. Most readers will know Bill Clinton served two terms, though the final two years of his second term were, arguably, compromised by the Lewinsky scandal and threats of impeachment. The first of two Clinton case studies was the disintegration of former Yugoslavia. Yugoslavia was part of the Eastern or Soviet Bloc though, unlike say Eastern Germany, it was not controlled directly by the Soviets or the Soviet Red Army. Tito managed to keep some independence against the Soviets though Yugoslavia was vulnerable to USSR machinations.

When former Yugoslavia began to disintegrate in mid-1991, Serbia and Slovenia first experienced conflict. Serb leaders tried to forestall disintegration and the Serbian military attempted to keep Slovenia yoked to Serbia by force. Just months later, a similar situation occurred with Croatia.

Whether Serbia was entirely to blame, which was a common narrative in Western media, is another matter and one on which this book takes no position. What was interesting was the third case having to do with Serbia and a former portion of Yugoslavia, Bosnia (actually, Bosnia-Herzegovina) falling into a state of conflict with Serbia.

In the Bosnia-Serbian case study, only nominal novelty in terms of NSC principals committee was seen. Namely, in the post-Cold War era, the United States (and a Democratic president, no less) using military power to force the Serbs to negotiate. As noted in the case study, President Clinton was unable to get the NSC principals committee consensus he so wanted and both Anthony Lake (Clinton's first NSC adviser) and Ambassador Richard Holbrook engaged in some terse bargaining with the Serbs. It may have been partly for reasons of foreign policy as well as for reasons of domestic politics. Either way, there was some novelty in the process though it was not especially important.

However, in the case of the war against Bosnia, the case study illustrated a new phase of militarization of U.S. foreign policy. The case study demonstrated an increased willingness in the post-Cold War era to militarize foreign policy, something utterly contrary to candidate Clinton's campaign pledge to focus on the U.S. economy like a laser beam. It is a particularly interesting case study in that it shows the tremendous continuity in U.S. foreign policy: from Truman through George H. W. Bush and again from Clinton through Obama, the United States has continued to expand presidential prerogatives at the expense of Congress and to militarize U.S. foreign policy and both changes have been located in the NSC.

(Perhaps the reader has noticed how often candidates for the presidency make bold claims. Once in office many bold claims remain unrealized. The cynic might be tempted to conclude that candidates will say anything to get elected, and there would be some truth to such a claim. However, the matter seems somewhat more complex. Presidential role is something that has evolved over time. The American people come to see the presidency in some way; those expectations place constraints on what presidents can do in office. Candidates are far less constrained by role considerations.)

The second Clinton case study was the administration's response to the rise of transnationalism. Al Qaeda attacked the United States on September 11, 2001. The case was selected due to the author's awareness that President Clinton created a new subgroup in the NSC for transnational threats. The original director of what became known as the transnational threat directorate (also called the counterterrorism security group or CSG) was Richard Clarke. Clarke had two staffers initially, both experts on religious extremism, Daniel Benjamin and Steven Simon.[14] The group of three did incredible things in preparing the United States for al Qaeda and other transnational threats to the United States. But they constituted a small entity inside the NSC and the NSC itself is a bureaucratic lightweight compared to State and Defense.

Nevertheless, the CSG accomplished remarkable things during the Y2K threat and the millennium attacks (which they helped prevent). Indeed, Richard Clarke was so adept at throwing bureaucratic elbows (and making himself invaluable to NSC principals) that he was elevated to the NSC principals committee and became a powerful voice there. I should note, also, that then DCI George Tenet declared war on al Qaeda in late 1998 (though not until after the U.S. embassy attacks in Kenya and Tanzania that fall). Sadly, more could have been done and probably should have been done.

Anyone who has read the 9/11 Commission's Final Report will have realized that in addition to the Clinton administration needing to do more, the transition from Clinton to Bush resulted in the new Bush administration underperforming for several months and not getting the Bush NSC principals up to speed on the al Qaeda and Afghanistan threat until just days before the attacks happened. That is another story for others to tell but the relevant chapters that demonstrate the continuity mentioned are the 9/11 Commission's Final Report Chapters Six, Seven, and Eight.[15]

Among other things, readers of that report will find that the Clinton administration came very close to using UAVs (drones) to kill bin Laden before the Bush administration came into office. In two cases, the president or others called it off at the last minute due to concerns over killing noncombatants. Another thing the reader will find in that report is while the subgroup of the NSC was busy tracking al Qaeda (and others) as was the CIA, there were also bureaucratic turf battles that prevented a more effective effort. For instance, CIA and Defense argued about who should pay for the missiles the government eventually figured out how to attach to UAVs. (UAVs originally were surveillance only.) Nor were the bureaucratic shenanigans confined to one administration: they occurred in both Clinton's last couple of years and into W. Bush's first year.

For present purposes, however, the issue is whether the NSC was used in a novel way. Nominally, it constituted novel use. (President Clinton, for instance, created the National Economic Council inside the NSC.) But as to the question about whether America's response to transnationalism was another example of militarization of U.S. foreign policy, the answer was yes. Without belaboring the point, recall that when the Cold War ended, the chattering class in Washington (elites and attentive public) were talking about peace dividends and reinvesting at home. The Clinton administration was partly elected on getting America's economy healthy again. Nevertheless, as president, Clinton clearly marked another iteration of militarization that has continued since.

That leaves only the Obama administration's "surge" in Afghanistan, the last of the case studies examined. It is worth noting that the George W. Bush administration toppled Saddam Hussein, sending U.S. troops into Iraq in March 2003. In 2006, an attack on a Shi'ite mosque in Samarra, Iraq, precipitated a civil war between Shi'a and Sunni in Iraq. Whatever one thinks about the decision to invade Iraq initially, President Bush made a relatively bold decision in late 2006-early 2007. It was to "surge" troops temporarily in Iraq.

At the time, most Democrats and the public had soured on the war in Iraq. In fact, the Iraqi Study Group (which included James Baker and Brent Scowcroft, two incredibly important Republicans from H.W. Bush's tenure) recommended finding a way out of Iraq rather than doubling down. President George W. Bush made the difficult decision to "surge" troops and it was an unpopular decision even in his own Republican Party.

President Barack Obama was elected in November 2008 and inaugurated in January 2009. As a candidate, Barack Obama campaigned for largely domestic issues. (Doubtless, the reader realizes that as far as presidential campaigns go, Democrats tend to run on domestic revitalization as a precondition for strong foreign policy whereas Republicans tend to run on strong foreign policy as necessary for domestic tranquility.) But candidate Obama could not avoid the Iraq War controversy; he, therefore, made a political statement during the campaign about Afghanistan (where al Qaeda directed 9/11) being a "war of necessity" whereas, he asserted, Iraq had been a "war of choice."[16]

Upon becoming president—another recurring motif of U.S. foreign policy—Obama learned how different the world was from what he campaigned for and was forced to address the world he inherited, not the world he imagined. In early 2009 (late February), the Obama administration announced an increase in troops in Afghanistan. It turned out that the request for more troops had languished since the Bush administration without being addressed. Thus, when Obama came to office he was forced to decide rather quickly to send some 21,000 additional troops to Afghanistan just to keep from losing there.[17]

Through a series of events President Obama was forced to address Afghanistan again much sooner than he had expected to do. First, the decision to send 21,000 was relatively unproblematic. After all, Obama had campaigned for Afghanistan being a war of necessity. Second, in spring 2009, multiple NSC and/or military advisers, including then secretary of defense Robert Gates and then chairman of the Joint Chiefs Admiral Mike Mullen informed President Obama that they believed the United States had the wrong commander in the field in Afghanistan (it was then general David McKiernan). Secretary Gates and Chairman Mullen recommended a change to General Stanley McChrystal, a protégé of sorts of General David Petraeus (from the Bush "surge" in Iraq). Third, after McChrystal replaced McKiernan, the former conducted a 60-day review (common with such a change of command). Eventually, General McChrystal's review resulted in a request for some 40,000 additional troops.

The result of all these factors (and others not mentioned) was a round of NSC principals meetings that began in mid-September and ended in late November 2009, in which Obama and his NSC principals met some nine times to discuss Afghanistan. The ultimate decision Obama made was to approve 30,000 additional troops (with the possibility of 10% additional enablers) in what the administration billed as a "surge" in Afghanistan. Whether Obama intended to mimic President Bush is unclear. We will have to await the president's (and others') memoirs. However, on December 1, 2009, President Obama announced a "surge" in Afghanistan that would last 18–24 months. It ended up looking very similar to President George W. Bush's Iraq surge.

Again, what this meant in terms of the comparative questions should be straightforward. The NSC, in particular, the NSC principals committee was used in a novel way but only when compared to the earlier increase of troops in 2009. It met and argued for more than eight weeks. The Pentagon presented a united front (with a few exceptions, one being General Cartwright, Chairman Mullen's deputy). Obama's political advisers (mostly Rahm Emanuel but Vice President Biden and Obama's then NSC deputy adviser, Tom Donilon) believed the military was trying to roll a new president and they resisted the increase. From the public record, Obama held his own company and did not decide until Thanksgiving or so. (He did, however, use the two factions or camps in an arguably novel way inside the NSC to combat the other without fully betraying his own views.[18])

It was likewise easy to make the case that President Obama contributed—as we have seen several president do—to the militarization of U.S. foreign policy. In fact, Obama used the Status of Forces Agreement (SOFA) signed by President George Bush (2008) and its dates to remove U.S. troops from Iraq. (For example, the December 2011 date, after which U.S. combat troops would be withdrawn from Iraq, was signed by President Bush in 2008.) While withdrawing troops from Iraq, Obama was moving them into Afghanistan, the exact opposite of what George Bush did in late 2002 and early 2003, when he withdrew troops from Afghanistan to send them to Iraq.

HOW THE NATIONAL SECURITY ACT OF 1947 AFFECTED THE BALANCE BETWEEN THE PRESIDENCY AND CONGRESS?

One thing should be clear from the forgoing summary of the cases. Namely, the presidency has become more powerful over time than Congress in terms of foreign policy. The founders never intended such a thing. On the contrary, they believed that no single branch, whether legislative, executive (or judicial) ought to be able to take the United States to war without consent of another branch. One simply needs to look at Articles I and II of the Constitution where Congress' and the president's foreign policy prerogatives are enumerated, respectively. At least initially, the founders desired that Congress be more powerful in terms of foreign policy than the presidency.

Article I, Section 8 (Clauses 10 through 14) spelled out Congress' prerogatives clearly. Congress has the responsibility to punish maritime crimes (10), to raise military forces as needed and to declare war (10 and 11), as well as various responsibilities during wartime. Article II, Section 2 (Clause 1) the president is the commander in chief "when called into the actual Service of the United States," which seems to indicate when Congress declares war.

The trouble is since World War II Congress has not declared war. Instead, it passes sense of the Senate resolutions and/or ex post facto bills that approve what the president has already done. In fact, it was Eisenhower and Johnson respectively (as noted earlier) who established the precedent (Taiwan Straits and Gulf of Tonkin) that Congress will rubber stamp almost anything the president has taken upon himself to do.[19] In short, as the presidency has become more powerful in terms of foreign policy, Congress has inevitably atrophied in power. The founders never intended such an asymmetry in power to develop. The contrary is nearer the case. That is, if anything the founders intended Congress to have more power (the Constitution gives the Senate the duty to advise and to consent in important offices in foreign policy and treaties).

Whether this is good or bad is beside the point. It is demonstrably distinct from what the founders created. No debate occurred in Congress or in the public sphere as to whether the founder's balance ought to be altered. Instead, the imbalance has occurred slowly, incrementally. As the Cold War commenced, Congress realized its inherent weaknesses: it consists of 535 member divided into committees and subcommittees where almost everyone gets to be Mister or Madam Chairmen. Moreover, as congressional elections (particularly the Senate but increasingly in the House too) have become more expensive, the House or Senate member spend disproportionately more time raising campaign funds for reelection. It means that certain staffers are really making some of the important decisions for the House and Senate. Thus, it has been relatively easy for Congress to yield to the president as "crises" occurred during the Cold War, particularly once nuclear weapons created a balance of terror between the United States and the former USSR. That has continued after the Cold War from a sort of inertia.

What is more, few Americans seem to realize the situation is not what was created by the Constitution or the first 100-plus years of precedent. In fact, Americans are blithely ignorant of their own history. Likewise, they tend to be ignorant of the National Security Act and its creations. On occasion, Ron Paul (or more recently Rand Paul) talked of the War Powers Act as if it was the culprit. In fact, the War Powers Act was an example of Congress trying to wrest power back from the presidency but unsuccessfully. The ultimate compromise of the War Powers Act was to give to the president 60 days (which can be renewed for an additional 30) of almost unfettered power to move U.S. military troops anywhere the president feels sufficient threat exists. However, the National Security Act of 1947 set the militarization of foreign policy in motion long before the War Powers Act.

That otherwise intelligent legislators blame the powerful presidency on the War Powers Act is a misunderstanding of America's foreign policy history. If House and Senate members do not fully appreciate what has happened in terms of the balance of foreign policy powers, how can anyone expect the average American to appreciate it? There is no evidence that the National Security Act of 1947 was ever kept a secret. On the contrary, initially, at least it was publicized during the debate Congress undertook.

Therefore, the explanation must reside elsewhere. Those who created the National Security Act realized what they were doing and they sought bipartisan consensus to do it. But since then as generational turnover has continued, the original debate has faded into history. The debate occurred as the Cold War was just commencing and Americans were frightened—as were many policy makers—about the USSR and its expansionist tendencies. People wanted a powerful presidency to manage "crises" so they accepted the expansion of presidential power as well as permanent military and intelligence communities that experienced tremendous growth as the Cold War continued. They got what they accepted and only rarely has the change in U.S. foreign policy been acknowledged, much less debated intelligently.

Why then did a debate not occur after the Cold War when the threat of Soviet expansionism was no longer an issue? After all, a brief debate about a "peace dividend" occurred in 1991–1992. During both President George H. W. Bush's and President Clinton's respective administrations, a flurry of new threats seemed to proliferate. Thus, the peace dividend debate was short lived. Then the U.S. embassy bombings (fall 1998), the attack on the USS Cole (2000), and 9/11 all occurred. Scarcely anyone has the motivation (or the courage) to question whether the United States requires such a huge, permanent military and intelligence community or whether it continues to need a powerful presidency. The result is few Americans (even policy-making elites and the attentive public) are aware of the National Security Act and almost no one questions the current state of affairs. Insofar as they do, they focus on ancillary arguments as the War Powers Act.

THE NATIONAL SECURITY ACT OF 1947 AND THE RISE OF THE AMERICAN SECURITY STATE

So, the National Security Act of 1947 presented the United States with the necessary conditions for the rise of the American Security State. It did not present sufficient conditions, however. Rather, the events of the Cold War provided them. Each time a new confrontation or "crisis" with the Soviets or one of their proxies arose, Congress yielded additional ground to the NSC inside the presidency and to the Pentagon and intelligence community, respectively. Additionally, Congress is simply institutionally at a disadvantage (as noted earlier) in terms of a strong voice. Two parties—for the most part—control Congress in perpetuity. They divide the spoils of incumbency.

The National Security Act of 1947 did not create the American Security State alone. But it did start the change of trajectory in U.S. foreign policy and that change eventually produced the American Security State. Nor has anyone pushed back sufficiently, which might have caused its atrophy once it began emerging. Creating a permanent Defense Department (which also unified the various branches) has led to a predictable result: America has a permanent military ready to go anywhere under nearly any circumstances so long as its civilian masters tell it to go. From the very beginning, decisions were made to divide the military-industrial complex (Eisenhower's phrase in his farewell speech) into as many key congressional districts and states to make it nearly impossible to degrade it at some subsequent point. The result is a permanent military hegemony.

Likewise, the National Security Act created the CIA (and brought tactical military intelligence under "civilian" control). But in doing so, it has created a permanent, massive intelligence community that has now grown to 17 different agencies (with no little redundancy among them). In 2004, following the Intelligence Reform and Terrorism Prevention Act, the latest bureaucratic layer was created: the Director of National Intelligence and the office of the director of national intelligence (DNI and ODNI respectively).[20] The intelligence community (IC) grew steadily during the Cold War but it has accelerated its growth and scope since the Cold War ended.

Like a permanent military, a permanent intelligence community has consequences. Tens of thousands of employees and many tens of thousands of contractors are dependent on the permanent IC. Like the military-industrial complex, the IC-industrial complex has been spread out in several states and congressional districts making it very difficult to decrease its size. To be clear, nowhere in these pages was it suggested that either the military or intelligence community are too big. Certainly, the United States has real threats in the world. The question is how have these institutions affected U.S. foreign policy? Clearly, the institutions created by the act resulted in the militarization of U.S. foreign policy; a preponderance of evidence supports the conclusion. Whether militarization of U.S. foreign policy has been good or bad must be left to others. Similarly, others will have to address the cost-benefit analysis of militarization.

Along with the empowered NSC inside the presidency, the three institutions created by the National Security Act of 1947 have, unquestionably, changed America's role in the world. Where once the United States was a second-rate power and content to be so and to stay out of European affairs (what was euphemistically known as isolationism), America has become the world's foremost hegemonic power with responsibilities in all corners of the globe. That so few Americans understand how this happened is troubling given America is also, arguably, the world's foremost democratic republic. Ignorance among the masses and attentive public about their own history is intolerable.

WHY DO SO FEW AMERICANS KNOW ABOUT THE NATIONAL SECURITY ACT OF 1947?

Another question is why so few Americans know of the history of the rise of the American Security State? First, recall that bipartisan consensus that arose as the Cold War commenced led to the National Security Act of 1947. Nor did those who formed the consensus hide what they were doing. On the contrary, they debated it and the public could have followed the debate as it occurred in 1946 and into 1947. Therefore, the reason so few Americans know about it, must lie elsewhere.

The simplest explanation is lack of institutional memory as generations came and went. The 80th Congress (first session) was eventually replaced by the 81st and 82nd and later the 90th and today by the 115th Congress. Each session lasts one year and each Congress consists of two sessions. As the House and Senate members retire or are voted out of office, others come in to replace them. A good deal of turnover occurred over the years and even important statues such as the National Security Act are forgotten naturally enough.

Additionally, as the Cold War consensus implies, consensus about the threat the Soviets posed was widely held among policy makers and by the masses. People were genuinely afraid of Soviet expansion. One need only remember Sputnik and the fear it engendered about nuclear bombs being delivered from the heavens. By the time the Cold War ended, none of the original policy makers were around to address whether the Cold War creations (those created by the National Security Act) needed to be revisited. So, one reason so few Americans know is lack of institutional memory.

Another reason is Americans tend not to follow foreign policy. The Iowa pig farmer or the New York investment banker is concerned about what affects him or her and less concerned about foreign policy (unless it directly affects him or her). In fact, Americans are notoriously ill-informed regarding foreign policy. Study after study demonstrates Americans' fickleness or outright ignorance when it comes to U.S. foreign policy.[21] Walter Lippmann called the American public the "bewildered herd."[22] The American public does not bear all the blame, however,

The media bear some responsibility. Very few Washington reporters understand the National Security Act of 1947 and the few who have written about it seem more interested in how one administration or another may have used it for its own purposes.[23] The Washington Press Corps is in the business of breaking news. They are not historians nor are they especially interested or rewarded by digging into America's political history. Finally, the media tend to cover spectacular events. "If it bleeds it leads" is an aphorism that adequately describes what drives the media, including the cable news networks. It is difficult not to see that the media have contributed to the ignorance of the American public in terms of U.S. foreign policy.

Another issue has to do with how candidates become president. Candidates run for presidency and are often ignorant of detailed knowledge of U.S. foreign policy. Once the candidate gets elected, he is often overwhelmed by the power of the presidency and the expectations of office (role expectations).[24] Then the president serves a term or two and when he writes his memoirs the NSC or the IC or the military is not likely to be the focus. Rather, the focus is what wonderful things the particular president did while in office. Thus, few presidential memoirs address the NSC or other aspects of the National Security Act.

In fact, each president tends to want to protect the prerogatives of the next president (role again) and particularly the next president who belongs to the party the previous president represented. Thus, there is little incentive for ex-presidents (all of whom know just how powerful they were relative to Congress and how much more powerful the NSC is versus Congress) to raise issues about the very institutions that allowed his presidency to be successful.

Even in academia, there are few who write about the National Security Act of 1947. I have listed them in my bibliography and cited them at appropriate places in the narratives above. I have written four books that mention the NSC and the National Security Act, three of which focused on particular aspects of the act. (This is the third.) The truth is, it is hard to get scholarly work on the National Security Act published, due to the mechanics of publishing.[25] Moreover, few publishers are cognizant of the act and its importance to U.S. foreign policy and they therefore tend to ignore proposals to publish scholarly work on the role the National Security Act has played in U.S. foreign policy. (Likewise, reviewers often know little about the act.)

In short, there exist any number of reasons the story of the National Security Act of 1947 has slipped through the cracks. It has been nobody's responsibility to publicize what was created in 1947 and how it has led to the rise of the American Security State. I have never found evidence of persons attempting to bury the story. On the contrary, when the act was passed, there was no reason to think the story would become buried in the Library of Congress. In fact, the White House has kept a web page on the NSC part of the act almost since the White House went online in mid- to late 1990s. Why more American do not read it or check into it is unclear?

HOW HAS THE UNITED STATES BLUNDERED
INTO THE NATIONAL SECURITY STATE?

What can be said with some confidence is few if any of the original members of the Cold War consensus realized that what they created would lead to the rise of the American Security State. Rather, President Truman and his advisers (Clark Clifford, Secretary Marshall, and Secretary Acheson and others) and key members of the Senate (particularly, Senator Vandenberg) simply thought they were creating what was necessary to prevent the Soviets from expanding beyond what the Soviets had already taken as World War II concluded. There appears to be no evidence that any of them thought the institutions they helped create would outlive the Cold War and change U.S. foreign policy forever.

The National Security Act of 1947 was seen as a stopgap expedient to forestall additional Soviet victories. When the Allies of World War II (including the Soviets) approached Berlin, the Soviet Red Army had grown considerably (and largely to the generosity of FDR's lend-lease program). The Soviets occupied what would soon become East Germany and the United States, British (and the French to a lesser extent) what would become West Germany. The Soviets grabbed parts of Poland and there was little either FDR or Truman (or for that matter, Prime Minister Churchill) could do about it at Yalta and Potsdam. Moreover, each had wrongly concluded that he could handle Stalin. Each of them soon stood corrected.

The fact is the United States more or less blundered into what has become the American Security State without any specific plan to create it. While multiple presidents and policy makers believed the United States needed to have the flexibility to respond to Soviet aggression, no evidence exists that suggest any of them desired to create the American Security State. It simply grew out of the same expediencies that led to the National Security Act of 1947.

A DEBATE IS NEEDED

The argument presented herein was never intended to judge the National Security Act of 1947 or any of the institutions it created. Rather, this book has sought to highlight how critical the National Security Act was in affecting U.S. foreign policy. However, that the United States has become the world's hegemonic power is undeniable and that its status as such is contrary to the Constitution that created the government (i.e., the power behind the hegemony) seems an important issue. Every four years as presidential elections are held, one may wait in vain to hear debates about whether the creations of the National Security Act of 1947 should continue or whether the militarization of U.S. foreign policy is appropriate. While marginal debates are occasionally raised during said elections, very little substantive debate has occurred around the National Security Act of 1947. One waits in vain to hear substantive talks of U.S. foreign policy. The only candidates who mention American imperium are those who have no chance of being elected (such as Ron and Rand Paul). Time will tell whether that changes in the Trump administration.

Even if one accepts that the American Security State is a good or necessary thing (for the order of world politics), a debate is still worthwhile. The American Security State has opportunity costs associated with it. Thus, Americans need to have an open and honest debate on whether the costs are worth the benefits. If America is the world's foremost democracy, the peculiar state of affairs highlighted in this book seems inexcusable.

Another problem, finally, is that both political parties (the Republican and Democratic Parties) have become incumbent parties. Noted earlier were the stables of foreign policy experts each party has and how they get recycled in subsequent administrations. There are benefits from this recycling of foreign policy expertise. (A similar thing happens in parliamentary systems.) However, during the life of the National Security Act of 1947 (it turned 70 years old in June 2017), roughly equal numbers of Republicans and Democrats have cycled through the White House and NSC (and as leaders in Defense, State, etc.). Beginning with Truman, the Democrats are Truman, Kennedy, Johnson, Carter, Clinton, and Obama. The Republicans are Eisenhower, Nixon, Ford, Reagan, H. W. Bush (Bush 41), and W. Bush (Bush 43). What can one reasonably infer from this?

One may reasonably infer that neither Democrats nor Republicans wish to upset the status quo. Put differently, both Democrats and Republicans are content with the American Security State. Nor is their reasoning faulty. Once in power, the president is filling the role of presidency first and foremost (and leader of his party only secondarily). Both Democratic and Republican presidents, therefore, like having the imbalance between the executive and legislative branches in their favor. And no president of either party has yet been in a hurry to consider the continued results of the American Security State.

CHAPTER 7

The National Security Act and the Militarization of U.S. Foreign Policy

Wherever the standard of freedom and independence has been or shall be unfurled, there will her heart, her benedictions and her prayers be. But she goes not abroad in search of monsters to destroy. She is the well-wisher to the freedom and independence of all. She is the champion and vindicator only of her own. She will recommend the general cause, by the countenance of her voice, and the benignant sympathy of her example.

—John Quincy Adams, Speech on Independence Day, United States House of Representatives, July 4, 1821

In the election this fall, which will go far to determine the conduct of the United States in the next twenty-five years, we stand for the election of President Lyndon B. Johnson. We admire the President for the continuity with which he has maintained our foreign policy, a policy which became a world-wide responsibility at the time of the Marshall Plan.

—Edward Weeks, "The Election," of LBJ, *The Atlantic*, October 1964, http://www.theatlantic.com/magazine/archive/1964/10/ the-1964-election/303598/

INTRODUCTION

The previous chapter addressed the various theses of this book. In particular, Chapter 6 demonstrated that the institutions created by the National Security Act of 1947 created necessary conditions—if not the sufficient conditions—for the United States to jettison "isolationism" and to begin growing into the American Security State (the world's hegemonic power or what some have called Pax Americana elsewhere[1]). In this chapter, the intent is to step back and consider the said evolution in terms of the chronological typology specified earlier.

It should be noted that others have used various chronologies for U.S. foreign policy, very different from the one employed herein. For this book the intention was to accept that by the end of World War II, the United States had become a world power of some import. Therefore, it was the book's plan to consider the continuation of this growth over the course of the Cold War. In thinking about the Cold War, one can divide it into any number of categories. But in the previous chapters, it was reasoned that the early Cold War (roughly from 1947 through the 1950s) was a distinct first period of the Cold War. The reasoning was straightforward. By the time the National Security Act of 1947 became law, U.S. policy makers realized they were involved in a grave (some believed existential) struggle with the former USSR but they had little idea how long that might last. (In fact, there was evidence that policy makers believed eventually the European empires, call it Pax Europaea, might return relieving the U.S. of its temporary inconvenience.)

The second part of the Cold War was the main part of the Cold War, lasting from the early 1960s through the 1980s (though even in that case a period of détente existed briefly). This was a period of frequent proxy wars between the Soviets and the Americans. During the second period of the Cold War, U.S. policy makers realized they were in a long-term struggle with the Soviets that had no foreseeable end in sight. Importantly, during this second period, the proliferation of nuclear weapons tempered any initial notions either superpower might have held about vanquishing its opponent by warfare. Nuclear war came to represent nuclear annihilation of both superpowers and in such a context traditional notions of success vanished. (Indeed, the nuclear strategy that came to characterize the main part of the Cold War was called Mutually Assured Destruction, or MAD.)

Finally, somewhere during the late 1980s and early 1990s, the Cold War ended. (By August 1991, the failed coup spelled a final collapse of the USSR but the Berlin Wall came down in 1989 and the Soviet Red Army relinquished its role as a protector of fraternal socialist states before 1991 so the end of the Cold War may reasonably be dated differently, depending on one's purpose.) Near the end of the Cold War, during President George H. W. Bush's tenure, the president called for a New World Order in which dollars earmarked for containing the USSR might be reprogrammed domestically in various ways. There was talk, at least initially, about a "peace dividend" during the immediate post-Cold War period.[2] Thus, this latter period is particularly important in terms of the militarization thesis as it represented a transitional period from the Cold War to the post-Cold War period.

The focus of this book was both the Cold War and post-Cold War periods. It is important to understand, however, America's foreign policy history prior to World War II and even the 20th century. Somewhere between the Spanish-American War (late 19th century) and World War II, the United States firmly rejected its previous isolationism. (Whether the United States was objectively isolationist prior to the 20th century is debatable but not worth arguing here. For any number of reasons, many Americans believed the United States was an isolationist power from its origins until the late 19th or mid-20th centuries. More important, an isolationist block existed in Congress that checked U.S. ambitions globally.)

By the time World War II occurred—in 1939 for Europe but not until Pearl Harbor in December 1941 for America—the FDR presidency had already reversed isolationism. Even prior to Pearl Harbor, President Roosevelt gave the Four Freedoms and lend-lease speeches making it relatively clear that FDR believed the United States must face fascism directly, even if Americans still resisted.[3] Whether or not the United States was an isolationist power before World War II, what is beyond debate is that the United States became an important world power as war destroyed Europe. (It took some time for the American public to fully support America's new powerful role in world politics.) The period is important because it spelled the end of European empires (in particular, the mighty British Empire or Pax Britannica). It has been argued that the United States eventually filled the void left by Pax Britannica's atrophy.

World War II along with the Cold War era formed the second period of U.S. foreign policy if one accepts the conventional wisdom. The United States rather quickly became an important world power soon followed by the United States emerging as one of two superpowers. During the Cold War era, in particular, the world was divided into the First World (the Western industrialized democracies led by the United States and its NATO allies), the Second World (the Eastern industrialized command economies led by the USSR and its allies) and the nonaligned world or what became known, somewhat pejoratively as the Third World. (Later, the least developed of the Third World were sometimes referred to as the Fourth World.)

The post-Cold War era is another period commonly seen as distinct for U.S. foreign policy as it is the period in which the United States became a *unipolar* power (or simply, a *hegemonic power*). Without the USSR to check U.S. foreign policy the United States *continued* to militarize foreign policy, as this book has demonstrated. Some of the pundits and policy makers thought the United States might throttle back on its leadership, if not exactly return to its "isolationist" roots. However, the opposite happened: the United States, in effect, doubled down on hegemony. So the question is why?

It is likely the case that many reasons including the ones I have not fully considered led America to its post-Cold War hegemonic continuation. However, a tentative answer is the following. Instead of one big thing to worry about, U.S. policy makers began to worry about many small things, indeed nearly everything that happens on the planet intersects with U.S.

interests—that is the nature of hegemony. There are very few parts of the globe where the United States does not have direct "interests" or at least treaty alliances and indirect interests. (Again, it is the nature of hegemony.)

Early in the post-Cold War era, the disintegration of former Yugoslavia and Somalia (recall Black Hawk Down) began impressing policy makers with the chaotic nature of the world politics. As Yugoslavia continued to tear itself apart with the return of ultranationalism so too did the United States begin to become acquainted with transnational Jihadists, in particular, what became al Qaeda and its various franchises. (As of this writing, al Qaeda has morphed into various al Qaeda franchises and even the Islamic State in Iraq and the Levant, ISIL. Indeed, the leader of ISIL, Abu Bakr al-Baghdadi was the second leader of al Qaeda of Iraq before morphing into ISIL.)

The point is that instead of the world becoming a less tense and violent place, the United States increasingly saw itself—meaning its policy makers, its attentive public, and eventually its masses—as *indispensable* to peaceful and proper operation of world politics. Both the Republican and Democratic Parties agreed that the United States was necessary if world politics was going to function properly. Thus, rather than disengage, the United States engaged even more than during the post-Cold War. As it did so, the USSR was not there to temper it and America's engagement became increasingly militarized over time. It was the beginning of history—rather than its end as some had predicted—and it has been a violent history indeed.

THE MILITARIZATION OF U.S. FOREIGN POLICY

The Early Cold War Years

As the reader will recall, the case study chapters were divided into the Cold War (the beginning or 1950s, Chapter 3) followed by Chapter 4 (the Cold War, 1960s-1980s), and the post-Cold War period (including the transitional George H. W. Bush administration). In the first of the three periods, during the first decade after the National Security Act of 1947, two different presidencies occupied the White House: one a Democrat (President Truman) and the other a Republican (President Eisenhower) who served two full terms. The NSC, the department of defense, and the CIA (what became the Intelligence Community or IC) were new but they all expanded bureaucratically.

The NSC went from a policy-making backwater (before the Korean War), where policy papers were churned out but Truman did not attend the NSC meetings, to become the hub or apex of U.S policy making. Initially, President Truman allowed his executive secretary to preside over the NSC meetings. This was important because until the Korean War President Truman continued to make foreign policy the old-fashioned way, by way of his cabinet or a subgroup of his cabinet that included President Truman, the newly created secretary of defense and, importantly, Truman's secretary of state Marshall (who was eventually replaced by Dean Acheson).[4]

With the outbreak of the Korean War that all changed. The NSC became the main locus of foreign policy making in the Truman administration, setting a precedent that would continue through today (with a couple of brief exceptions highlighted in the case studies). Even when the Korean War became stalemated, Truman used his NSC—what evolved in time as the NSC principals, the statutory members and advisers, as well as a few others—as the new locus of policy making. These were busy years in which the Soviets provoked—as Truman and his NSC principals saw it— confrontations and what became known as proxy wars around the globe in parts of the Third World. Thus, once the locus of policy making moved to the NSC setting, it never moved back.

Likewise, the U.S. Department of Defense and the secretary of defense became two critical bureaucratic powers. Previously, the old War Department had always played a secondary role to the secretary of state and the State Department in presidential cabinets. After Korea, the Defense Department grew into a bureaucratic giant that came to eclipse even the U.S. State Department (and the secretary of defense eclipsed the secretary of state). Defense Department's budgets was many times (10 or more) larger than States' and the Vietnam War, in particular, made Defense into the most important bureaucracy in the executive apart from the NSC principals committee. By dint of its budget and the number of employees, Defense grew to dominate foreign policy making. Thus, it is scarcely surprising that U.S. foreign policy would become militarized over time as Defense grew into the most important cabinet bureaucracy.

Less dramatically, the intelligence community (IC) grew bureaucratically. During the Cold War it expanded considerably. The original civilian leader of the IC was the director of central intelligence (DCI) who served both as the director of the CIA and, ostensibly, the civilian leader of the entire IC. However, with Defense controlling roughly 80 percent of the IC budget, the DCI never in fact was able to exert control over the various IC entities whose budgets were approved through yearly defense appropriations (even when secret or black budgets). Nevertheless, the IC grew and expanded over time and the partnerships between Defense and the IC helped both bureaucracies to expand their respective bureaucratic muscles.[5]

For instance, it was the first decade after the National Security Act of 1947 became law that the United States began using covert and paramilitary operations, largely conducted out of CIA, to get rid of governments the United States found troublesome. Whether they were allies of the Soviets or just too "leftist," the CIA participated in the overthrow of Iran's democratically elected Mossadegh government (1953), along with British intelligence. The following year, CIA (with the U.S. Information Agency, State) overthrew the Arbenz government in Guatemala. The precedent of covert, paramilitary operations was set. Virtually every subsequent president has used the precedent.

Virtually every president after Eisenhower has used covert and/or paramilitary operations. Covert actions proved addicting to presidents and it is not difficult to see why. Namely, when presidents use covert operations they do not need to get the consent of Congress. Initially, presidents told no one outside the NSC principals (usually a NSC subgroup of the principals with a "need to know"); but in time as some of these operations came to light (as they always do in time), new oversight committees were created in both the House and the Senate. Even with the oversight committees, however, presidents found it much easier to operate covertly than overtly. "Findings" are permitted that allow presidents to tell only the so-called Gang of Eight (the two leaders of the House and Senate respectively and their minority partners, along with the chairs and vice chairs of the House and Senate intelligence oversight committees). Telling just eight is far easier than having policy debated in both chambers and subjected to the political process the founders envisaged.

In short, the first decade (or more accurately, the first 13 years) following the National Security Act saw the militarization of U.S. foreign policy as the NSC principals engaged in "crisis management" against an active USSR that played to win the Cold War. The Cold War was seen as a zero-sum game by both sides: only one side could win. Therefore, the U.S.-led First World and the USSR-led Second World both militarized the foreign policies of their respective blocs. There were very few voices, until the Vietnam War became unpopular who challenged the empowered presidency. Both the Defense Department and the IC played important subsidiary roles to militarize America's foreign policy.

The Main Cold War Years: 1960s through 1980s

During the main years of the Cold War (1960s, 1970s, and 1980s) the American Security State expanded further. The number of proxy wars increased and were conducted in Africa, Latin America (both South and Central America), Cuba, and across vast parts of Asia. Atomic then thermonuclear (nuclear weapons) increased in degree of sophistication and in terms of capacity to end life on earth. As the stakes increased, new and novel uses of the NSC, the military, and the intelligence community (IC) continued to proliferate. Congress deferred even more to the president and the NSC; and even during the few years in which détente existed, the tensions of the Cold War only decreased marginally. (For instance, the United States kept bombers with nuclear weapons in the air 24/7 ready to penetrate Soviet airspace. It likewise kept intercontinental ballistic missiles [ICBMs] targeted on the Soviets and nuclear submarine-launched ballistic missiles [SLBMs] ready to strike the Soviets on the president's authorization.)

As noted earlier, nuclear weapons (and other weapons of mass destruction or WMDs) helped to create the "crisis management" mind-set of the Cold War's high-stakes policy making. Leaders in either party realized that Congress was two big and bulky to make quick decisions in such high-stakes contests as those played between the United States and the USSR, especially when WMDs might be involved. While the United States typically held a technological edge over the USSR (somewhere between three and five years), it was always understood the Soviets would catch up. So the Cold War consensus emerged that allowed the NSC inside the presidency to expand, increasingly, its power at least until the "emergency" period ended. Once the Cold War lasted 40-plus years, there was no one left around on Capitol Hill who remembered these changes were intended as stopgap expediencies. Thus, the changes remained.

The End of the Cold War

But what happened after the Cold War ended? Recall that in late summer 1991, Premier Gorbachev's changes were well underway. He had implemented two programs called *perestroika* and *glasnost* in the mid-1980s and by 1989 change was gaining momentum, though how it would turn out was not clear. Gorbachev announced the Soviet Red Army would no longer enforce Soviet control over its previous satellites (East Germany, Poland, the Baltic States, and former Yugoslavia) and soon (fall 1989) the Berlin Wall began to crumble.

Change was happening quickly in the USSR, so quickly that reactionary forces sought to reverse Gorbachev's progress and that resulted in a failed coup attempt by disgruntled hard-line military officers (and communist party members) in the USSR. The result was the end of Gorbachev's changes and a brief period of civil unrest in Russia. Then former satellites and even former parts of the USSR began spinning away from Russia's control as the USSR imploded on itself. This in turn led to Yugoslavia breaking away and the disparate parts of former Yugoslavia seeking their own independence and leading to wars between Serbia and Slovenia, Serbia and Croatia, and eventually Serbia and Bosnia-Herzegovina and Kosovo respectively. (It also led to Czechoslovakia eventually breaking into a Czech and a Slovak Republic.)

In policy- and lawmaking circles in the United States, only after it became clear the USSR existed no more could change occur. Indeed, in the 1989–1991 period (when it first seemed, then became clear the USSR was no more) a ubiquity of "new thinking" occurred in and out of government. Francis Fukuyama published the *End of History* and became famous with his assertion that liberal democracy won the Cold War. Samuel Huntington—already famous—published his *Clash of Civilizations* thesis in *Foreign Affairs* and in book format. And Benjamin Barber published "Jihad versus McWorld" in *The Atlantic Monthly* (now *The Atlantic*). Political science and the "punditocracy" thoroughly debated all the new thinking about the post-Cold War world. But what happened next was not quite what those purveyors of punditry expected.[6]

Instead, the world continued much like it had during the Cold War only adding new concerns. With the disintegration of Yugoslavia, nationalism reared its ugly head again. Nationalism had been buried beneath ideological and power struggles between the superpowers during the Cold War, so it had been a while since the attentive public in the West had worried about nationalism. However, the centripetal forces tearing Yugoslavia apart, alone, were significant. Policy makers and elites had been lulled into a sense that nationalism was no longer a worry. But it was not just the reemergence of nationalism that followed 1991 alone that reanimated leaders at either end of Pennsylvania Avenue.

Indeed, while Yugoslavia was torn by ethnic and religious strife a new "ism" appeared, one that Americans were ill-prepared for. It was *transnationalism*. The United States had been involved in a proxy war in Afghanistan, as most readers surely realize, during the 1980s. The old USSR invaded Afghanistan to prop up an ally and Soviet occupation led to jihad by Afghanistan tribal elements (the mujahedeen) and Muslims from afar who came to fight the Soviet infidels. During the Cold War the calculus was simple: an enemy of my enemy was my friend. The United States supported all kinds of undemocratic and even antidemocratic forces for the simple reason they were anti-communist or anti-USSR. The United States, therefore, helped arm the mujahedeen because doing so materially hurt the Soviets. The thinking may have been more than a little myopic as what eventually emerged from the mujahedeen was al Qaeda (or what we think of today as violent extremism or Jihadism).

By the mid-1990s, jihad had spread from Afghanistan to Bosnia to elsewhere and it was clear the phenomenon was growing. In fact, the U.S. Marines were attacked in Lebanon in fall 1983 by suicide bombers (though Shi'a rather than the Sunni jihadists of 1993 forward). In the mid-1990s, a new kind of Jihadism had emerged: they were Sunni and they held a fundamentalist view of the Koran and Mohammed's words (known as Salafism or *Salfi*); many were associated with Saudi Arabia's Wahhabi version of Sunni Islam, a virulent version. Many of them believed they had the right to declare other Muslims as heretics, or what was known as *takfir* (*takfiri*) so that the emerging phenomenon was quite literally a Sunni-Salafi-Wahhabi-Takfiri phenomenon that became known as Jihadism.[7]

By the mid- to late 1990s, many in policy- and lawmaking circles had begun to sense the danger of Jihadism. Nevertheless, for various reasons—including, America's Bill of Rights, that is, its civil liberties—law enforcement did not pursue Jihadism even when they traveled through or lived in the United States. (Another complication was the FBI is America's domestic intelligence agency, insofar as it has one, and because it is both a law enforcement and an intelligence agency, it had very specific rules of evidence—in federal code, rule 6E—that kept the two functions separate.)

Some realized al Qaeda (and bin Laden, specifically) had begun threatening America outright, certainly by 1998. It was in late 1998 that al Qaeda pulled off a virtually simultaneous attacks on two U.S. embassies, one in Kenya and one in Tanzania. That caught everybody's attention and in fact DCI George Tenet declared war on al Qaeda later that year.

In a case study (Chapter 5), some of these developments were presented because they were relevant to how U.S. foreign policy changed during the 1990s. For instance, the case study noted that President Bill Clinton created a new entity inside the NSC called the counterterrorism security group (CSG) also known as the transnational directorate run by Richard Clarke and staffed by a couple of others. The political problem was President Clinton was in his final two years and was embroiled in various impeachment attempts and some fairly unpleasant politics in Washington. The result was his administration took note of al Qaeda and began responding but did too little.

Despite knowing about al Qaeda, many of us simply could not conceive of al Qaeda attacking the United States as it did on 9/11 despite the U.S. embassy attacks in 1998. How could we so easily dismiss al Qaeda? In fact, those of us who were raised during the Cold War had come to see states as the only important actors in the global system. Nation-states, only, had armies and navies and the material wherewithal to attack another nation-state. During the Cold War, the world had seen terrorism (of various kinds) but the acts were staged to get attention, to publicize some cause or another. Many of us simply became blind to non-state actors being able to conduct an attack (at least like 9/11) on the United States. After all, the United States was the most powerful nation-state in existence.

Moreover, even al Qaeda's attacks had always been on America's facilities abroad. That is, where America projected power into far-off reaches of the globe (and necessarily kept forces for force protection). Many of us had lived so long with the idea of the USSR attacking American from outside its borders that it became difficult to imagine some small group capable of such an attack. As noted earlier, conventional wisdom and popular culture prior to 9/11 pointed toward a chemical or biological attack on New York City. Thus, many of us thought al Qaeda a threat but not quite the threat it proved on 9/11. We simply could not conceive of what al Qaeda did on 9/11. It was literally beyond the scope of our imaginations.

So despite Clinton's record of preparing the United States for al Qaeda—which has both positive and negative aspects—President Clinton was unable to move the nation from its Cold War paradigm. Nevertheless, as President Clinton prepared to leave office he had done some important things inside the NSC to prepare the United States for al Qaeda. Inside the CIA, director George Tenet likewise began to move the IC bureaucracy. But neither was able to move the ship of U.S. foreign policy, which moves like a massive aircraft carrier unless and until it gets set in a different and distinct direction.

President Clinton was, of course, replaced by President George W. Bush and the transition was marked by the Supreme Court ruling that cut the transition almost in half. (Recall, both Al Gore and George W. Bush claimed the 2000 election and the Supreme Court settled it in the latter's favor.) Other complications arose. Inside the Bush administration a fight between traditional Republicans (Colin Powell's State) and the neoconservatives (in the NSC principals committee including Vice President Cheney and others) probably delayed the Bush administration from responding in a more timely way. Thus, it is fair to say the Bush administration also did too little. President Bush's NSC deputies had developed policy options in September and the NSC principals were preparing to meet with the attacks on New York and Washington occurred on 9/11.[8]

By the end of the 1990s, these two things, nationalism and transnationalism, created yet another consensus (albeit much more short lived than the Cold War consensus) that became part of the Bush Doctrine. The Bush Doctrine—the administration would make no distinction between those who commit terrorist acts and those states who harbor them—was simply a restatement of a Clinton policy but it did demonstrate that consensus had again formed that U.S. foreign policy was entering another dangerous period and that previous talk about peace dividends was misplaced.

The rest is history (hopefully, well known). The United States responded to 9/11 with war in Afghanistan (though not a case study included herein, it was an example of novel use of the military with air and special forces combined in the post-Cold War era) in October 2001. By late 2002 (or early 2003), the Bush administration conflated 9/11 with Saddam Hussein publicly and the United States therefore invaded Iraq in spring 2003, setting another post-Cold War precedent of regime change (the United States had done so covertly during the Cold War but this was novel in its post-Cold War setting). President Bush was replaced, after two terms, by President Barack Obama who made a Bush-like "surge" in Afghanistan on December 1, 2009 (one of the case studies).

The world is still amid the post-Cold War period and U.S. foreign policy continues to be increasingly militarized. The United States considers itself the "indispensable" nation to making the world work properly and there is little reason to think U.S. foreign policy will be demilitarized in the foreseeable future. An election occurred in November 2016 and we will have to see how President Trump views the American Security State, though early signs are his rhetoric and his actions are at odds, thus likely resulting in more of the same.

What are we to conclude? It is apparent that the United States has continually militarized its foreign policy for several decades. The Cold War was widely seen by Americans as an imperative and reason for the United States to do so. But we have seen through various phases of the Cold War that new impetuses provided new reasons to militarize foreign policy.

Even after the heartbreak of the Vietnam War, the United States (after a respite of a couple of years) began militarizing foreign policy again.

During the Cold War, a remarkable continuity in U.S. foreign policy has existed. Continuity is defined as gradual change in the goals and objectives of U.S. foreign policy—that is, incremental change only. Dramatic change would belie continuity. (Presidential candidates spew all kinds of rhetoric but once they become president and *role* expectations set in they act remarkably alike in terms of foreign policy irrespective of political party.)

Continuity can be seen in the following as well. During the entirety of the Cold War, six Republican presidents militarized U.S. foreign policy: two terms of Eisenhower, almost two terms of Nixon, a little more than one term of Ford, two terms of Reagan, and one term of Bush 41. During those same Cold War years, four Democratic presidents militarized foreign policy: what remained of Truman's second term (1949–1953), nearly one term of Kennedy (1961 to late 1963), the remainder of Kennedy's term by Johnson and then another term in his own right, and Carter. In those years, Congresses have come and gone and the balance of power had shifted and shifted back again. (The National Security Act became law during the 80th Congress and today we are in the first session of the 115th Congress.)

President after president (and it seems to matter little which party they ostensibly represent) has done it and since the Cold War ended (1991)—while President George H.W. Bush was in office—three post-Cold War presidents have militarized foreign policy: two terms of Bill Clinton (D), two terms of George W. Bush (R), and two terms of President Barak Obama (D). Militarization of U.S. foreign policy occurs irrespective of which party controls the White House or Capitol Hill. (We are witnessing the first term of President Trump but it is early at this writing. Nevertheless, candidate Trump ran on defeating "Islamic terrorism," so it seems plausible to think President Trump will also militarize U.S. foreign policy.)

To be clear, during the various phases of the Cold War and again since the Cold War ended, policy makers have increasingly militarized U.S. foreign policy. They have done so incrementally and one consequence has been the public has rarely had public debate about the role of the United States in the world today. Rather, both parties have accepted the foreign policy orthodoxy that without the United States to make things run properly, the world would go to hell in a handbasket. This may or may not be true. What is true is that both parties have done their respective parts to ensure such a debate does not occur (not secretly or coyly or slyly but openly).

This leads to another issue that bears on this book's theses. Is the American public so ill-informed that policy makers and lawmakers regularly dupe them? Is the public the bewildered herd led by political elites that Walter had Lippmann asserted?[9] It is beyond this book's scope but, alas, the public seems easily manipulated and distracted, whichever best serves policy makers. Americans seldom follow policy (especially foreign policy) unless it has a direct and clear affect on their lives and well-beings. Americans love to exercise their right to complain about politicians (lawmakers, policy makers) yet they do not know with precision what their politicians are doing.

In short, in the world's most important democracy, arguably, something has gone amiss with democratic theory. Democratic theory holds (among other things) that people will vote in their own interests. It holds that voters will educate themselves about important topics and hold their leaders accountable for not making wise decisions. Instead, America's electoral system has turned into political theater, in which performing seals (candidates) bark out sound bites—ones that have been created by political consultants and tested by professional pollsters for their resonance with certain demographics of voters. One need read only *Game Change* (about the 2008 presidential election) or *Double Down* (about the 2012 presidential election) to understand just how broken the system is. Narrative drives movement and narrative is part truth—sometimes a seed of truth—with political fiction to create what the media will report about a given candidate.

To what extent the same holds true with public policy is unclear and beyond this book's scope, the system appears broken there as well. What is clear is that in terms of foreign policy, Americans are raised to be functionally illiterate about who and how foreign policy is made. They are socialized from the time they begin learning American history into compliant purveyors of political orthodoxy. They tend not to read. They tend to get their news from television (the main goal of which is to sell advertising). And they tend to know very little about what their government does in their name, whether in terms of foreign policy or public policy.

How long can America retain its hegemony—supposing it should for the moment—when its political system is in such a shamble? It reminds this author of the period of England's Golden Jubilee (late 1880s) when, unbeknown to politicians and lawmakers in the United Kingdom, England was on its way out. It assembled a massive armada to show the world the old aphorism ("The sun never sets on the British Empire") at the very time the sun was beginning to set on the British Empire. How much longer can the United States sustain political dysfunction and imperium? Is America facing its jubilee as did the British in the late 1880s?

CONCLUSIONS

Militarization and the National Security Act

To reiterate, the United States was a secondary or tertiary power until the 20th century. Then a series of events put the United States into a different position. World War II left the European empires razed. Out of that surprising development two new superpowers emerged, the United States and the USSR. From about 1947 until about 1991, these two super-powers ran the world as a duopoly (a condominium where two members called the shots).

Understandably, the United States made some extraordinary decisions as the Cold War commenced. The Cold War consensus formed quickly and helped bury lingering isolationist sentiment in the United States. In consequence, both Democratic and Republican lawmakers and Demo-cratic policy makers passed an important new law, the National Security Act of 1947.

The act created three new institutions, all three of which contributed to the militarization of U.S. foreign policy. It created a permanent De-fense Department (from the previous War Department) in which all the armed forces were unified under a single secretary of defense. Having a permanent—rather than the previous ad hoc—military made it far eas-ier to see every challenge in terms of military solutions. Over time De-fense even eclipsed State, previously the most important cabinet agency in helping make foreign policy.

Likewise the act created a permanent intelligence community (IC). It began with taking the tactical intelligence in Navy and elsewhere and combining them with the newly created civilian intelligence agency, the CIA. Also, like Defense, in the IC a new civilian leader of CIA was created, the director of central intelligence (DCI) as the ostensible leader of all the IC, both civilian and military. Over time different parts of the IC resisted coming under the DCI and they managed to retain some independence. Also, like Defense, a permanent IC led to the militarization of U.S. foreign policy.

The IC like any other bureaucracy must justify its budget by making itself invaluable to policy makers. The IC was created to give timely in-telligence to the president and his NSC. By virtue of the fact that Defense controlled about 80 percent of the IC over time made the IC more likely than not to see threats similarly to the way Defense saw them. The his-tory of the IC is one of parochial and petty fights between its various enti-ties often driven by insignificant, bureaucratic fights between Defense and others.

The third thing the National Security Act did was to create inside the executive office of the presidency the National Security Council. Like De-fense and the IC the logic was unimpeachable. Of the three branches of government, which was best set up to direct foreign policy, the Congress or the executive office of the presidency? The answer was the latter so the NSC was put under the presidency (despite the messy balance the found-ers created). The NSC has become the apex or most important locus of high-level foreign policy making and national security policy making.

As power accrued to the NSC and therefore the presidency, some other part of the government had to yield power. Congress did so and did so willingly given the high stakes of the Cold War. By the Vietnam War, Congress began having second thoughts but it was too late. The increased power the presidency had accumulated was not going to be bartered away for petty privileges. A tension between the two branches—the Congress and the presidency—began and it continues to this day.

There is evidence that those who passed and signed the National Security Act of 1947 did so as a temporary means to contain the Soviets. If true, the implication is that once the Soviets were no more, some of the extraordinary institutions created by the act might be disassembled and things turned back to former times. In this book, we have discussed how President George H. W. Bush talked about reprogramming some of the annual appropriations back into domestic spending.

However, the Cold War's end did not spell an end to the National Security Act's creations. Instead, a series of events caused policy makers and lawmakers to search for new monsters. Nor were new monsters difficult to find. Ugly nationalism in former Yugoslavia provided one set of examples. As the United States increasingly involved itself in Yugoslavia's destruction, CNN and others broadcast pictures of prisoners of war reminiscent of Nazi death camps. By the mid-1990s, another series of external impetuses moved U.S. foreign policy: the growing and looming threat of transnational religious extremist (Sunni Islam's Jihadism).

For both Democratic and Republican administrations, it was far easier to vilify these external threats than to dismantle institutions that had become part and parcel of America's economy. (Let me be clear. The armed forces and the intelligence community are "socialism" in the true sense of the word. The government entirely controls the means of production. Even the defense contractors [private firms] are controlled by the government.)

Politicians tend to take the path of least resistance. (Who doesn't in life?) Therefore, we have seen a continuation of the militarization of U.S. foreign policy well beyond the Cold War, now some two decades plus beyond. It seems very unlikely that will change anytime soon.

Inputs

Let us finally return to the inputs (independent variables) noted in Chapter 1. They were external-systemic, societal, governmental, individual, and role. The external-systemic is perhaps easiest to trace on the militarization of U.S. foreign policy.

Once the United States became a power invested in maintaining the status quo of the system, what happens outside of U.S. borders becomes homogenized for policy makers. Whether it is Saddam invading Kuwait or the 2008 economic meltdown of the global economy, the question becomes a binary one: does it threaten the status quo or does it not?

President after president comes to office (many with different management styles and different personalities) and once in office becomes vested in the policies his predecessor established. Virtually all external stimuli to U.S. foreign policy are processed this way and the NSC principals respond in ways to ensure—to the extent they can ensure it—that the United States continues to maintain the status quo. The system favors the United States so maintaining it becomes the response of administration after administration.

Both in the previous chapter and this one, problems with societal inputs to U.S. foreign policy have been mentioned. America is certainly a pluralistic society. It has a free press and civil liberties guaranteed by the Bill of Rights. But there are difficulties in the transmission of public opinion to policy makers as well as the vigilance of the public in terms of foreign affairs. The media themselves have manifold problems. Over time the public defers to policy makers. There are few people around who are old enough to remember when America was not an important protector of the status quo and each year their numbers diminish. The result is remarkable obedience to those in power when it comes to protecting America's security. Despite proliferation of media beyond traditional means, Americans seem less informed than during the Cold War. The public seems essentially inert when it comes to foreign policy.

In terms of government machinery—the bureaucracy—the main bureaucracies created by the National Security Act of 1947 were created to contain the USSR during the Cold War. Once the Cold War ended they did what bureaucracy does when it is rendered obsolete. They found new monsters to slay. The NSC, the Defense Department, and the intelligence community (IC) have all grown steadily over time. In fact, Defense and the IC have grown more robustly in the post-Cold War era than during all but the beginning of the Cold War. The other bureaucracies that are involved from time to time in U.S. foreign policy (from Commerce to Agriculture to Justice) defer to the powerful bureaucracies. The result is continuity.

As noted repeatedly, it matters little which party is in power. Once in power they become incumbent parties. Therefore, though one may see some diversity in the top slots (of the bureaucracy) the president, vice president, secretaries of defense and state, and so forth have remarkably similar backgrounds. Yes, Barack Obama shows that an African American from a broken home can become president. (But even Barack Obama was a Harvard lawyer, that is, a fairly typical president not unlike other presidents.) Thus, individual differences have rarely evidenced themselves in U.S. foreign policy.

That leaves role, which has been mentioned at various times in the previous chapters. Role is difficult to measure but seems quite important in the continuity seen in U.S. foreign policy. Whatever differences existed between say candidate Jimmy Carter and candidate Ronald Reagan or candidate George W. Bush and candidate Barack Obama, once in office they become remarkably similar in outlook. They assume the role of the presidency (not party or individual) and they tend to do what their predecessors did. The result again is continuity.

THE NEXT PRESIDENT

The question becomes whether one might reasonably expect to see something different in the future? After all, at this writing, America (and many of its enemies and allies) await President Donald Trump and his policies. Trump appears to be less loyal to party politics—perhaps less to incumbency?—and he has demonstrated some independence from strict party loyalty. First, Trump has been aligned with both Republicans and Democrats at various times during his political career. Second, he seems far less disciplined than most presidents-elect. He continued to respond and react on Twitter, apparently with little input from his foreign policy advisers during the campaign and since. In fact, it is not clear that Trump knows the importance of the NSC, though he has appointed two NSC advisers (Mr. Flynn has already been replaced by Mr. McMaster).

Certainly, President Trump has taken unpopular positions among the mainstream of either the Republicans or the Democrats. His positions on immigration have alarmed many as have his familiarity (if not outright admiration) of Vladimir Putin. But it should be remembered that those "extreme" positions, if they are extreme, were proffered mostly during the primary process. The few advisers he has appointed or nominated so far—in terms of foreign policy—seem to be within the compass of past appointees-nominees. Time will tell.

For better or worse, the United States has been on a course of imperium since roughly after World War II. During the Cold War and since the United States has continued to militarize foreign policy, the president has continued to grow more muscular as the Congress has, concomitantly, atrophied. Unless and until Americans realize the trajectory the United States is on in terms of foreign policy, the debate it badly needs to have cannot take place. Eventually—at least if other empires are prologue—the American Security State will struggle to find the resources to continue empire, while maintaining itself as an important democratic state in global affairs. America's resources are not infinite. The only question is when its resources will become so exhausted that it will no longer be able to have the debate. The choice will be made externally.

To be clear, nowhere in this book was it asserted that those who drafted and passed the National Security Act of 1947 did so to create imperium. Rather, it was taken as a stopgap measure and to contain the Soviets. The institutions thereby created proved successful in containing the USSR. But the Cold War consensus also led the United States into the Vietnam War.[10] Somewhere by the late 1960s or early 1970s, a debate about the change of trajectory in U.S. foreign policy was due. Yet no such debate occurred. A brief entrenchment—called the Vietnam "syndrome" by some—gave way to a renewed Cold War and continued militarization. Toward the end of the Cold War, it appeared a debate might finally occur but, alas, yet again events conspired to prevent it. At the very least that debate is well overdue at present.

Notes

PART I

1. The National Security Act of 1947 created the three institutions cited above. However, it was not until the Reorganization Act of 1949 that the National Security Council (NSC) was permanently fixed in the executive branch.

CHAPTER 1

1. Franklin D. Roosevelt, "Fireside Chat," May 26, 1940. University of California, Santa Barbara, The American Presidency Project, http://www.presidency.ucsb.edu/ws/index.php?pid=15959 (accessed December 8, 2016).

2. Franklin D. Roosevelt, "Fireside Chat," December 29, 1940. University of California, Santa Barbara, The American Presidency Project, http://www.presidency.ucsb.edu/ws/index.php?pid=15917 (accessed December 8, 2016).

3. Franklin D. Roosevelt, "Address to Congress Requesting a Declaration of War," December 8, 1941. University of California, Santa Barbara, The American Presidency Project, http://www.presidency.ucsb.edu/ws/index.php?pid=16053 (accessed December 8, 2016).

4. I first saw the Kegley-Wittkopf text in its third edition. I have only a subsequent edition in my possession now and will use it. See Eugene R. Wittkopf, Charles W. Kegley, and James Scott, *American Foreign Policy: Pattern and Process*, sixth edition (Belmont, CA: Thomson-Wadsworth, 2003), p. 14. In earlier editions, the same text was coauthored by Wittkopf and Kegley only. Accordingly, they wrote U.S. foreign policy "embraces the goals that the nation's policymakers seek to attain abroad, the values that give rise to those objectives, and the . . . instruments used to pursue them."

5. Wittkopf and Kegley, *American Foreign Policy*, pp. 14–15. See James Rosenau, "Pre-Theories and Theories of Foreign Policy," in James Rosenau (ed.), *The Scientific Study of Foreign Policy* (New York: Nichols, 1980), pp. 114–167. I hasten to add that

Rosenau and others studying what they called comparative foreign policy asserted that the same inputs affected all nation-state's foreign policy. For present purposes, however, let us assume they affect U.S. foreign policy. I should also note that my mentor in graduate school was Charles F. Hermann, one of a group of foreign policy scholars who, with Rosenau, formed what became known as comparative foreign policy studies. They were interested in using then new technologies (the computer that many college campuses had) to quantify the foreign policy of all the system's many factors and to make generalizations about foreign policy generally.

6. In the recent presidential election, some accused candidate Donald Trump of having less than a proper presidential temperament. Those critics were largely saying that Donald Trump did not fit the role of the president, whether they realized it or not.

7. I am reversing a famous quote by America's sixth president, President John Quincy Adams, whose speech to the U.S. House on the 50th anniversary of the American Revolution (July 4, 1821) said, America had "abstained from interference in the concerns of others" and that wherever "the standard of freedom and independence" had been unfurled "there will be [America's], her benedictions and her prayers" and then said, "But she goes not in search of monsters to destroy. . . ." The Miller Center, University of Virginia, http://millercenter.org/president/speeches/speech-3484 (accessed August 20, 2015).

8. For example, Pax Britannica ruled a vast colonial system. The United States by contrast seems far less likely to covet others' resources or if it does it buys them rather than takes them.

9. Notable exceptions exist. For my generation, Bob Woodward has made a living reporting and writing tell-all biographies of U.S. foreign policy. Forty years ago, there were no Bob Woodward's around.

10. For a more recent example, FDR used an argument made by Dean Acheson in the *New York Times* as justification for giving U.S. destroyers to Great Britain despite the Neutrality Acts and congressional refusal to cut a deal with United Kingdom for access to Caribbean Islands. See Doris Kearns Goodman's *No Ordinary Times* (New York: Simon and Schuster, 1995), Chapter 6 "I Am a Juggler," p. 283, eBook edition.

11. *Oxford English Dictionary*, Mac Edition, Version 2.2.1 (copyright, 2004–2014).

12. It may be worth noting that Senator Paul (like his father) wrongly ascribes the rise of America's National Security State to the War Powers Act (1971). In fact, the War Powers Act was an attempt by Congress to wrest back power that backfired and demonstrated just how powerful the presidency had become. Rather than constrain the presidency the War Powers Act created an all-powerful president for 60 (and possibly 90 days). It is somewhat mystifying that Senator Paul carries on about the War Powers Act and appears ill-informed of the National Security Act of 1947.

13. See M. Kent Bolton, *U.S. National Security and Foreign Policymaking after 9/11: Present at the Re-Creation* (Lanham, MD: Rowman & Littlefield, 2008), see Table 3.1, p. 43 (years 1991, 1992, and 1993).

CHAPTER 2

1. Doris Kearns Goodwin, *No Ordinary Time: Franklin and Eleanor Roosevelt* (New York: Simon and Schuster), Chapter 24 "Everybody Is Crying," pp. 688–689 of 997, eBook edition.

2. David McCullough, *Truman* (New York: Simon and Schuster, 2015), Chapter 8 "Numbered Days," pp. 410–412 of 1229, eBook edition.

3. See Loch Johnson, *American Foreign Policy and the Challenges of Leadership* (Oxford: Oxford University Press, 2015).

4. FDR died in April 1945 just two months after the Yalta Summit. Thus, both FDR and Churchill were replaced by new leaders between the end of Yalta and the end of Potsdam, respectively.

5. Some revisionist historians forget that in early 1949, Stalin called capitalism and communism incompatible and war between the two inevitable. See David McCullough's *Truman* (New York: Simon and Schuster), Chapter 11, p. 589, eBook edition. Where McCullough writes, "in a rare public address in Moscow on February 9, Stalin declared that communism and capitalism were incompatible and that another war was inevitable."

6. See "Arthur Vandenberg Biography," United States Senate, http://www.senate.gov/artandhistory/history/common/generic/Featured_Bio_Vandenberg.htm (accessed May 25, 2016).

7. I have written about the Cold War consensus elsewhere as have others. I first saw the Cold War consensus articulated in Richard Melanson's *American Foreign Policy since the Vietnam War*, third edition (New York: M.E. Sharpe, 2000). Even before Melanson's two scholars who studied the Vietnam War articulated the consensus, though they did not call it precisely thus. See Leslie Gelb and Richard Betts, *The Irony of Vietnam: The System Worked* (Washington, DC: Brookings, 1979).

8. Harry S. Truman, *Memoirs by Harry Truman: Volume Two, Years of Trial and Hope* (New York: Doubleday, 1956), p. 120.

9. Truman, *Years of Trial and Hope*, pp. 331 and 337, respectively.

10. George F. Kennan, "The Sources of Soviet Conduct," *Foreign Affairs*, July 1947. Kennan published his analysis in Foreign Affairs anonymously using the pseudonym "X."

11. Kennan, "The Sources of Soviet Conduct."

12. The U.S. National Archives, *The U.S. Constitution*, Article II, Section Two (first paragraph) and Article I, Section Eight, respectively, http://www.archives.gov/exhibits/charters/print_friendly.html (accessed October 13, 2013).

13. See Dean Acheson, *Present at the Creation: My Years in the State Department* (New York: W.W. Norton & Company, 1969); Clark Clifford (with Richard Holbrooke), *Counsel to the President: A Memoir* (New York: Random House, 1991).

14. Clifford, *Counsel to the President*, pp. 156–157.

15. Clifford, *Counsel to the President*, p. 157.

16. Clifford, *Counsel to the President*, p. 158.

17. Clifford, *Counsel to the President*, p. 159.

18. Clifford, *Counsel to the President*, p. 160.

19. Clifford, *Counsel to the President*, p. 161.

20. M. Kent Bolton, *U.S. National Security and Foreign Policymaking after 9/11: Present at the Re-Creation* (Lanham, MD: Rowman & Littlefield, 2007), pp. 53–58.

21. Bolton, *U.S. National Security and Foreign Policymaking after 9/11*, Chapter 4.

22. Three are worth noting. John Prados, *Keepers of the Keys* (New York: William Morrow and Company, 1991) and Loch Johnson and Karl Inderfruth, *Fateful Decisions: Inside the National Security Council* (Oxford: Oxford University Press, 2004). Also, a memoir of a former NSC staffer was written but a memoir is not a study. See David Rothkopf, *Running the World: The Inside Story of the National Security Council and the Architects of American Power* (New York: Public Affairs, 2004).

23. It would be more accurate to say that the National Security Act of 1947 and the Reorganization Act of 1949 together created all these institutions including placing the NSC inside the executive branch of the presidency but I shall not spend time on the Reorganization Act of 1949. The National Security Act has been amended several times since including the Intelligence Reform and Terrorism Prevention Act of 2004 mentioned multiple times in this text.

PART II

1. See Alexander L. George, "Case Studies and Theory Development: The Method of Structured, Focused Comparison." Paper Presented to the Second Annual Symposium on Information Processing in Organizations, Carnegie-Mellon University, October 15-16, 1982.

2. Richard A. Melanson, *American Foreign Policy since the Vietnam War: The Search for Consensus from Nixon to Clinton* (London: M.E. Sharpe, 2000), pp. vii-x.

3. To be clear, the NSC principals and deputies committees did not exist per se until the George H.W. Bush administration. However, what evolved by the early 1960s was what I shall call the NSC principals—meaning, the members and advisers specified in the National Security Act of 1947 and additional ad hoc (rather than statutory) members. For instance, anyone who has read about the Cuban Missile Crisis is aware that the Kennedy administration created an ad hoc committee called the executive committee (known as the ExCom), which was effectively NSC principals as well as some NSC deputies and others. Johnson continued this practice and what may be called roughly the NSC principals and other committees as well as growing NSC staffers existed thereafter. Thus, in some of the earlier case studies, I will use NSC principals and NSC members synonymously. The reader will see in the earliest case studies I simply list Question 1 (A, B, and C) and discuss the NSC changes in fairly brief terms.

CHAPTER 3

1. Harry S. Truman, *Memoirs by Harry S. Truman, Volume I: Years of Decision* (New York: Doubleday, 1955). In the first chapter of volume I, Truman described a brief meeting with Roosevelt in late February (possibly February 27, 1945). The meeting was to discuss Roosevelt's upcoming speech to a Joint Session of Congress to explain the deals struck at Yalta just weeks earlier. Then Truman briefly met with Roosevelt again on March 1, 1945, the day of the speech as the president arrived on Capitol Hill. Truman says he was terribly concerned about how Roosevelt looked and was anxious to relieve him of burdens so his health would return (as it had on similar occasions). Truman wrote: Roosevelt "left Washington for the South [Georgia] on March 30, 1945." Then in a new paragraph that consists of one sentence wrote, "I never saw or spoke with him again," 1–4; quotes from p. 4.

2. Truman, *Years of Decision*, p. 13.

3. David McCullough, *Truman* (New York: Simon and Schuster, 1991), Chapters 8 and 9, eBook edition. The quote of Stimson is in the first five pages of Chapter 9, 730.

4. That the People's Republic of China and the USSR formed a monolith proved wildly pessimistic as they worked together but also clashed in many ways. However, they were perceived as monolithic until the late 1950s.

5. See John Prados, *Keepers of the Keys* (New York: Morrow and Sons, 1991), compare Chapters 2 "Fits on the Table" and 3 "You Could Depend on Him." Likewise, David Rothkofp, *Running the World: The Inside Story of the National Security Council and the Architects of American Power* (New York: Public Affairs, 2005), p. 57.

6. M. Kent Bolton, *U.S. National Security and Foreign Policymaking after 9/11: Present at the Re-Creation* (Lanham, MD: Rowman & Littlefield, 2007), pp. 59–63.

7. Prados, *Keepers of the Keys*, p. 63.

8. Prados, *Keepers of the Keys*, pp. 54–56.

9. Harry S. Truman, *Memoirs by Harry S. Truman, Volume II: Years of Trial and Hope* (Garden City, NJ: Doubleday, 1956), pp. 241–242.

10. Meaning Forrestal with Johnson. See McCollough, *Truman*, Chapter 15 "Iron Man," p. 1537, eBook edition.

11. McCullough, *Truman*, p. 1570.

12. Truman, *Years of Trial and Hope*, p. 328.

13. Truman, *Years of Trial and Hope*, p. 332.

14. Truman, *Years of Trial and Hope*, p. 333.

15. Truman, *Years of Trial and Hope*, p. 333.

16. See Bolton, *U.S. National Security and Foreign Policymaking after 9/11*, pp. 81–63.

17. Stephen E. Ambrose, *Eisenhower: Solider and President* (New York: Simon and Schuster, 1990), p. 716 of 1365.

18. The Defense Department featured a piece on America's first 14 chairmen of the Joint Chiefs in August 1999. The list began with General Omar Bradley, America's first and concluded with General Sheldon in Clinton's second term. See Defense Department, "The Chairmen of the Joint Chiefs of Staff," August 10, 1999, http://www.defense.gov/news/newsarticle.aspx?id=43048 (accessed July 22, 2015).

19. Ambrose, *Eisenhower*, p. 589.

20. Robert E. Cutler, "The Development of the National Security Council," *Foreign Affairs*, April 1956, http://www.foreignaffairs.com/articles/71255/robert-cutler/the-development-of-the-national-security-council (accessed June 12, 2009).

21. See Townsend Hoopes, *The Devil and John Foster Dulles* (New York: Little, Brown & Company, 1971).

22. Ambrose, *Eisenhower*, p. 640.

23. Ambrose, *Eisenhower*, pp. 680–683.

24. Ambrose, *Eisenhower*, pp. 680–683.

25. Ambrose, *Eisenhower*, pp. 683–684.

26. Ambrose, *Eisenhower*, p. 684.

27. Ambrose, *Eisenhower*, p. 685.

28. Harry S. Truman, *Memoirs by Harry S. Truman, Volume I: The White House Years: Mandate for Change, 1953–1956* (New York: Doubleday, 1956), p. 421.

29. Richard H. Immerman, *The CIA in Guatemala* (Austin: University of Texas Press, 1982) and John Prados, *President's Secret Wars* (New York: William Morris and Company, 1986). They disagree on some specifics; while Immerman says August, Prados thinks it was a slow-building decision over the summer.

30. M. Kent Bolton, "How Decision Time and Degree of Anticipation Affect the Decision-Making Process as U.S. Decision Makers Confront Various Foreign Policy Challenges," PhD Dissertation, The Ohio State University, 1992, pp. 374–381.

31. Eisenhower, *The White House Years: Mandate for Change, 1953–1956*, p. 424.

32. Richard H. Immerman, *The CIA in Guatemala* (Austin: University of Texas Press, 1982), pp. 156–157.

33. President Eisenhower's Farewell Address, "Reading Copy," Dwight D. Eisenhower Presidential Library and Museum and Boyhood Home, https://www.eisenhower.archives.gov/research/online_documents/farewell_address/Reading_Copy.pdf (accessed June 7, 2016).

34. Dwight D. Eisenhower, Transcript of Dwight D. Eisenhower's Farewell Speech, January 16, 1961. See Dwight D. Eisenhower Library and Museum, http://www.eisenhower.archives.gov/research/online_documents/farewell_address.html (accessed February 20, 2015).

CHAPTER 4

1. Robert S. McNamara will forever be associated with the Vietnam War but under his leadership, the Defense Department grew into a massive bureaucracy with many more employees and a budget that dwarfed the State Department by 10 times. The secretary of defense, likewise, became more important than the secretary of state during the Kennedy and Johnson administrations. Importantly, for the present study the NSC advisor, McGeorge Bundy also became a full-fledged participant in what had evolved into the NSC principals.

2. These ideas came from Senator Henry M. Jackson's Subcommittee on National Policy Machinery, Organizing for National Security, three volumes, published by the U.S. Senate, "Committee on Government Operations," 86th and 87th Congresses (Washington: Government Printing Office, 1961). I mentioned Senator Jackson's report briefly in a previous chapter.

3. Jackson, "Committee on Government Operations."

4. Robert S. McNamara and Brian Van De Mark, *In Retrospect: The Tragedy and Lessons of Vietnam* (New York: Times Books, 1995), pp. 13–14.

5. The NSC principals committee was not formally created until President George H. W. Bush but in the Kennedy administration subgroups of NSC members met that presaged the NSC principals committee to some extent.

6. Arthur M. Schlesinger Jr., *A Thousand Days: John F. Kennedy in the White House* (Boston: Houghton Mifflin, 1965), p. 210. The chapter "Gathering Forces" is particularly good on the Kennedy brain trust.

7. See Cecil V. Crabb Jr. and Kevin V. Mulcahy, *Presidents and Foreign Policy Making: From FDR to Reagan* (Baton Rouge: Louisiana State University Press, 1986), p. 260.

8. McNamara, *In Retrospect*, pp. 94–95. Chapter 3 "The Fateful Fall of 1963" where the fiasco of the Diem coup is discussed and where Rusk is shown as indecisive and unable to control his own employees, Roger Hilsman and Ambassador Henry Cabot Lodge, who McNamara concludes pushed the Diem coup, while NSC principals were out of town one weekend. Incidentally, the story does not wash. The weekend the NSC principals were away was in August 1963. The coup did not occur until early November, just three weeks before Kennedy was assassinated. If neither Rusk nor other NSC principals, including the president, failed to get Hilsman and Lodge under control, the entire NSC principals committee appears incapable of bending the two men to the NSC's will. That is more an indictment of the NSC than of Dean Rusk.

9. U.S. State Department, Historical Documents, *Foreign Relations of the United States Volume XXIV*, "Laos Crisis," Document Two, Date January 3, 1961, https://history.state.gov/historicaldocuments/frus1961–63v24/d2 (accessed February 26, 2015).

10. Schlesinger, *A Thousand Days*, p. 235.

11. Irving Janis, *Groupthink: Psychological Studies of Policy Decisions and Fiascoes* (Boston: Houghton Mifflin, 1971).

12. Janis, *Groupthink*, pp. 15–17. I should note that others question whether Robert Kennedy attended. In Peter Wyden's *Bay of Pigs: The Untold Story* (New York: Simon and Schuster, 1979), p. 289; the author says the attorney general was not there.

13. Janis, *Groupthink*.

14. The *Pentagon Papers* come in multiple editions, including a *New York Times* and *Washington Post* edition. They are collections of documents begun during the time of McNamara in Pentagon, under the editorship of Leslie Gelb. The version used, hereafter, is the original volumes published by the Government Printing Office. U.S. Defense Department, *United States-Vietnam Relations, 1945–1967*, edited by Leslie Gelb, Books Three and Four (Washington, DC: Government Printing Office, 1971). I will refer to them as the *Pentagon Papers* because they became known by that name. But I wish to distinguish between the assemblage of documents published with editorial comments by the aforementioned newspapers and the original 13 volumes.

15. McNamara, *In Retrospect*.

16. Stephen Ambrose, *Eisenhower: Soldier and President* (New York: Simon and Schuster, 1991), Chapter 14, "McCarthy and Vietnam."

17. McNamara, *In Retrospect*, p. 29. Both the block quote and the paraphrase are about underlying assumptions.

18. National Archive, *Pentagon Papers*, http://media.nara.gov/research/pentagon-papers/Pentagon-Papers-Part-IV-B-5.pdf, p. ii (accessed May 19, 2015).

19. DOD, U.S.-Vietnam Relations (*Pentagon Papers*) Book Two, Part VI, B, 3. Although I have the hard copies of all the volumes, for ease of use I will cite the National Archives Copies online at http://www.archives.gov/research/pentagon-papers/.

20. National Archive, *Pentagon Papers*, http://media.nara.gov/research/pentagon-papers/Pentagon-Papers-Part-IV-B-5.pdf, p. 1 (accessed May 19, 2015).

21. McNamara, *In Retrospect*, p. 52. Averell is spelled Averill elsewhere.

22. McNamara, *In Retrospect*, pp. 52–54.

23. McNamara, *In Retrospect*, pp. 53–54.

24. National Archive, *Pentagon Papers*, http://media.nara.gov/research/pentagon-papers/Pentagon-Papers-Part-IV-B-5.pdf, p. vii (accessed May 19, 2015).

25. National Archive, *Pentagon Papers*, http://media.nara.gov/research/pentagon-papers/Pentagon-Papers-Part-IV-B-5.pdf, p. viii (accessed May 19, 2015).

26. I found no evidence the U.S. was complicit in the assassination of Diem. On the contrary, the NSC members seem to have been shocked by the brutal assassination. One might argue the CIA (or at least one or two CIA operatives) were involved in some way or foresaw the assassination but I found no evidence of it directly.

27. McNamara, *In Retrospect*, p. 311. The chapter is called, appropriately, "Estrangement and Departure: May 20, 1967-February 29, 1968," and McNamara makes clear he was increasingly estranged from the president. But he also hints earlier in the chapter that once McGeorge Bundy left, things deteriorated.

28. Jack Valenti, a political adviser to Johnson gave an interview to the George Washington University's National Archives Project. In it he talks of his conversation with President Johnson after several successive coups whereupon Valenti

said: "And I can remember sitting with him one day when he got news that there was another coup in Vietnam and another general ha[d] ascended to the power platform and he frustrated said, hot-damn I'm getting sick and tired of this God-damn coup shit in Vietnam, it's got to stop." National Archives, Episode 11, Vietnam "Interview with Jack Valenti," http://nsarchive.gwu.edu/coldwar/interviews/episode-11/valenti2.html (accessed May 20, 2015). The interview from the beginning may be found on http://nsarchive.gwu.edu/coldwar/interviews/episode-11/valenti1.html.

29. McNamara, *In Retrospect*, p. 129; McNamara says the two covert missions were approved in January 1964. The next page (130) describes the DeSoto missions.

30. McNamara, *In Retrospect*, pp. 129–131.

31. McNamara, *In Retrospect*, p. 132.

32. McNamara, *In Retrospect*, p. 141. The *Pentagon Papers* account is essentially the same minus the updated information (no second attack). See National Archives, *Pentagon Papers*, V.C. 2 (b), http://media.nara.gov/research/pentagon-papers/Pentagon-Papers-Part-IV-C-2b.pdf, pp. 1–15 (accessed May 18, 2015).

33. National Archives, *Pentagon Papers*, IV.C.2(c), http://media.nara.gov/research/pentagon-papers/Pentagon-Papers-Part-IV-C-2c.pdf (accessed May 18, 2015), p. v.

34. McNamara, *In Retrospect*, pp. 159–160.

35. McNamara, *In Retrospect*, p. 158.

36. McNamara, *In Retrospect*, pp. 160–161.

37. McNamara, *In Retrospect*, p. 162.

38. McNamara, *In Retrospect*, p. 163.

39. McNamara, *In Retrospect*, pp. 164–65.

40. McNamara, *In Retrospect*, p. 165.

41. McNamara, *In Retrospect*, pp. 167–168, "Fork-in-the-Road" Memorandum, paragraphs I through V.

42. McNamara, *In Retrospect*, pp. 167–168, "Fork-in-the-Road" Memorandum, paragraph VI.

43. McNamara, *In Retrospect*, pp. 167–168, "Fork-in-the-Road" Memorandum, paragraphs VI through VIII.

44. McNamara, *In Retrospect*, p. 168.

45. McNamara, *In Retrospect*, p. 169.

46. Crabb and Mulcahy, *Presidents and Foreign Policy Making*, p. 251.

47. Stephen E. Ambrose, *Nixon: The Triumph of the Politician, 1962–1972* (New York: Simon and Schuster, 1997), Chapter 7 "The Primaries," p. 357, eBook edition.

48. Alexander L. George, *Presidential Decisionmaking in Foreign Policy* (Boulder: Westview Press, 1980), p. 155.

49. George, *Presidential Decisionmaking in Foreign Policy*, p. 155. Also see Seymour M. Hersh, *The Price of Power: Kissinger in the Nixon White House* (New York: Summit, 1983), pp. 28–29. Morton Halperin's role is discussed by Hersh.

50. M. Kent Bolton, *U.S. National Security and Foreign Policymaking after 9/11: Present at the Re-Creation* (Lanham, MD: Rowan & Littlefield, 2007).

51. Bolton, *U.S. National Security and Foreign Policymaking after 9/1*, especially Chapter 4.

52. Ambrose, *Nixon*, p. 615 (default, two-page view).

53. Ambrose, *Nixon*, p. 626 (default, two-page view). Also, see Joan Hoff, *Nixon Reconsidered* (New York: Basic Books, 1994), p. 177. Nixon is quoted telling

Haldeman, "I call it my madman theory Bob, I want the North Vietnamese to believe I've reached the point where I might do anything to stop the war," p. 177.

54. Ambrose, *Nixon*, p. 626 (default, two-page view).

55. Ambrose, *Nixon*, p. 626 (default, two-page view).

56. Ambrose, *Nixon*, p. 627 (default, two-page view).

57. Ambrose, *Nixon*, pp. 627–628 (default, two-page view).

58. Ambrose, *Nixon*, pp. 630–631 (default, two-page view).

59. Paul Bedard, "Reagan's Son Claims His Dad Had Alzheimer's as President: Doctors Dismiss Claims the Gipper Suffered from Alzheimer's Disease While in the White House," *U.S News and World Report*, January 14, 2011. Online version available at http://www.usnews.com/news/blogs/washington-whispers/2011/01/14/reagan-son-claims-dad-had-alzheimers-as-president (accessed May 12, 2015).

60. Debra Whitefield, "Analysts Debate Value of Firm Hand: Aloof Reagan Style, Flaw or Model of Management," *Los Angeles Times*, March 12, 1987, http://articles.latimes.com/1987–03–12/news/mn-9321_1_management (accessed May 21, 2015).

61. See Richard A. Melanson, *American Foreign Policy since the Vietnam War: The Search for Consensus from Nixon to Clinton*, third edition (New York: M.E. Sharpe, 2000). Melanson wrote that apart from opposition to the Law of the Sea Treaty, withholding arrears from the UN and Libya (and a good deal of conservative rhetoric), "the Reagan presidency appeared devoid of a foreign policy." He also wrote that the "troika" of Meese, Deaver, and Baker kept foreign policy on a short tether (pp. 136–139). He also concluded that Reagan's "hands-off leadership style, left the White House Troika" Weinberger, Casey, and first secretary of state Alexander Haig vying for control of foreign policy (p. 139); it is no great leap to infer it continued into the subsequent few years during which Iran-Contra occurred.

62. John Tower et al., *The Tower Commission Report* (New York: Bantam-New York Times, 1987), p. xviii.

63. To the best of my recollection, *The New Republic* was the first to use the moniker of Iranamok back in 1987. My recollection is they held a contest and someone came up with the name as being more appropriate than the Iran-Contra scandal. The only reference I found for it was from the inimitable Eric Alterman, "Inside Ollie's Mind," *The New Republic*, February 6, 1987. http://www.newrepublic.com/article/89594/inside-ollies-mind-oliver-north (accessed May 22, 2015).

64. This has long presented a contradiction in U.S. foreign policy. On the one hand, the United States values democracy and democratic governance. On the other, during the Cold War, the United States supported regimes that were anticommunist, that were anything but democratic. In fact, in the post-Cold War era, the United States had struggled with the same dilemma.

65. John Tower, Edmund Muskie, and Brent Scowcroft, The President's Special Review Board, the Full Text, *The Tower Commission Report* (New York: Bantam-New York Times, 1987), p. xi.

66. John Tower, Edmund Muskie, and Brent Scowcroft, The President's Special Review Board, the Full Text, *The Tower Commission Report* (New York: Bantam-New York Times, 1987), pp. 23–30.

67. Bob Woodward, *Veil: The Secret Wars of the CIA 1981–1987* (New York: Simon and Schuster, 1987).

68. Woodward, *Veil*, p. 169.

69. Woodward, *Veil*, p. 283.

70. Woodward, *Veil*, p. 284.

71. Ann Wroe, *Lives, Lies and the Iran Contra Affair* (London: IB Tauris, 1991).

72. See Department of Defense, The Economy Act Orders, 31 USC, §1535 and 1536, http://comptroller.defense.gov/Portals/45/documents/fmr/archive/11aarch/11a_03_042000.pdf (accessed May 22, 2015).

CHAPTER 5

1. See M. Kent Bolton, *The Logic of World Politics in the New World Dis-Order* (San Diego: Cognella Press, 2014). Particularly, the chapter on American ethos.

2. The figure accounts for inflation. It comes from M. Kent Bolton, *U.S. National Security and Foreign Policymaking after 9/11: Present at the Re-Creation* (Lanham, MD: Rowman & Littlefield, 2007), pp. 41–45.

3. George H. W. Bush and Brent Scowcroft, *A World Transformed: The Collapse of the Soviet Empire, the Unification of Germany, Tiananmen Square, the Gulf War* (New York: Alford A. Knopf, 1998), pp. 19–20.

4. Bush and Scowcroft, *A World Transformed*, pp. 21–22.

5. Bush and Scowcroft, *A World Transformed*, p. 21.

6. As noted in earlier chapters, the NSC principals had evolved earlier than the Bush administration though they were called by various other names. Early in the H. W. Bush administration the NSC produced a work product. In the Bush 41 administration, the work product was called National Security Presidential Decisions and NSPD 1 may be found at the Federation of American Scientists website, U.S. presidential decisions, https://fas.org/irp/offdocs/nspd/nspd-1.htm (accessed June 2, 2016).

7. Bob Woodward, *The Commanders* (New York: Simon and Schuster, 1991), pp. 86–87.

8. The DCI no longer exists. The 2004 Intelligence Reform and Terrorism Prevention Act (an amendment to the National Security Act of 1947) created a new position that supplanted the DCI. The new position is the Director of National Intelligence. See Bolton, *U.S. Foreign and National Security Policymaking after 9/11*.

9. Woodward, *The Commanders*, p. 91.

10. Woodward, *The Commanders*, p. 140.

11. See Cornell Legal Information Institute, 50 U.S. Code § 3093, "Presidential Approval and Reporting of Covert Actions," https://www.law.cornell.edu/uscode/text/50/3093 (accessed June 21, 2016).

12. Woodward, *The Commanders*, pp. 146–171.

13. Nick Williams Jr. and Daniel Williams, "Iraq Threatens Israel with the Use of Nerve Gas," *The Los Angeles Times*, April 3, 1990, http://articles.latimes.com/1990–04–03/news/mn-702_1_gas-attack (accessed May 24, 2015).

14. Woodward, *The Commanders*, pp. 226–227.

15. Bush and Scowcroft, *A World Transformed*, pp. 302–303.

16. For those wondering, yes the same Robert Gates who later became President George W. Bush's (Bush 43) second secretary of defense. In fact, he stayed on during the first couple of years of the Obama administration. If one studies U.S. foreign policy, one sees pretty quickly the same pools of foreign policy "experts" return to government time and again. It is another reason for continuity in U.S. foreign policy.

17. Woodward, *The Commanders*, p. 227.

18. Woodward, *The Commanders*, p. 228.

19. Woodward, *The Commanders*, p. 229.

20. Woodward, *The Commanders*, p. 229.

21. Woodward, *The Commanders*, p. 231.

22. Woodward, *The Commanders*, pp. 232–234.

23. Woodward, *The Commanders*, pp. 236–237.

24. Woodward, *The Commanders*, p. 237.

25. Woodward, *The Commanders*, p. 238.

26. Another holdover was Richard Clarke who eventually became an NSC principal in the Clinton administration. But he was a relatively low-level staffer when Clinton took over the presidency.

27. See Presidential Review Directive/NSC-1, "U.S. Policy Regarding the Situation in Former Yugoslavia," January 22, 1993. The copy I found can be seen at the Federation of American Scientists, Intelligence Resource Program, http://fas.org/irp/offdocs/prd/prd-1.pdf (accessed May 11, 2015).

28. See Presidential Review Directive/NSC-1, "U.S. Policy Regarding the Situation in Former Yugoslavia," January 22, 1993, p. 1.

29. William G. Hyland, *Clinton's World: Remaking U.S. Foreign Policy* (Westport, CT: Praeger, 1999) (Kindle Locations 437–440).

30. Hyland, *Clinton's World* (Kindle Locations 452–454).

31. Hyland, *Clinton's World* (Kindle Locations 460–463).

32. See Dusko Doder, "Yugoslavia: New War, Old Hatreds," *Foreign Policy*, June 19, 1993, http://foreignpolicy.com/1993/06/19/yugoslavia-new-war-old-hatreds/ (accessed July 28, 2016).

33. Hyland, *Clinton's World* (Kindle Locations 523–525).

34. BBC News, "Russia Condemns NATO at the UN," http://news.bbc.co.uk/2/hi/europe/303127.stm (accessed December 13, 2016).

35. Hyland, *Clinton's World* (Kindle Locations 527).

36. Hyland, *Clinton's World* (Kindle Locations 517–518).

37. Hyland, *Clinton's World* (Kindle Locations 520).

38. Hyland, *Clinton's World* (Kindle Locations 537).

39. I have defined jihadi terrorism as a uniquely Sunni-Salafi-takfiri phenomenon. While there are other religious terrorists (in Islam, Christianity, and Judaism), the issues the United States has had with Iran and Hezbollah are much more in the realm of traditional foreign policy challenges. They are considered by the U.S. government state-sponsored terrorists and therefore traditional statecraft (deterrence, overt threats, retaliation, etc.) are useful. For Sunni-Salafi-takfiri jihadis, they are transnational (crossing multiple state borders) and their ideology is such that they embrace martyrdom, making traditional instruments of statecraft problematic. In 1983—as noted elsewhere here—the U.S. Marines (and French Paratroopers) were attacked in Lebanon. Again, however, they were considered state-sponsored terrorists.

40. Daniel Benjamin and Steven Simon, *Age of Sacred Terror* (New York: Random House, 2002), p. viii, eBook edition.

41. Benjamin and Simon, *Age of Sacred Terror*, p. 230.

42. See the National Commission on Terrorist Attacks (the 9/11 Commission), The 9/11 Commission Report, http://www.911commission.gov/report/911Report.pdf (published and accessed July 7, 2004), Chapters 6 and 7.

43. The 9/11 Commission Report, pp. 213–214.

44. The 9/11 Commission Report, p. 277 "Time Runs Out."

45. "The 9/11 Commission Report," The 9–11 Commission, http://www.9–11commission.gov/report/911Report.pdf (accessed July 7, 2004).

46. The reader may recall that I noted earlier that the director of national intelligence (DCI) was supplanted by the newly created director of national intelligence (DNI) as a result of the 2004 Intelligence Reform and Terrorism Prevention Act (IRTPA).

47. The trilogy was, Bob Woodward, *Bush at War* (New York: Simon and Schuster, 2003), *Plan of Attack* (New York: Simon and Schuster, 2004), and *State of Denial* (New York: Simon and Schuster, 2007).

48. See Bob Woodward, *Obama's Wars* (New York: Simon and Schuster, 2010), Chapter 7.

49. Robert Gates, *Duty: Memoirs of a Secretary at War* (New York: Alfred A. Knopf, 2014), p. 773, eBook edition. The quote reads: "I would learn only later that this was the first time a wartime commander had been relieved since Truman fired Douglas MacArthur in 1951."

50. Bob Woodward, *Obama's Wars*, pp. 117–118.

51. Bob Woodward, *Obama's Wars*, Chapter 14 and Chapters 15–20, especially pp. 278–281, 289–292, and 299–309.

52. Robert M. Gates, *Duty*, Chapter 10, pp. 686–792. See 743 for his thinking on resignation.

CHAPTER 6

1. The proliferation of the intelligence community was demonstrated by Dana Priest and William Arkin, "Top Secret America," *Washington Post*, July 2010, http://projects.washingtonpost.com/top-secret-america/ (accessed again on December 14, 2016).

2. See *The War Powers Act*, Library of Congress, https://www.loc.gov/law/help/war-powers.php (accessed December 14, 2016).

3. The end of the Cold War can be dated differently. By the time Premier Gorbachev announced the Soviet Army would no longer maintain "socialism."

4. M. Kent Bolton, *U.S. National Security and Foreign Policymaking after 9/11: Present at the Re-Creation* (Lanham, MD: Rowman & Littlefield, 2008), pp. 41–45.

5. Alexander George, "Case Studies and Theory Development: The Method of Structured, Focused Comparison," Paper Presented to Second Annual Symposium of Information Processing in Organizations, Carnegie-Mellon University, October 15–16, 1982.

6. David Collier, "Understanding Process Tracing," *PS: Political Science and Politics* 44, no. 4 (2011): 823–830. Or see Stephen Van Evera, *Guide to Methods for Students of Political Science* (Ithaca, NY: Cornell University Press, 1997).

7. Bolton, *U.S. National Security and Foreign Policymaking*, pp. 41–45.

8. Credit for the "perfect disaster" belongs to Irving Janis, *Groupthink: Psychological Studies of Policy Decisions and Fiascoes* (Boston: Houghton Mifflin, 1961).

9. Robert McNamara and Brian Van De Mark, *In Retrospect: The Tragedy and Lessons of Vietnam* (New York: Times Books, 1995), p. 321.

10. Stephen E. Ambrose, *Nixon Volume II: The Triumph of a Politician, 1962–1972* (New York: Simon and Schuster, 1997), Chapter 14 "Transition and Inauguration, November 6, 1968-January 20, 1969."

11. Ambrose, *Nixon Volume II*, Chapter 14.

12. Somewhat more interesting is the fact that "plugging leaks" about Vietnam and even Korea (in spring 1969) resulted in the creation of the "plumbers." The plumbers were to fix internal leaks in the administration and the cover up of many of their activities along with some campaign irregularities led directly to Watergate.

13. John Tower, Edmund Muskie, and Brent Scowcroft, The President's Special Review Board, the Full Text, *The Tower Commission Report* (New York: Bantam-New York Times, 1987), p. xvii.

14. An excellent book detailing what the CSG-TNT accomplished is Daniel Benjamin and Steven Simon, *The Age of Sacred Terror* (New York: Random House, 2002).

15. The 9/11 Commission, *The 9/11 Commission Report*, Chapter 6 "From Threat to Threat," Chapter 7 "The Attack Looms," and Chapter 8 "The System Was Blinking Red." I have the original PDF version published by the 9/11 Commission on July 7, 2004, then available at http://www.9–11commission.gov/report/911Report.pdf (I believe it is now available at the National Archives).

16. Sheryl Gale Stolberg, "Obama Defends Strategy in Afghanistan," *New York Times*, August 17, 2009, p. A6.

17. Stolberg, "Obama Defends Strategy in Afghanistan," p. A6.

18. The best account so far is Bob Woodward, *Obama's Wars* (New York: Simon and Schuster, 2010). Former secretary of defense has written his memoirs and he has a chapter that largely agrees with Woodward's observations, though a few differences in the two accounts exist. See Robert M. Gates, *Duty: Memoirs of a Secretary at War* (New York: Alfred A. Knopf, 2014), see Chapter 10 "Afghanistan: A House Divided."

19. As of this writing, there has been no woman elected as president. The odds look relatively favorable for Hillary Clinton.

20. See http://www.odni.gov/index.php and http://www.dni.gov/index.php. They point to the same website. Under Intelligence Community and Members of the Intelligence Community, the reader will see all the seals of the agencies and read about their missions.

21. Ole R. Holsti, *Public Opinion and American Foreign Policy* (Ann Arbor: University of Michigan Press, 1996). Also John E. Rielly, ed., *American Public Opinion and US Foreign Policy, 1987* (Chicago: Chicago Council on Foreign Relations, 1987). Also, Eugene Wittkopf, *Faces of Internationalism: Public Opinion and American Foreign Policy* (Durham, NC: Duke University Press, 1990).

22. Walter Lippmann, *Public Opinion* (New York: Transaction Publishers, 1946).

23. Reporters like Bob Woodward have written about the NSC principals of various administrations and even addressed amendments to the National Security Act (such as the Goldwater-Nichols Act) but have not put the pieces together in their reporting. It is probably because Woodward's purpose was to expose foibles of specific administrations and not unearth the story of the National Security Act. Dana Priest and others have also written about one or two things created by the act. See Bob Woodward, *The Commanders* (New York: Simon and Schuster, 1991).

24. So far only men have been elected president so he is the appropriate pronoun.

25. I want to take this opportunity to again thank Praeger Security International (http://psi.praeger.com/help.aspx) for the opportunity they gave me to write this book. I have desired to write it for some 20 years.

CHAPTER 7

1. M. Kent Bolton, *U.S. National Security and Foreign Policymaking after 9/11: Present at the Re-Creation* (Lanham, MD: Rowman & Littlefield, 2008), Chapters 3 and 4 and throughout.

2. For instance, Loch Johnson divides U.S. foreign policy into its "formative years," which he dates from the origins until the Spanish-American War in the late 1890s, the Cold War, and what he calls the "fractured world" of the post-Cold War. See Loch K. Johnson, *American Foreign Policy and the Challenges of World Leadership* (New York: Oxford University Press, 2015), see Chapter 2. I have used essentially the same typology with the adjustment that not until World War II did U.S. foreign policy unalterably change. Bolton, *U.S. National Security and Foreign Policymaking after 9/11*, Chapters 1–4.

3. See Doris Kearns Goodwin, *No Ordinary Time: Franklin and Eleanor Roosevelt* (Simon and Schuster, 1995), especially Chapter 8 "The Arsenal of Democracy."

4. President Truman actually had three secretaries of state over the course of his presidency. Recall, Truman finished out Roosevelt's term when FDR died in April (just three months into his fourth term) and he inherited Secretary James Francis Byrnes who served until 1947 when Truman replaced him with Secretary George Marshall. Marshall served as secretary of state through 1949 when Truman made him special ambassador then eventually secretary of defense. The State Department keeps a chronology of its former secretaries. See U.S. Department of State, Former Secretaries of State, http://www.state.gov/secretary/former/ (accessed April 4, 2015).

5. One reason the IC's growth was less dramatic was because it was hidden from the public. Nevertheless, enough has been published to know that it grew into a behemoth whose budget was more in line with the State Department (which has an agency in the IC called INR) than Defense. After 9/11, however, the IC grew dramatically if still hidden or partly hidden. Perhaps the best journalistic coverage was by Dana Priest (former national security reporter) and William Arkin. The series was published during the summer of 2010, called Top Secret America. See *The Washington Post*, http://projects.washingtonpost.com/top-secret-america/ (originally accessed in late June 2010) but re-accessed in September 22, 2016.

6. Samuel P. Huntington, "The Clash of Civilizations?" *Foreign Affairs*, Summer 1993, https://www.foreignaffairs.com/articles/united-states/1993-06-01/clash-civilizations (accessed December 15, 2016). Benjamin R. Barber, "Jihad vs. McWorld," *The Atlantic*, March 1992, http://www.theatlantic.com/magazine/archive/1992/03/jihad-vs-mcworld/3882/ (accessed December 20, 2014). The "punditocracy" was first coined by Eric Alterman, *Sound and the Fury* (Cornell: Cornell University Press, 1999).

7. See Daniel Benjamin and Richard Simon, *Age of Sacred Terror* (New York: Random House, 2003).

8. Bolton, *U.S. National Security and Foreign Policymaking after 9/11*.

9. Walter Lippmann, *Public Opinion* (New York: Greenbook Publications, 2010).

10. In particular, see Leslie Gelb and Richard K. Betts, *The Irony of Vietnam: The System Worked* (Washington, DC: Brookings, 1979). Though the authors never claim Vietnam was the militarization of U.S. foreign policy directly, they indirectly made the case that the Cold War consensus led to the Vietnam War.

Bibliography

Acheson, Dean G. *Present at the Creation*. New York: W.W. Norton & Company, 1969.

Adams, John Quincy. Speech to the U.S. House on the 50th Anniversary of the American Revolution. July 4, 1821. The Miller Center at the University of Virginia. Accessed August 20, 2015. http://millercenter.org/president/speeches/speech-3484.

Alterman, Eric. "Inside Ollie's Mind." *The New Republic*. February 6, 1987. http://www.newrepublic.com/article/89594/inside-ollies-mind-oliver-north.

Alterman, Eric. *The Sound and the Fury: The Washington Punditocracy and the Collapse of American Politics*. New York: Perennial Books, 1993.

Ambrose, Stephen E. *Nixon, Volume Two: The Triumph of a Politician, 1962–1972*. New York: Simon and Schuster, 1989. eBook Edition.

Ambrose, Stephen E. *Eisenhower: Soldier and President*. New York: Simon and Schuster, 1990. eBook Edition.

Bedard, Paul. "Reagan's Son Claims His Dad Had Alzheimer's as President: Doctors Dismiss Claims the Gipper Suffered from Alzheimer's Disease While in the White House." *U.S. News and World Report*. January 14, 2011. Accessed May 12, 2015. http://www.usnews.com/news/blogs/washington-whispers/2011/01/14/reagan-son-claims-dad-had-alzheimers-as-president.

Benjamin, Daniel, and Steven Simon. *The Age of Sacred Terror: Radical Islam's War against America*. New York: Random House, 2002. eBook Edition.

Bolton, M. Kent. "How Decision Time and Degree of Anticipation Affect the Decision-Making Process as U.S. Decision Makers Confront Various Foreign Policy Challenges." PhD Dissertation, The Ohio State University, 1992.

Bolton, M. Kent. *U.S. National Security and Foreign Policymaking after 9/11: Present at the Re-Creation*. Lanham, MD: Rowman & Littlefield, 2008.

Bolton, M. Kent. *The Logic of World Politics in the New World Dis-Order*. La Jolla, CA: Cognella Press, 2013.

British Broadcasting Company. Europe "Russia Condemns NATO at UN." BBC News. March 25, 1999. Accessed July 28, 2016. http://news.bbc.co.uk/2/hi/europe/303127.stm.

Bush, George, and Brent Scowcroft. *A World Transformed: The Collapse of the Soviet Empire, the Unification of Germany, Tiananmen Square and the Gulf War*. New York: Alford A. Knopf, 1998.

Clifford, Clark M., and Richard C. Holbrooke. *Counsel to the President: A Memoir*. New York: Random House, 1991.

Collier, David. "Understanding Process Tracing." *PS: Political Science & Politics* 44, no. 4 (2011): 823–830. doi:10.1017/s1049096511001429.

Cornell University Law School. Legal Information Institute. "50 U.S. Code § 3093—Presidential Approval and Reporting of Covert Actions." LII/Legal Information Institute. Accessed June 21, 2016. https://www.law.cornell.edu/uscode/text/50/3093.

Crabb, Van Meter Cecil, and Kevin V. Mulcahy. *Presidents and Foreign Policy Making from FDR to Reagan*. Baton Rouge: Louisiana State University Press, 1988.

Cutler, Robert. "The Development of the National Security Council." *Foreign Affairs*. October 11, 2011. Accessed June 12, 2009. http://foreignaffairs.com/articles/71255/robert-cutler/the-development-of-the-national-security-council.

Doder, Dusko. "Yugoslavia: New War, Old Hatreds." *Foreign Policy*. June 19, 1993. Accessed July 28, 2016. http://foreignpolicy.com/1993/06/19/yugoslavia-new-war-old-hatreds.

Eisenhower, Dwight D. Dwight D. Eisenhower Presidential Library and Museum and Boyhood Home. Eisenhower, Dwight D. "President Eisenhower's Farewell Address." National Archives and Records Administration. Accessed June 7, 2016. https://www.eisenhower.archives.gov/research/online_documents/farewell_address.html.

Eisenhower, Dwight D. Dwight D. Eisenhower Presidential Library and Museum and Boyhood Home. Eisenhower, Dwight D. "President Eisenhower's Farewell Address." Reading Copy. National Archives and Records Administration. Accessed June 7, 2016. http://www.eisenhower.archives.gov/research/online_documents/farewell_address/Reading_Copy.pdf.

Gates, Robert Michael. *Duty: Memoirs of a Secretary at War*. New York: Alfred A. Knopf, 2014. eBook Edition.

Gelb, Leslie H., and Richard K. Betts. *The Irony of Vietnam: The System Worked*. Washington, DC: Brookings Institution, 1979.

George, Alexander L. "Case Studies and Theory Development." 1982. MS, Paper Presented to the Second Annual Symposium of Information Processing, Carnegie-Mellon University, Pittsburg, PA.

George, Alexander L. *Presidential Decisionmaking in Foreign Policy: The Effective Use of Information and Advice*. Boulder, CO: Westview, 1982.

The George Washington University. "The National Security Archives." Interview with Mr. Jack Valenti. June 3, 1966. Accessed May 20, 2015. http://nsarchive.gwu.edu/coldwar/interviews/episode-11.html.

Goodwin, Doris Kearns. *No Ordinary Times: Franklin and Eleanor Roosevelt*. New York: Simon and Schuster, 1995. eBook Edition, pp. 688–689 of 997.

Halperin, Mark and John Heilemann. *Double Down*. New York: Penguin eBook, 2013.

Heilemann, John, and Mark Halperin. *Game Change: Obama and Clintons, McCain and Palin and the Race of A Lifetime*. New York: Harper-Collins ebook, 2012.

Hersh, Seymour M. *The Price of Power: Kissinger in the Nixon White House*. New York: Summit Books, 1983.

Holsti, Ole R. *Public Opinion and American Foreign Policy*. Ann Arbor: The University of Michigan Press, 1996.

Hoopes, Townsend. *The Devil and John Foster Dulles: The Diplomacy of the Eisenhower Era*. New York: Little, Brown & Company, 1971.

Hyland, William G. *Clinton's World: Remaking American Foreign Policy*. Westport, CT: Praeger, 1999. Kindle Edition.

Immerman, Richard H. *The CIA in Guatemala: The Foreign Policy of Intervention*. Austin: University of Texas Press, 1998.

Janis, Irving Lester. *Groupthink: Psychological Studies of Policy Decisions and Fiascoes*. Boston: Houghton Mifflin, 1972.

Johnson, Loch. *American Foreign Policy and the Challenges of Leadership*. Oxford, England: Oxford University Press, 2015.

Johnson, Loch, and Karl Inderfurth. *Fateful Decisions: Inside the National Security Council*. New York: Oxford University Press, 2004.

Kennan, George F. "The Sources of Soviet Conduct." *Foreign Affairs*. July 1947. Accessed March 16, 2015. https://www.foreignaffairs.com/articles/russian-federation/1947-07-01/sources-soviet-conduct.

"Laos Crisis." Historical Documents, Foreign Relations of the United States. January 3, 1961. Accessed February 26, 2015. https://history.state.gov/historicaldocuments/frus1961-63v24/d2. Volumes 1–12.

Lippmann, Walter. *Public Opinion and Foreign Policy in the United States*. London: Allen and Unwin, 1952.

McCullough, David. *Truman*. New York: Simon and Schuster, 2015. eBook Edition.

McNamara, Robert S., and Brian Van De Mark. *In Retrospect: The Tragedy and Lessons of Vietnam*. New York: Times Books, 1995.

Melanson, Richard A. *American Foreign Policy since the Vietnam War: The Search for Consensus from Richard Nixon to George W. Bush*. Armonk, NY: M.E. Sharpe, 2005.

The National Archives of the United States. The National Archives and Records Administration. "The Constitution of the United States." Accessed October 13, 2013. https://www.archives.gov/founding-docs/constitution.

The National Archives of the United States. The National Archives and Records Administration. *The Pentagon Papers*. June 23, 1971. Accessed May 19, 2015. https://www.archives.gov/research/pentagon-papers. Volumes 1–12.

The National Archives of the United States. The National Archives and Records Administration. "Presidential War Powers." War Powers | Law Library of Congress | Library of Congress. http://www.loc.gov/law/help/war-powers.php.

The National Commission on Terrorist Attacks (the 9/11 Commission). *The 9/11 Commission Final Report*. July 7, 2004. Accessed July 4, 2004. http://www.9-11commission.gov/report/911Report.pdf.

Office of the Director of National Intelligence. "Intelligence Community: Members of the Intelligence Community." No publication date. Accessed January 22, 2017. https://www.odni.gov/index.php/intelligence-community/members-of-the-ic.

Prados, John. *Keeper of the Keys*. New York: William Morrow & Company, 1991.

Prados, John. President's Secret Wars: CIA and Pentagon Covert Operations from World War II through the Persian Gulf War. Chicago: Ivan R. Dee Publisher, 1996.

Reilly, John E. *American Public Opinion and U.S. Foreign Policy, 1987*. Chicago: Chicago Council on Foreign Relations, 1987.

Roosevelt, Franklin D. "Address to Congress Requesting a Declaration of War." From the University of California, Santa Barbara. The American Presidency Project. December 8, 1941. Accessed December 8, 2016. http://www.presidency.ucsb.edu/ws/index.php?pid=16053.

Roosevelt, Franklin D. "Fireside Chat." From the University of California, Santa Barbara. The American Presidency Project. May 26, 1940. Accessed December 8, 2016. http://www.presidency.ucsb.edu/ws/index.php?pid=15959.

Roosevelt, Franklin D. "Fireside Chat." From the University of California, Santa Barbara. The American Presidency Project. December 29, 1940. Accessed December 8, 2016. http://www.presidency.ucsb.edu/ws/index.php?pid=15917.

Rosenau, James. "Pre-Theories and Theories of Foreign Policy" in James Rosenau, *The Scientific Study of Foreign Policy*, 114–167. New York: Nichols, 1980.

Rothkopf, David. *Running the World: The Inside Story of the National Security Council and the Architects of American Power*. New York: Public Affairs, 2004.

Schlesinger, Arthur M. Jr. *A Thousand Days. John F. Kennedy in the White House*. Boston: Houghton Mifflin, 1965.

Stolberg, Sheryl G. "Obama Defends Strategy in Afghanistan." *The New York Times*, August 17, 2009. A6.

"Top Secret America." *The Washington Post*. Published July 2010. Accessed December 14, 2016. http://projects.washingtonpost.com/top-secret-america.

Tower, John, Edmund Muskie, and Brent Scowcroft. *The Tower Commission Report: The Full Text of the President's Special Review Board*. New York: Bantam Books, 1987.

Truman, Harry S. *Memoirs by Harry S. Truman, Volume One: Years of Decision*. Garden City, NY: Doubleday, 1956.

Truman, Harry S. *Memoirs by Harry S. Truman, Volume Two: Years of Trial and Hope*. Garden City, NY: Doubleday, 1956.

The United States Congress. 86th Congress, Second Session and 87th Session, First Session. Congress. Senate. Committee on Government Operations. *Organizing for National Security*. Washington, DC: Government Printing Office, 1961.

The United States Senate. "Arthur Vandenberg Biography." Accessed May 25, 2016. http://www.senate.gov/artandhistory/history/common/generic/Featured_Bio_Vandenberg.htm.

The U.S. Defense Department. *United States-Vietnam Relations, 1945–1967*. Edited by Leslie Gelb. Washington, DC: Government Printing Office, 1971.

The U.S. Department of Defense. Comptroller Office. *The Economy Act Orders*, 31 USC, § 1535 and 1536. http://comptroller.defense.gov/Portals/45/documents/fmr/archive/11aarch/11a_03_042000.pdf. Retrieved May 22, 2015.

The U.S. House of Representatives. *The National Security Act of 1947*. Committee on the Armed Services. 80th Congress, Second Session. July 26, 1947. (Also known as Public Law 253.)

The U.S. House of Representatives. *The Reorganization Act, 1949*. Public Law 109. 81st Congress, First Session. Approved June 29, 1949. Found at the Truman Library.

Van Evera, Stephen. *Guide to Methods for Students of Political Science*. Ithaca, NY: Cornell University Press, 1997.

The White House. The National Security Council. "U.S. Policy Regarding the Situation in Former Yugoslavia." Presidential Review Directive/NSC-1. Published by the Federation of American Scientists, Intelligence Resource Program. January 22, 1993. Accessed May 11, 2015. http://fas.org/irp/off docs/prd/prd-1.pdf.

The White House. The National Security Council. "NSPD-1: Organization of the National Security Council System." NSPD-1: Organization of the National Security Council System. Published by the Federation of American Scientists, Intelligence Resource Program. Accessed June 2, 2016. https://fas .org/irp/offdocs/nspd/nspd-1.htm.

Whitefield, Debra. "Analysts Debate Value of Firm Hand: Aloof Reagan Style, Flaw or Model of Management." *Los Angeles Times*. March 12, 1987. Accessed May 21, 2015. http://articles.latimes.com/1987–03–12/news/ mn-9321_1_management.

Williams, Nick Jr., and Daniel Williams. "Iraq Threatens Israel with Use of Nerve Gas: Mideast: Leader Denies Nuclear Capability But Says He Would Destroy 'Half' His Adversary If Attacked." *Los Angeles Times*. April 3, 1990. Accessed June 21, 2016. http://articles.latimes.com/1990-04-03/news/ mn-702_1_gas-attack.

Wittkopf, Eugene R. *Faces of Internationalism: Public Opinion and American Foreign Policy*. Durham, NC: Duke University Press, 1990.

Wittkopf, Eugene R., Charles W. Kegley, and James M. Scott. *American Foreign Policy: Pattern and Process*. Belmont, CA: Wadsworth, 2003.

Woodward, Bob. *Veil: The Secret War of the CIA 1981–1987*. New York: Simon and Schuster, 1987.

Woodward, Bob. *The Commanders*. New York: Simon and Schuster, 1991.

Woodward, Bob. *Bush at War*. New York: Simon and Schuster, 2002.

Woodward, Bob. *Plan of Attack*. New York: Simon and Schuster, 2004.

Woodward, Bob. *State of Denial*. New York: Simon and Schuster, 2007.

Woodward, Bob. *Obama's Wars*. New York: Simon and Schuster, 2010.

Wroe, Ann. *Lives, Lies and the Iran-Contra Affair*. London: IB Tauris and Co., 1991.

Wyden, Peter. *Bay of Pigs: The Untold Story*. New York: Simon and Schuster, 1979. http://www.trumanlibrary.org/calendar/viewpapers.php?pid=1144.

Index

About the Author

M. KENT BOLTON is a professor of political science and global studies at California State University San Marcos. Professor Bolton has taught world politics, U.S. foreign policy, and national security courses for 23 years at CSUSM. Prior to taking his position at CSUSM, he taught at George Washington University (1992–1994) and Arizona State University. He has written three books that focused on various aspects of the National Security Act of 1947 and a textbook on world politics. He has also written sundry articles, chapters, and op-ed pieces. He lives in Carlsbad Village in northern San Diego County.

www.ingramcontent.com/pod-product-compliance
Lightning Source LLC
Chambersburg PA
CBHW050431280326
41932CB00013BA/2073